THE TREE OF INNOCENCE

Michael Scott

Fisher King Publishing

The Tree of Innocence
Copyright © Michael Scott 2015
ISBN 978-1-910406-07-6

All rights reserved. No part of this publication may be reproduced or distributed in any form or by any means, or stored in a database or electronic retrieval system without the prior written permission of Fisher King Publishing Ltd. Thank you for respecting the author of this work.

Published by
Fisher King Publishing
The Studio
Arthington Lane
Pool-in-Wharfedale
LS21 1JZ
England

CONTENTS

Preface	1
Introduction	5
One - **Becoming Awake**	10
Two - **The Freedom to be Mortal**	25
Three - **Original Sin**	40
Four - **Revisiting Intelligence**	53
Five - **Into the Unknowable**	69
Six - **The Poisoned Chalice**	84
Seven - **Changing the Rules**	103
Eight - **I Am God**	121
Nine - **The Cleansing**	135
Ten - **Blissful Unknowing**	150
Eleven – **Zibaldone**	166
Twelve - **An Accident Waiting to Happen**	181
Thirteen - **The Tree of Innocence**	200
Fourteen - **The Giant Hare**	220
Fifteen - **Superstition**	237
Sixteen - **The Ego-Self-Personality**	249
Seventeen - **What Comes Next?**	260

Preface

'The Watching Vastness'
The easiest way forward would be to imagine that I am the spokesman of an alien genius, or perhaps a genius alien that arrived on earth before life began and, like an intelligent but imperceptible dark matter, has brooded upon the biosphere for a few billion years. We can hypothesise that the presence of this alien consciousness (alien only in the sense that it didn't originate on planet earth) has become almost apparent to a very, very, recent indigenous arrival, the hominid tribe.

We should have a name for this billions-of-years-old consciousness, the ancient equivalent of modern global surveillance, as it is convenient for me to refer to my supposed authority, the force that drives the dummy, me. I could call it The Ventriloquist, but that would be inaccurate as it doesn't speak, either directly or indirectly. It doesn't put words in my mouth nor, for that matter does it infiltrate my mind with thoughts. I think it functions by electronic osmosis, in much the same way as nutrients pass through cell membranes in living organisms.

More loftily, I could imagine this watching vastness as the Void or the Emptiness, as in Buddhist or Taoist philosophising. I rather like the idea of the Void and would like to adopt it as my source of everything and nothing. But I doubt if I can get away with anything so concrete, comforting as it may be.

The urge to identify *something* seems to be common to all hominids as if it is endemic in the machinery of our consciousness. My intuition, i.e. my brief from the Void, is that this is an error in hominid design, and unique to the unfortunate tribe. But that may be my misunderstanding of the intelligent dark matter, or the photonic billions, or the quantum field, or whatever this Void actually might be.

Maybe it is the intention of the alien genius; keeping me and all the other messengers in mushroom-rearing obscurity.

Anyway, on slender evidence and shaky foundations, the hominids have been imagining cosmic masters for some thousands of earth-years - not very long, but rather significant to the hominids. They might as well listen to me as much as the others. Who are these others?

The Messengers

This is the whole point. The messengers are the hominids that have been trying to impart knowledge to other hominids for a few thousand years. There is, in the hominid mind, a conviction that the universe actually exists and really *means* something. It seems to be an exclusively hominid, possibly only a human, characteristic. Therefore, when I say 'alien consciousness', meaning something 'out there', a Void or a 'Ground of Being', it is a specifically hominid perception, as far as this human mind knows. Communicating this perception by speech or writing is a practice that typifies the hominids (well, the humans, as we don't possess records of views of the other hominids), and it is not always remembered by the human persons that these ideas are exclusively the product of the minds of the messengers. They, I, might claim to have received the knowledge from beyond our own minds, but that has never been actually proved. How could you prove it?

Knowledge

This is the issue. It seems to be restricted to three kinds. First there is the apparently endogenous knowledge whereby we instinctively understand the biological rules of existence. This is the kind of knowledge that all forms of life possess. Second there is the added knowledge that we have to learn in order to exist. This is more problematic than the instinctive knowledge. Human beings put enormous energy into trying to distinguish between these two kinds of knowledge; it is called the nature/nurture debate.

The Messengers may be involved in these two kinds of knowledge, but they are usually not too concerned about the origin of the knowledge. It stays more or less at the biological level. More or less. Confucius was a conspicuous messenger who taught good behaviour but, as far as I know, he did not dabble in the 'supernatural'. Gautama Buddha was another messenger who confined himself to rules of behaviour that were basically logical and human-centred. Epicurus was similar, except that he mentioned Voidal elements, calling them the gods, though stressing their unimportance in human affairs.

Even in these examples, however, there is the difficulty of establishing the authority of the messenger or the authenticity of the message. The same must be said for all the other millions of messengers who, while not straying into the third brand of knowledge, the Void, still claim authority that is without apparent substance. They proclaim beliefs, they claim knowledge, and other humans are expected to take all this knowledge on trust. There is argument, strife, revolution and even war in these areas of knowledge.

In the third form of knowledge, often loosely named 'spiritual', the authority and authenticity criteria are stretched to breaking point. The possible existence and nature of the Void is endlessly and overwhelmingly debated, beliefs are formulated, violence is usually involved. We humans, the latest version, 'sapiens', has maimed, tortured, and killed many millions of our race in the name of the beliefs within the third knowledge. The human animal is a killing machine, like so many of the other animals on planet earth. If, as a 'messenger', I was actually serving some superhuman master, I would be humiliated by the behaviour of my race. So much so, that I think I would die of disgrace.

After these discursive remarks, I should state my actual position:

I have no authority. I am not a messenger. I have no supernatural master. The only reason for other hominids to take passing notice of me is that I have two essential qualities lacking in the great panoply of self-appointed messengers -

I do not nurture or cherish beliefs beyond those essential for basic decency.

I do not have, and know that I do not have, any unquestionable knowledge.

These are rare qualities in teachers, politicians, priests, and all the other self-styled messengers in our species. If they do not put you off, as a reader, you may like to know that:

The purpose of this book is to question whether we have made a mistake in putting KNOWLEDGE on a pedestal and worshipping it as our ultimate saviour.

Introduction

The Awakening Root

Scientists may have secret pleasures. Being rational, super-logical, by profession, they still harbour emotions and even ecstasies. Maybe they start with joy and move on to hard analysis. Growing up seems to demand being serious. Not all of us are totally converted by that societal norm.

I confess to a pair of deep-seated joys in botany which still shine within me even in my advanced maturity. First, the more obvious one of seeing a plant, perhaps of uncertain identity, produce its first flower. The transformation never fails to thrill me. And since the classification of plants is heavily biased towards flower-structure, the emergence of the flower often initiates new wonder and new work upon the relationship between plants. The second thrill is earlier in time. As a boy I loved to put seeds on wet filter paper and watch for the first sign of life, the emergence of the white, fragile, rootlet. As Darwin once wrote, *'It is hardly an exaggeration to say that the tip of the radicle... acts like the brain of one of the lower animals; the brain being situated within the anterior end of the body, receiving impressions from the sense-organs, and directing the several movements.'*

I like the way he shrewdly implies that consciousness exists so widely in nature that it even operates in an exploring plant rootlet. As a metaphor, I think of the germinating seed as a young human animal. The radicle is the first part of it to emerge as a growing entity into the external environment. This is also a radical event for the individual organism. In the radicle is the awareness of the world and it must guide the growth process.

It could also be regarded as the leading point of the genotype or the potential essence of the being it foreshadows. As the thrusting new 'ego' of the organism, it follows a path of knowledge inculcated into its cells by the chemical messenger, DNA. This is not knowledge as we might claim to know it, but when the plant becomes the fully formed phenotype we can only applaud the extraordinary power of the data in the cell nuclei. The word 'essence' is useful, because it specifies that any organism is both more and less than its genotype. Without our individual genotype, we human organisms could not be formed, nor could we function. Yet the instruction manual encoded in the DNA is not the whole story of who and what we are. We must also remember that such knowledge is imperfect. We are not beings without limitations. No organism is. In our case, our most prized characteristic, our intelligence, is also our primary weakness. We do not have perfect knowledge. A skeleton in our racial closet that will be examined throughout this book.

Thinking further about the fragile radicle, it epitomises the fragility of life; the same fragility that hovers in the existence of all living things. Everything the radicle encounters is a threat or an opportunity. If it is lucky, it comes to no harm and the development continues with the unfurling of the first leaves, the cotyledons, which are eventually followed by the true leaves in the form of the plumule. It is now a seedling. Its world is still a mixture of positive and negative forces. There is much work to be done before the organism becomes a fully developed plant.

The detail is different but the process is similar for the human infant. It is less obvious what constitutes its 'radicle', as all of its structure is imbued with its essence. The baby is radicle, cotyledon and plumule all in one. To a large degree its growth process and its behaviour are ordained in its genetic constitution, which is coeval with its essence. But the big difference between plant seedling and human infant is that the latter has more potential for radical behaviour as opposed to mere growth of radicle and plumule. It is the radical element in the infantile human that is its strength and its vulnerability. This is the capacity to respond to external influences; many of those will be hostile or harmful. The young human is ill-equipped to distinguish good from bad. Its essence may be perfect within itself, but its real world is not, at least in terms of safe growth and maturing. In other word, it depends on luck much as the plant seedling does.

There is another immense difference between plant and animal. Generally, the seedling is on its own - its parents do not assist or obstruct its development. But the human infant is unable to survive on its own and must have help to grow and be safe. This help is not guaranteed, nor is the nature and quality of it and it may not even exist. The radical feature of human development is that it is both a matter of chance and of infantile intention. Our individual beginnings are a lottery of diverse agencies, and they are not made any more reliable by notional safety factors or mythical supernatural rescuers. We are all damaged in the process of infancy. It is merely a question of how and how much. The first radical factor to consider, therefore, is to review the assumptions made culturally about the process of early human development in each individual.

Awareness of Error
I consider that we vastly underestimate the hazards of our first few years of childhood. The radicalism here is the understanding that human childhood circumstances are inevitably sub-optimal. I am not suggesting that we pour resources into correcting this, as I think such efforts are made futile by lack of knowledge. What I am urging is that we accept, take for granted, that our individual early development is made in adverse circumstances. We all suffer, whatever stories we tell

ourselves. Our basic structure, our phenotype, and the way we develop in response to the environment, are all sub-optimal at least, and self-defeating at worst. We are all sub-standard products even when we appear to be beautiful and/or talented.

To a self-congratulatory species like mine, this viewpoint must seem like treachery or disloyalty, or some such moral judgement. But this is because we obfuscate reality. Much as we might bemoan the bad behaviour of human kind, it never seems to occur to us that this is how we are made. It almost seems that the hangover from intense religious zealotry makes us protective of our nature because we think we are the likeness of the creator of the universe. So we may be 'fallen', but are actually perfect. This is a serious untruth.

There is, however, a second suggested radical idea, i.e. that none of this matters very much. 'Survival of the fittest', clumsy term that it is, should be interpreted in the sense of fitness being a measure of compatibility rather than physical supremacy. There can never be a perfect fit between organism and environment. It is always approximate, because nature is inherently approximate. There is never perfect balance in the lottery of life. In other words, the whole biosphere is sub-optimal, however wonderful or terrible it seems, it is just not, ever, perfect. It cannot be because of the way time works in relation to space and its contents. Change is always happening. And life streams away from us into the past, so the present never arrives, only fragment by fragment of the unknown future.

What matters is that we should accept our initial struggle and be aware that most of it is beyond our conscious recall. So the third radicalism is to understand that there isn't much we can do in terms of retrospective healing. This understanding would be particularly innovative. We spend so much time and effort trying to understand, even to discover, past experiences. Ask someone how they feel and they tend to recount the things in their life which they believe to have been crucial to them. More often than not, the tendency is to scroll, that is, to repeat the same pivotal stories about ourselves. There may be some benefit in this, but it can't be much in terms of transformation. Conversely, the habitual recitation is probably harmful in that it may be reinforcing an error of perception. I suggest that the life-story procedure should be abandoned in favour of honest examination of the moving scene of present behaviour, with no manufactured reasons or excuses.

If these three radical concepts are valid, what would it mean for our collective and individual behaviour? The answer to this lies in the human potential to behave with enhanced awakeness and compassionate humility. It may not seem a very radical idea, but it is, because virtually no-one behaves in this way. My objective here, in the closing section of my life, is to describe why and how it is my promise to myself for dealing with my competitiveness, my dogmatism, and my background feeling of duress and despair. It will require a form of awakeness and humility that has so far eluded me and which I must now pursue and enact as best I can, in the interests of a new serenity in my life to replace the old neuroses.

To summarise:

1. We are inevitably sub-optimal, a natural condition implicit in our biology.

2. It doesn't much matter, because our lives are ever-changing anyway.

3. So drop the life-story and focus honestly on behaviour in the moving present.

4. Recognise that knowledge is the most limited and risky of our possessions.

One
Becoming Awake

Where to Start?

I think I have already started, but this may be a good point to assert that I do not intend to try to go back and adjust my infantile experiences and responses. The problem does not lie in the past. It is in the living present moment. Each thought and action I have now, and the way I write it down, is my new radicalism and I want to ignore the past and the future as they are beyond my potential to act. I *know* virtually nothing, but I should be able to *be* as I wish. The truth is that there is virtually nothing to stop me carrying out that process.

If I am to heal, which is a dubious concept anyway, because neither I, nor anyone else, can know exactly what my wholeness might be, I have to be able and willing to *change*. My experience of the processes of so-called healing, whether by counselling, medicines, or loving advice, is that there is too little commitment (in the recipient of the process) to new modes of thinking or behaviour. There is an entrenched refusal to change in the psyche. It is as if the mind has such investment in itself, with the emphasis on self, that however great the need for a different way of being, the default position is inertia. Over and over again, in the healing program, the need to change is experienced as a terrible threat. The personality seems to be saying, 'Whatever you do, don't destroy me!', as if it sees itself as the one valuable entity in the life-picture.

Unfortunately, it does see itself that way. The personality, the amalgam of habit and belief that we carry about like a snail-shell, or the armadillo's leathery armour, or the hedgehog's spines, is the manufactured product we have created out of the debris of damaged essence. It is also the raw material of our emotional response to life's gifts and punishments. I behave as though this personality is the actual me. Obviously, or so I must believe, the personality is sacrosanct. So, regardless of its toxic content, I try to preserve it intact despite the fact that it is this personality that is preventing me from becoming real and whole. All the retreats, encounter-groups and meditations in the world are not able to alter our resolve to stay as we are, while pretending we want to be different. In my experience, the mysterious process of coming awake is the only way out of the impasse.

First Steps

The hard fact is that I have to start here and now. The past is irrelevant; the future is unattainable and unknowable. Every moment of the **moving present** is my material. What has gradually become apparent to me is that I am more or less new-born every millisecond. This is my window of opportunity. The first step of my individual radicalism is, therefore, the absolute realisation that all my existing habits, beliefs, experiences, emotions, fears, pains, anger, happiness, guilt, regret, all of these, are out of date. I pass my use-by date every micro-moment. This takes some accepting.

The surrender to reality is an overwhelming experience if it is successful. The extent to which nothing actually matters is suddenly seen as infinite. I am likely to feel, 'After all these years I am merely potential again.'

The beautiful Void appears to surround me. I am reborn as the permanent nothing. I am liable to try to scurry hurriedly back into my armadillo shell. Freedom strikes me as too much to bear. But, in reality, I know I can't stay in the safety of my confining shell. That illusion is over. That unreality is finished. I have to stay awake. My eyes must open after all the years of sleep. Now that I really see the world, much as I dislike most of it, I cannot stop seeing it again. I am edging into reality.

The Reality is Fear

Ironically, the sharp lurch into reality brings a hidden jungle of fear into view. It is ironical because there must be an innate assumption that the enlightenment that coincides with, or is the result of, awakening will show a more beautiful and fulfilling world. It is not part of the contract that one gets a terrible scare. But wakening is not easy and its fruits may be bitter, for a while, until their true value emerges. What was not realised, before coming awake, was that the human individual is motivated by the desire to neutralise or deny the basic fears inherent in existence.

As I edge into reality, slowly and spasmodically waking up, I have to confront these fears as they line up before me like a firing-squad. Around and within me are the defences and placebos that I have mustered during my life to keep me safe and happy. These antidotes to fear are powerful analgesics; they drug the consciousness, so that the whole personality collapses into more or less stable-seeming stasis.

This system depends on devising a way of smothering the fear. The method becomes a habit, the habit becomes a belief, and the actual fear is reduced to a sickly, soft-focus, pervasive anxiety. In other words, evasion by diffusion doesn't work. Therefore, as I emerge into awake reality, I have to take off the covers and look the fear in its true face. How counterintuitive this feels after decades of futile denial. I have to face the monster now that it is no longer hidden behind bamboo doors. In this approach, I cannot rely upon a secure state of inner being, because there isn't one. Instead I have to follow a process of surrender, or recognition, a way of seeing the horror for what it is and not caring very much. Is that possible?

Fear of Death

This is the most important fear, heavily disguised, usually denied in all sorts of subtle ways, and it is extremely complex. In one sense our future death is the most certain factor in human life, because we must know it's going to happen. But it is totally unknown in terms of when or how, unless we opt for suicide. And knowing whether or not to commit suicide is also a knowledge problem. Death is truly a knowledge quicksand.

As it lies in the unknown future, death is known as an objective fact but not yet as an experience except by imagination and observation of others. It is debatable whether the objective fact is actually knowledge at all. Indeed, this question goes to the core of the knowledge enigma. The knowledge that death is at the end of life is in-the-head knowledge, like book-learning. This is a piece of pseudoknowledge, inasmuch as it is something we assume about the future and therefore is inherently dubious. True knowledge of death would come with the experience itself, but would depend on the nature of the experience. Here again, knowledge is elusive, it is not possible to know how aware one will be when death happens.

A more arrant type of pseudoknowledge is the litany of supposed examples of life-after-death. Obviously a person can die and then revive. Modern medical technology makes recovery from death rather common. But the person involved is not dead, and there must be great scepticism about any of these occurrences being life after death. True death doesn't come and go as in ER wards. When it comes, it stays.

Fear of death is atavistically buried in species history, and is also deep in personal emotions. Nothing is more frightening than death, unless it is the pain which often precedes the main event. But, again, those of us who are alive do not know death because it is hiding in the future.

Paradoxes of Death

Death makes a mockery of knowledge, exposing the theoretical and flimsy structure in the human psyche. We are even cavalier about it, almost mocking it in our own perceptions. It is often seen as a paradoxical potential resolution of problems. The death of a rich man releases assets to the world he has left. A despised person is removed from the scene by timely extinction.

How often does a death please others, even as they utter ritual regrets? In extreme and astonishing slaughter, entire masses of people may simultaneously be wiped out. This must be desired by somebody and perpetrated by many. And there is also the ugly reality that the whole human race dies completely during a lifetime. The human population of the world is constantly being replaced. Those alive today will all be dead by the early years of the next century, if not before.

There is also the gruesome fact of ritual death, as a spectacle or a religious rite. It is not so long ago that criminals in England were publicly executed. Martyrs are heroes who have been killed for their beliefs. Whole nations may be involved in the slaughter of other nations as in the big wars of the twentieth century. Many people like to kill, especially given ritual licence to do it.

Christianity is a cult that hinges on death, the sacrifice of their god in the person of his son.

The South American Pagan faiths killed on an epic scale. It is hard to resist the suspicion that death in all these contexts is pleasurable to the survivors. Do we not all enjoy death as spectacle or fantasy? Is this not part of the partially submerged human impulse, the basic animal desire for blood? Do we not know what killers we all are, given the circumstances?

The Fearing and the Knowing

The fear of death rears like a cobra in the mind and feelings of a person if a symptom appears which might foreshadow terminal illness. So we are periodically reminded of its immense personal importance, and severely troubled by illness in those we love. Thus abandonment and isolation are also attendant upon the fear of death. We may be aware that death could imply freedom, a state more complex than we might relish, as it means taking responsibility in some new way or leaving others to a different life. Most of all, perhaps, is the damage done to our sense of meaning, our need to feel a purpose in existence. Yet, despite all this potential havoc, we keep going and keep worrying about other matters. We behave most of the time as if death did not exist.

We use time-worn strategies. We focus on self-boosting factors such as work, our specialness, our essential companions, our causes, our desires, so that the chimaeric self we lug about and celebrate as our unique personality, is also a package of absurd, death-denying, death-defying, fantasies. What we seem incapable of doing is actually recognising the reality of the approaching demise. We may indulge in denial to the extent of imagining some paranormal miracle, like reincarnation, resurrection, spirit-survival, or any other weird fantasy. The occasional overlord may have the equivalent of an emperor's terracotta army. There is now little recourse to the practice of including food and jewellery in magnificent coffins. More likely is the will that contains instructions as to how the world should behave after we have passed. We may not be clinically deranged. But we are insane enough to behave spasmodically, even frequently, as if we are not actually going to die.

Radicalising Death

What could be revolutionary, truly transformative, in our experience of the death-fear? What would it be like genuinely to regard death as neither enemy nor friend, for example, but merely an acquaintance, a person nearby and neutral? Would that make a difference to our moment by moment being?

What if we could witness the signs of dying in ourselves and others without panic? Ageing is not usually bracketed with dying, it seems, but what if it were? I think that that equation is in our unconscious and our emotions, but that we fail generally to experience consciously our disintegrating appearance as part of the dying process. This means that we see death as a future event rather than a current reality, the fact that it is with us in every moment. This blindness, this denial, actually causes or intensifies the fear of death while apparently pushing it far into the background of existence.

Death as Drama

Another way of denying the reality of death is to weave it into stories and fantasies. Killing people is probably the most popular entertainment we have. It is probably a close-run comparison, but we seem more content to witness a human death on film than human sexual congress, as can be proven by merely watching the products of innumerable studios. In a sense, sex is real and death isn't, so we are uneasy with the first and relaxed with the second in the form of consumable fantasy. *Real* death, as in a school massacre or a train crash is much more disturbing even if watchable in a different emotional context. And thus the complexities and the complexes multiply.

Yet the arts can offer a different way of seeing death. It is a risky business. By its nature, art, whether literature, music, or visual, is not nature. It is a construct. It invites the observer/listener to change consciousness and find new resonances in existence. The risky part is that the work may be taken too literally, or even totally misunderstood. It may not be clear whether a funeral march is simply a dirge or, contrarily, a glorification the combative spirit. Like any knowledge, creations in the arts are unreliable. This is to be expected. But does it not militate against the virtue of a possible relief system?

Can the theatre come to our aid in facing death's reality with equanimity instead of trying to evade it? Some drama, perhaps, for some people. But which plays, and in what way could they help? The deaths in Shakespeare's works, for example, have never helped me deal with my own fear. In a way they are too intellectual. And obviously they have to provide entertainment for playgoers.

As with the old Greek horror plays, I experience a sense of the ludicrous and absurd more than the great terminus itself. I have been in the cast of 'The Tempest', 'Twelfth Night', 'Macbeth', 'Measure for Measure', and 'Othello', in amateur readings, and have not enjoyed the experience because of the lack of genuine engagement with the emotions. In a recent reading of 'Othello', an essentially dark and sinister play, in which most of the leading characters die rather unpleasantly, our cast broke out in giggles three quarters of the way through. And the cast consisted of people who claim to love and admire the bard.

Whose Drama Is It?

In a sense, I have to make, and act within, my own drama. Writing for others, or being written for, is a hazardous knowledge-system because the receivers are diverse and often dysfunctional in relation to the text presented to them. It is the same with music and painting. This entails superficiality, because the deepest issues have to be glossed for acceptance. For this, or other reasons, art fails generally to engender transformation, especially in relation to emotions deeply in denial. It could be argued that religious art is a more effective process, as it is specifically dedicated to progressive change, at least in theory. But I am sure that religious knowledge is an extreme form of false knowledge, so however powerful the drama, it is inevitably hollow. Maybe it works for a religious believer, but this raises other knowledge problems as will be discussed later. The falseness should be seen in the dependence upon an icon rather than upon oneself. And icons are just not real

Writing to one's own being is one way of finding inner reality, towards coming awake, free of pseudoknowledge. Maybe it's the best way, together with poetry. We can see, for a start that death is the only absolute fact in our confused existence. All the other things, like work, affiliations, causes, obsessions, addictions and imagination, are kept in front of our psychic vision to make the world seem worthwhile. But the background hiss in life is that nothing is worthwhile because our ticket is running out. I may put great effort into projects and relationships but the daemon on my left shoulder repeats the mantra, 'Remember that this will all pass and there will be nothing of you left except a few words and images and you will soon be forgotten'.

The radical possibility is that I may be able to demolish and go beyond this uneasy dialogue with myself. I am not sure how much of it is my own creation and how much the product of my culture, but if it has been *made* can it not be *unmade*? Part of my reason for wanting to do this is that I dislike living the acceptable lie. We deal with the fear of death by creating a myth. In general, this results in a life in twin hells. In one hell we are terrified but pretend we aren't and in the other we are depressed because we sense life is pointless because it is ephemeral. Why would we want to exist in a self-conceived world in which Dante's crazy inferno is reduced to a pair of witches' cauldrons.

There is huge anger in my drama. It is not just the anger of the defeated perfectionist, bad as it is, but is also, and more so, the anger of being misled, cheated, betrayed, by my sources of so-called knowledge. Even more fundamentally enraging to me is the futility, waste and fantasy of my fellow humankind, traits which have dogged me also throughout my life until now. Paradoxically, the imminence of my death has been clarifying and helpful in demolishing the fairy stories, good or bad. Into my drama, death's imminence has inserted a refreshing honesty. I assume this is commonly experienced. But I'm not sure. Maybe some of us think we must fight death, and win life back for ourselves. I do not understand this mentality. Why should life and death be two sides of a competitive struggle? Why is it not perfectly fine to let death take its course? Are we afraid of doctors and nurses being made redundant?

As I have said elsewhere and often, the sickness that really matters is not the one that kills me, but the one which makes me obsessed with my godlike and eternal self. I am not clear who invented that monstrosity, but I curse them for making us all foolish. In my drama, the demon king is the human self, or its icon, the ego. It must be these mad agencies that make death such an awesome event, so awesome that we ignore it and revere death to similar extremes of excess. How can I move out of their noxious embrace. Well, clearly, there must be some way of saying 'No' so as to reverse the decades of acceptance. It is not as easy as saying, 'Death's OK by me, bring it on', but that may be the headline. That question seems crucial: is death OK by me? Could the portrayal of death by the imagination be redesigned to show how good-natured it actually is? How would it look? Like a Summer afternoon or a Winter night? Is it not always shown as the latter? Even with churchy music and soft focus, isn't it really offered as a sort of nightmare? And a rowdy drunken wake is even worse, the antics of desperation.

The Definitive Human Idiocy.

I have suggested that my team of deep impulses, competitiveness, dogmatism, duress and despair, are where my asleepness resides and now I am adding the realisation that fear is the cement that holds them in place. The fear of death, or rather the denial of the fear, is one primary energy source for several other impulses. For example, in denying death and creating a sleep of the psyche, a phantom called 'ultimate rescuer' joins forces with another, the 'special me'. By having an ultimate rescuer, which is anything or any person that is chosen to represent security, and by being somehow special, a unique *self*, I can place the first great fear in a glass case and regard it as stuffed. As will appear, in due course, the other fears, of freedom, of isolation and of meaninglessness and of purposelessness have similar generic character to the fear of death, and they all enhance the effect of one another in muffling our awareness of reality.

Allied to the ego-myth of personal specialness, and the belief in one's personal power, there is the equally mythical faith in a supernatural agency which protects human beings. Obviously this chimaera has usually been a god of some kind, a myth that has existed throughout human history and which still flourishes in many cultures. It is also present, in secular form, in millions of psyches as a powerful protector, although it may not always be benign, as in the common case of a woman or child who mistakenly believes a particular man is their ultimate rescuer regardless of how awful his behaviour may be. Sometimes it is a doctor or priest who remains a shining figure for a person so long as the truth of their basic human weakness is not revealed. The variety is pretty well endless.

For many people there is eventually a collapse of the myth and resulting terror of actual reality, i.e. that an ultimate rescuer does not exist. Hero-worship is a similar error of imagination with frequently disastrous consequences.

Whatever the exact nature of the delusion, the important fact is that it is a delusion. The reality of death needs to be taken head-on not diffused into turbid channels of romance. Myths of personal power are also very dangerous because the reality comes as a profound shock, sometimes a fatal one. Risking all in the interests of truth, I would suggest that all the great heroes are potentially harmful ultimate rescuers. For example, the religious icons are preposterous confections, none more elaborate than the Krishnas, the Christs and the Buddhas. Similarly, leading figures like monarchs and military leaders may become icons of perfection, vastly overrated.

It doesn't much matter if we overrate the icons and the saviours, so long as we don't fall into the error of believing that they are really our saviours or our champions. The problem is that we evade the truth. In the case of death this is particularly unfortunate in that even if the believer can be proved to be mistaken, the belief may persist and become a cult or a power-struggle. Thus, the current of history shows the mayhem and murder that attends these beliefs, not to mention the accumulated despair of the billions who are not 'saved'. This leads to the question of why people are terrified of freedom.

Fear of Freedom

The demon king here is responsibility, in the sense that if I am free then I am responsible for what I do, even for what I am. As with the other devices, the need is to be safe and it is an unsafe feeling to be the author of one's own misfortunes. It should feel safer to be the author of one's successes, but that is a heady brew in that one success may signify the availability of many others. In other words, a person feels chosen for special functions and rewards. Either way, the projection of oneself out onto the table of chance is complex to say the least. Most of human beings take refuge in specialness of some kind. Again, illusions win over reality.

If we are told, however, that we are actually quite free though without divine or mundane unique guidance, we are terrified. It is as if a person is in a universal criminal court where everyone knows the truth about him and he feels unable to fool the universe - especially while the universe is paying attention. The primary feeling is of being exposed, unprotected and liable to any disaster that blows along towards him.

Therefore, as with fear of death, we invent a protector, but this one is a powerful servant or a majestic gift of personal perception. Again, this has terrible consequences because not only do we invent an impossible trust in our own ambit but invite, even fool, others to share the power. This myth edges on to the next, our omnipresent fear of isolation.

I Am Alone

If I manufacture a god or a personal gift I feel a false sense of security, in that I either have help or I have special powers. But what if I am fundamentally alone in the universe? Well, I have a thousand strategies to obscure that fact. I have my family, my tribe, my nation, my army, my comrades, my colleagues, my customers, etc, ad infinitum. But skid row beckons. I know I am in danger but refuse to face it, and insist upon the miracle of companionship. Yes, but what about death of comrades? What if the group turns against me? Can I trust my comrades? Should I court my enemies to be on the safe side? So I seek strategies of liaison and start worrying even more. So what, I will stand alone, in my pomp. But what is it all for?

Fear of the Void

At the end of the illusory rainbow stands emptiness. My ideas of purpose and meaning have been hammered and dissected. I stand in a cold, empty space and all I can do is sing 'Over the Rainbow'. The ultimate rescuer has morphed into three incomplete creatures, a cowardly lion, a tin man, and a scarecrow stuffed with straw. Here is the crunch question: why am I here? No-one tries to answer that question without inventing purpose or destiny. In my case, I tend to offer love, beauty and truth to myself, but in all honesty they are pretty insubstantial fare for the gluttonous ego.

Yet it is the question that must be answered before the end comes. It may then be, why have I been here? There is a perfectly satisfactory answer, but can the human mind take it. Before closing this chapter I want to say that it is hugely valuable to know what the question actually is, free from the flummery of all those illusions. One way of answering the 'overwhelming question', to use T. S. Eliot's portentous but gnomic phrase, though hardly it's answer, is that it doesn't matter one way or the other. It doesn't really matter if the world ends, as it certainly will one day. But the 'not mattering' is really the point. If I am free, if I am not afraid of dying, if I am content with my own company (though welcoming to others), and if I don't care about meaning or purpose, then I am in a sort of no-lose situation. Maybe it's not nice to have no delusions, and all my skeletons will continue their damned rattling till I am a heap of ashes, but I am potentially rather free. I quite like the thought.

Is there more to be said? The Unknown hovers there, side by side with the unknowable, and their presence should be enough to keeps me interested as my own end approaches. I can understand why humankind has invented gods: there is this pervasive sense of 'something out there', and 200,000 years of human history hangs there too, with the idea of gods, like a cosmically-sized tapestry that we can't quite see. I think that the god-idea is mistaken, but only because it is defined and limited. The human imagination is still rather primitive, by which I mean it may be early days yet in the apparent expansion of something that we can call 'consciousness', or the Void, in which all is contained and nothing retained. Ideas like that swirl about without getting anywhere conclusive or illuminating. In what way, I wonder, does any of it actually matter? Is speculation all there is and all we will ever have in our human heads? In what way could that possibly matter?

It certainly will not solve anything to continue with the farce of knowledge, the self-inflated idea that we can escape the vice of imperilled existence by piling higher and higher heaps of knowledge, all of which are limited to the human mind. How could real freedom be obtained without first gaining the freedom from needing certainty

Two
The Freedom to be Mortal

Twenty-eight years ago I walked along the side of the great flow of water that I have come to regard as 'Freedom River', the brown, turbid, and often turbulent, Yorkshire Ouse, on a sunny November afternoon, and photographed the landscape around it as if seeing it for the first time.

It is not the river itself that seemed free, though I suppose it is, more or less, despite human interference. The freedom was, and is, in my being and my psychology. The river had been on the route of my Sunday morning walk for many years, but it had never looked like this before.

I knew I had been transformed and I liked the feeling, even though I was out of a job for the first time in my adult life. I dimly realised that I faced a new reality, one in which the opportunity to be free would constantly goad me, but I didn't realise the size and stress of the task. It has been a slow process, with many reverses. But as the freedom grew, so did the importance to me of each moment by moment task to be awake and free.

Now, in the repeatedly-new *Now*, existence offers a new freedom to overtop the accumulated freedoms since twenty-five years ago. This, if I can catch the essence of it as it rushes past my eyes, is more arduous than ever.

When I painted pictures of Freedom River I thought I might have moved into a new dimension of being and awareness. But this ever-changing-now is a new state of being entirely. If it isn't quite the full force of freedom that strikes me, yet, it is big enough to dominate my existence in a way the older freedoms never did.

The Focus of Old Age

It is partly the new power of old age and illness, the reality of *this* now that strikes like a cobra. I always knew that freedom could be testing, but was unprepared for it to be lethal. But of course, it must be. It is next door to the biggest and most denied horror, the coming of death, and the combined power of the two makes irresistible demands if I am awake enough to hear the alarms.

The two have to be hand in hand. If I am denying death I am balking at freedom. It's a paradox. It is a complex paradox, too, as human consciousness has this rare capacity to elaborate and complicate what may be simple, though no less fundamental, issues for other mammals. I am living within a medical labyrinth, for example, which is created by and for civilised human communities. It undermines my effort to live in the present and to accept death's reality as well as the facing of the terror of freedom. It allows, even commands, me to revert to normative denial and swamps me with future-directed anxiety.

As old age has caught up with me I have become so much less afraid of death, at some levels of my consciousness, that I rather welcome the prospect. But looking around at the people I know, I realise that, for them, death is such a monster that it really terrifies them. This means that they are both denying its reality as a nearby personal event, and fighting like mad to keep it at bay. It's hard to imagine a bigger knowledge muddle. An incident stands out. I recently lost a precious and very close friend to the monster with the hood and the scythe. I was accosted by an old, new-age, mutual acquaintance in a social setting. With a manic smile on his face he told me that the dead friend was just above us, sitting on a cloud, laughing at us, more alive than we were down on the ground.

It would be bad enough if this were merely a tasteless joke. But it wasn't a joke. For this man, death was merely a door into another world. Extinction it most assuredly was not. I just answered that I didn't share that view. But I went away pondering the mental consequences, indeed the existential consequences, of such a fanciful belief.

My parents, dead for decades, sometimes seem to visit me in my dreams. I can also raise them as images in my mind and often do. But my intelligence, such as it is, rates as miniscule the probability of these 'visits' being anything but phantoms created by my own mind. In fact, now that I am old and they are long gone, I enjoy these spectral encounters. Yet I do not expect nor hope to meet them soon in paradise.

The advantage of age is that the truth is more bearable. But it is hard to hold on to it, so great is the force of denial around me. And I am, it seems, less able to hold the truth securely when thinking of the death of people I love. I am afraid of the isolation and the rise of meaninglessness.

The Agony of Loss

Losing someone to death is fearful, but probably easier to face than the cosmic insult of one's own demise. Although it is hard not to blind oneself with hope, death must surely be less deniable when a loved one sinks into weakness and illness. It may be even more painful to see a loved one in terminal decline than to contemplate one's own extinction, but there is potentially more truth in the situation. Surely we get a more real image of death when we experience it second-hand but in deep passion. Another way of looking at it is to ask whether death should be far more of an interpersonal experience?

If so, we have a long way to go. The collective *knowledge* of mortality is corrupt and vitiated by hypocrisy. I have stopped going to funerals because they impact upon me with complete falseness. The ritual of religious mourning is extremely impersonal. If it is secular, the funeral will borrow sombre jollity from the religions that continue to mask the truth of our existence. The deceased, who no longer exists, may be present as a carcase and this relic is treated reverently before burning or burying. No-one knows how to grow in awareness in the fog of platitudes. The feasting afterwards is an insult to intelligence, because the denial is in full swing. Nothing is learned from the experience, not very often, anyway. We treat a funeral just as we treat life, prosaically, self-indulgently, meretriciously.

Death as Surrender

How could death have more meaning, how could it help us come awake? Is it not a prime opportunity for looking at our foolish assumptions, for demolishing our preposterous false knowledge?

As the end looms or insinuates, we live dangerously in the sense of walking like fools along the cliff-edge of death and freedom and not yet quite falling over, nor knowing what that falling might mean if and when we do it. We are, understandably, exhausted and more or less demoralised. Our worst behaviour is liable to break out when we could be transcending the petty limits of ordinary being.

The predicament is partly the absurd, even obscene, culture and its legal framework, which withholds essential freedoms such as comfortable assisted suicide if we want it. Our society is coercive and ruthless. We should not have to suffocate or strangle ourselves to achieve freedom from pain and fear. It seems laughable to work hard to face death and fear when our freedom is so negated. It is another ironic twist in the labyrinthine reality of death and freedom.

Looking at my own situation, I am appalled by the extent to which I am obsessed with the future. Ailments abound in my family, and our prospects are limited by increasing fragility. On the other hand, less afflicted friends seem reluctant to acknowledge our condition. People will visit and, apart from a few polite enquiries, will concentrate on their holiday plans, the exploits of their children, politics, television, anything but be with us in facing the reality to which age has brought us. We are afraid to discuss it, apart from medical gossip, because these friends do not signal a wish to be real and awake. There are exceptions, but all too often the talk is of quack medicines or unusual cures.

There is discussion of death, admittedly, but it is detached, the grief is suppressed, there is focus on remaining in contact with the dead in some way, however fanciful. I would like to explore the advantages of approaching death, to converse about the benefits of maturity that may only be achieved in this situation. Rather like the Tibetan concept of the bardo, particularly the idea of pre-death enlightenment and the changes in the psyche that can be achieved. Rather than a funeral, which is shutting the stable door after the soul has bolted, I would favour pre-death rituals and meditations plus, of course, access to painless termination. There's no chance of any of this, it seems.

Instead, there is this obsession with the future, fear of it, and utter focus on staying alive and getting well again. Is this an evasion of the chance of development for someone who wants, in principle at least, to be awake and be in reality? Or is it a fair and natural attempt to deal with fear of death and act freely?

It is undoubtedly the response of someone transfixed by self-importance, but are the fears of extinction not inherently self-important? Can one be awake, alive to the Void, and still be self-important? If so, what are the chances of real freedom, of simply not caring about the existential threats? Did we not *really* expect to die at around this time? How can we become real? How can we wake up and enjoy the final ride?

Fear of the Unknowable

This is perhaps the most important fear, never articulated, always enveloped in energetic hope and intent. The denial of fear is the default position, but how bizarre it is to deny that we can never know very much. Surrender to mystery is not our racial tendency. Humankind needs to *know* and will invent any madcap nonsense rather than admit total ignorance about, for example, the meaning or purpose of existence, or the question of whether we have immortal souls.

We use the word 'unknown' as a challenge to ourselves: we work, search, experiment, invent, create - anything to get more knowledge. But what if, instead of 'unknown', the word should be 'unknowable', meaning that the human mind can never know very much, and that most of the knowledge that we do have is dubious in veracity or value? Maybe the most important fear is actually the **terror of unknowability**. We are knowing animals, we have to know everything, yet in the one area we really care about we know nothing and can know nothing, except the very high probability that each of us will die. And we tend to be confused about that near-certainty - i.e. we might survive it miraculously in some form. But we don't *know* that, either. What an extremely unsatisfactory existence we have.

As we do for the main existential fears, death, isolation, etc., we also pay devoted attention to denying that we are terrified of unknowability. We do this by being obsessed with having and acquiring knowledge. It is hard to imagine anything more futile than this hunger for knowledge as it can never be sated.

Though perhaps even worse than that, is the questionable

assumption that *enough* knowledge would solve all problems and make clear what must be done and how to do it. What a forlorn hope and how absurdly arrogant as well. We don't successfully manage our response to the little we do know, and are always calling for more to help us out of our muddle. Individually, this keeps us more or less in continuous crisis, as in my need to comprehend my short future in the context of age and illness. It is as if I am begging some superordinate power to explain to me what is going on and how my life will run its course. It is basically an infantile, and all too human, need.

A Knowledge Audit

So how well have we done up to now? The assessment must be subjective, because there is a mixture of consequences of human activity, and considerable uncertainty about benefits versus costs. My own view is that the human experiment, or adventure, has been overwhelmingly disastrous, the main catastrophe being our headlong and generally accidental drive to make the planet uninhabitable, and we now know enough to realise that we are in deep trouble. There is much we could do to reduce the hazards, but we dither in our responses, making counterproductive moves and blaming anyone but ourselves for the state of existence we have made for ourselves. In a few thousand years of our most recent history, and especially in the last few hundred, when we have vastly increased our population, we have simultaneously achieved and broken the evolutionary mandate.

It is assumed, by persons of science, that the human genome, the genetic constitution of our species, has fulfilled an old mandate, not unlike an ancient politico/religious command, and we have gone forth and multiplied. The genes have no minds, so they do not deliberate, but by coincidence the old patriarchal mandate made biological sense when our species was a minor, weak, struggling, primate tribe.

It is nonsense now, of course, yet the old mandate continues to act, but against our survival. In normal biology, call it 'nature', the environment curtails such out-of-date genomes by simply killing the surplus. Having massively overshot the biological target, humankind still carries the urge to procreate to excess.

On the plus side, for reasons not altogether clear, perhaps some obscure function of the environment (or the collective unconscious!), the human race is now apparently breeding at mere replacement levels. That is good news if it is true. But, the damage may already have been done, as we are already too numerous for the planet to bear, perhaps by a factor as large as three or even four (i.e. there should be less than two billion of us instead of more than seven billion). There is already enough knowledge available to us to recognise our plight - indeed it has been available for years as a biological inevitability - yet it has not done much good. So at the global level, the audit shows our knowledge systems to be fatally flawed, primarily in the religious or social habits by which we still actively promote human fecundity.

Ingrained infantilism

It is odd, even counter-intuitive, that such a cerebral species as ours should behave so lunatically. We are undoubtedly clever and creative, yet we are also foolhardy and unwise. In a way we are, up to or beyond late adulthood, like boisterous children, headstrong, selfish, and demanding. The massive human brain, where knowledge is brewed up like quorn or dough, seems fundamentally out of touch with biological reality. It is as if the spirit of humankind announces to itself that it, the wonderful human master of the world, will make its own rules and impose them on the rest of the biosphere, using the sceptre of knowledge to impose its will.

Important as species-survival may be to anyone who loves the human race, there is this deeper problem of our ingrained infantilism: we have not become mature, generally as a species, nor individually, in most cases. We don't seem to recognise this overriding problem of our species. For example, I recognise the priority need to become awake, another way of describing personal maturity, but I struggle to advance in that direction. In effect, I have plenty of knowledge about the existential horrors, yet I lack the ability to deal with them. More and more knowledge hasn't helped at all. There is another element involved, maybe several, perhaps many. The problem seems to be beyond knowledge. I think it may be a question of a psychic dysfunction, maybe lack of will, or perhaps just basically poor design of the human creature in the imperfect evolutionary process. All the other dozen or so human species have become extinct, and ours nearly expired at one stage in its short history. We are not necessarily doomed, but we don't have a charmed collective life. Is there a better bet than mere accumulation of knowledge to give us a chance to become whole and durable?

The Killing Species

Any audit of humankind's achievements with knowledge, would include our tendency to care for each other and for selected members of the plant and animal kingdoms. There is compassion and kindness built into our knowledge-systems. We are not the only species to display kind behaviour, but it is widespread and deeply rooted in us. What, therefore, has gone wrong? Why do we so often break out into maniacal butchery? As mentioned above, we stay childish throughout life, which must account for some of our love of murder, because children can kill without realising their criminality. They are swayed as easily by hatred as by love, presumably. And maybe we never lose the childhood mind-set.

Yet there seems more to it than petulance. Murder on a vast, or tiny, scale must be influenced by beliefs about past and future, often embellished by folklore or social mores. Killing is frequently a stratagem for gain, obviously. But the aim can be hard to define. Why, exactly, did the Crusades happen? Why did Hitler, Stalin, Pol Pot, Churchill, Truman, and countless kings and aristocrats, deliberately kill millions of other humans? What was the knowledge motive in these atrocities.

Is it, implicitly, the satanic marriage between power-lust and defensive grandiosity, sanctified by an absolute belief that death is an unanswerable argument. Such massacres are usually in the name of a god, a creed, a dogma, a philosophy, or a superstition. Nothing and no-one is safe when these apocalyptic riders pound the landscape.

The psychiatric explanation ought to be convincing. After all, this appetite for killing is a symptom of disease or it means nothing. Admittedly, knowledge being what it is, there may just not be an explanation. Yet the condition known as schizophrenia, muddled though it may be, does indicate endogenous dysfunction. In non-human animals these tendencies to harm the other members of the species, i.e. results of the biological development mistakes, will tend to be bred out as the individuals will fail to breed for one reason or another. But humans do not quite obey that rule. It seems bizarre, but apparently leaders of industry tend to be psychopathic while psychopathic tendencies are welcomed in the armed forces (and who knows where else?). Interestingly a science-based survey of soldiers in the field was reported to have shown that some 70% of men deliberately missed when firing at the enemy. Only the psychopaths could be relied upon for a kill. Subsequent training-programs were allegedly adjusted to correct this error of behaviour.

Observation and Deduction

Our species is much given to curiosity, travel, documentaries, dramas, spectacles, rituals, and parades. We are an observing animal, rather akin to our dogs and cats in needing to explore the world. What do we make of it? How do we get into fixed habits of viewing, in which certain kinds of event or activity become addictive?

Maybe we can't resist football or crime dramas. Soaps and sagas enthral millions of us. History is a rich vein for the keen mining engineer, never mind that it has its bunkum-ish aspect. We particularly like to watch celebrities, a curious animal species if ever there was one, and most of us watch television news, apparently unaware of how much we are being manipulated. And a surprisingly large number of human animals like to watch non-human animals.

All of this observation must coagulate into specific mind-sets. Fashions of knowledge change with what is presented and how it is shown. A true republican must feel extreme nausea at the way royalty is presented, as if it were sacred or infinitely precious according to some weird alchemy. Not liking sport is a formula for endless irritation. Interest in politics is assumed but the actuality of politicians dismays. Even if one has a basic yearning for the spiritual, the antics of clerics invite derision or contempt. For the 'believers', promises of heaven are irresistible, however ludicrous. It is as if we live in a gigantic knowledge factory, making a vast array of products, some of which we casually, eagerly, or reluctantly, consume, with no possible understanding of what the diet is doing to us. Somehow, I can't perceive that human behaviour is enhanced by most of which is observed. I am mildly addicted to high quality crime dramas, for example, yet even the best leave me sad and bereft at some level of my being. It is partly the fact that I am foolish enough to watch them, that my life is empty enough to bother with them. But I have to do something to get off the treadmill of work and responsibility, so why not 'Wallander'?

History and Natural History

This is an interesting comparison of what might seem similar searches for knowledge.

Edward Gibbon and Gilbert White, almost exact contemporaries in the 18th century, covered between them the immense subject of behaviour: human-historical and animal-biological. But they were exceptional men. Most naturalists and most historians are pretty average, and it is better not to be too transfixed by their observations. But much of our knowledge-spectrum depends on such people. Is that wise?

History: does historical knowledge have any value? Why would the world of Henry VIII, even when dramatised in novels, make any difference to my state of being? Or, more importantly, *how* would it make any difference? Well, of course, all past events *affect* the present, a fact that gives history a value up to a point. But there are great contra-indications which somehow fail to put a limit on how much credit we give to the knowledge of the past.

The question of accuracy is obvious. No history can be accurate. An event in the immediate present is hard enough to describe with any degree of precision, however hard we try and however much evidence is sifted and whatever the investigative skills applied. Even harder is the attempt to discover causes. The further we go back, the greater the delusional or mythical content. We simply cannot trust the past, even our own supposed memory of happenings in our own lives.

Then there is the problem of how we should react. The two horrible wars of the last century still give us interpretational difficulty. The wide range of films and documentaries leave everything open to different understandings. Two historians recently clashed on whether it was right to go to war in these conflicts. Did America and Britain sacrifice so many men to fight Germany in the Normandy invasion so as to liberate France, or were they squaring up to the threat of Soviet expansionism? Was it a good thing for the world that Alexander the Great died before he could invade everywhere? Was it a disaster that Emperor Constantine decreed Christianity as the correct religion? Are we grateful as a species because Islam was established? Did the crusades achieve spiritual evolution? Are we British glad, after everything, to have basically German monarchs?

My point is that while history may be an amusing parlour game for aficionados, it is fairly useless as a guide to present human behaviour. Just as old buildings and ruined castles are probably charming to some, what use are they in giving us clues to becoming more civilised before it is too late?

Natural History

I prefer biology, the science of life, but natural history has the virtue of being beyond the laboratory, at least speaking metaphorically. In principle, natural history is an outdoor activity. But to be taken seriously as a form of knowledge, it would not be enough to be merely a bird-watcher, a butterfly-collector, or an admirer of wild plants. Two kinds of naturalists, then? The first kind is just a person who likes being 'out in nature'. The second kind is a searcher after new knowledge about our fellow organisms. These are different kinds of pleasure, too.

There are several things that can be said about naturalists in general. At least they look at and think about the biosphere that they occupy along with the plants and creatures they observe. But this does not necessarily mean that they are open to enlightenment of the spirit, in a poetic way, or to activism in protecting the natural environment. On the other hand, they do not have to be blinkered sentimentalists, liking one creature and disliking another, as do some feeders of birds who object to squirrels joining the feast.

The main value of natural history must be that its objective is far less exploitative than most other human activities. We may, as naturalists, get pleasure from the pursuit, but we don't, in general, cause any harm. We may even help other life-forms to survive and enjoy their lives. On balance, I would expect that most naturalists have such an intention.

Biologists on the other hand are a mixed bunch. In the Gaussian curve of purpose, I guess rather a large percentage of the qualified biological scientists do actually exploit, or help to exploit, the living world. I was once a botanist working in the agricultural supplies industry, and I became sickened by the entire arena. Now, I observe as a naturalist and am even more despairing of the way human beings use the land and sea and living organisms. Biologists do not generally seem to take up arms against this outrage. I feel that this as a failure of nerve and intent on their part.

Still, as a knowledge-system, natural history is on the whole benign and helpful to the great continuity of life. Unfortunately, they do not have the battalions needed to stop the destruction of the planet.

Does Humankind Expect to Survive?

From these few considerations, the inference must be that human beings are not safe upon this earth, largely because of their own stupidity. If knowledge were piling up in a useful form to make us more rational, it might save us. But the kind of knowledge we collect, and the way we use it, is narrowly self-centred and unlikely to promote our survival anyway.

The most eccentric and useless investment in knowledge, albeit with rather a glamorous image, is astrophysics. I cannot imagine why scientists are allowed to squander millions upon research into black holes and dark matter, nor why we keep on hurling metal objects into space. The immense gamble on getting human feet onto the moon's surface seems to me to have been straight out of 'Gulliver's Travels' or 'Alice in Wonderland'.

Another area of research expenditure which seems a very ineffective knowledge-generator is in the drugs industry. This touches fundamentally on the issue of mortality and our freedom to live or die. Keeping old people alive is utterly pointless as well as fascist, given that most of we old ones would 'go happily into that good night' if we were allowed the choice. It would need a shift of the cultural centre of gravity, but it could be a real gain in terms of our being. Another connection to the knowledge-madness would be that the solution to billions of starving people requires that we actively reduce our population, rather than drain the planet even further of its dwindling resources to produce more human food.

We Can't Predict

There is no way of predicting the future and not even politicians and their professorial advisers have the magic eye that shows what will happen tomorrow or next year. The credulity of the public all over the world still allows leaders to send people to fight other people somewhere or other. There is widespread famine. Our own country has nuclear submarines, many countries now have nuclear bombs. The seas are dying. The rain-forests are being extirpated. The ice melts. There are infernos and floods.

Has bad knowledge caused this apocalypse? Or just our insane need for immortality?

Three
Original Sin

An Example of Absurd 'Knowledge'

How Weird is This? (From BBC site online) *'Original sin is an Augustine Christian doctrine that says that everyone is born sinful. This means that they are born with a built-in urge to do bad things and to disobey God. It is an important doctrine within the Roman Catholic Church. The concept of Original Sin was explained in depth by St Augustine and formalised as part of Roman Catholic doctrine by the Councils of Trent in the 16th Century.'*

Like all religious diktat, this is intentionally absolute knowledge. From one authority, too, though these absolute decrees do come in many forms and from all kinds of human groupings. This particular verdict on humankind, like the adamantine certainty of Luther and Calvin, leaves no autonomy for anyone except the very highly-placed ecclesiastics like themselves. Original Sin is inbuilt because Adam and Eve supposedly couldn't resist the Tree of Knowledge of Good and Evil. It is, in my view, a criminal belief. Augustine should be posthumously defrocked for it. And excommunicated. Not that I would regard that as much of a punishment

There is a massive mountain of argument and speculation about this Christian fixation. Jews and Muslims won't have anything to do with it. It seems endemic in Catholicism. But Protestants, variably, tend to fudge the subject.

Before looking at 'sin' as a form of knowledge that has consciously or unconsciously ruled Western life for centuries, it may be instructive to explore the controversy of this particular form of it. My reason for doing so is that the 'original sin' fantasy is an alarming example of how knowledge can be insane and yet exert massive power. It shows how pseudoknowledge has ruled, and still rules, the world.

Here is a brief synopsis of alleged authoritative views on the subject:

God's reason for including the Tree of Knowledge (of good and evil) amongst the plants in Eden was to test whether Adam would choose to obey His instruction not to eat from it.

God told Adam that if he did eat from that tree he would definitely die.

God gave Adam (and Eve) the choice so that they would be free beings.

There was nothing actually wrong, i.e. evil, about the tree or its fruit and there is no likelihood that eating from it would have added to Adam's knowledge.

The act of disobedience was the whole point.

But it did give extra knowledge because the human couple perceived evil for the first time, so the sin of disobedience caused the world to fill with sin.

Why did God allow Adam and Eve to be tempted by the Devil? Because they had to make a choice. This was God's will.

It was this mistake, the disobedience, that made the world become horrible - sin, suffering, death, strife, sickness, etc.

The worst thing was that now every human would be born full of sin.

The worst long-term result was that God would have to kill his own son so that people could be made innocent - if they worshipped the dead son of God.

It is quite a story, even told simply in ten sentences.

The picture is one of madness. And if the perpetrators of the story were unaware of what an insane monster their god was, then I can only conclude that schizophrenia ruled in clerical writing circles. I made a poem out of the story, as if the Abrahamic deity were telling it - to his therapist, perhaps. The poem, satirical in intent, shows clearly that the entire basis for the biblical story (of the creation of original sin, particularly) is sheer megalomaniacal paranoia.

It is as if we have come across the material of a deranged stand-up comedian and that he turns out to have forgotten that everything he is and does is fictional. He no longer realises that he is merely an entertainer. But how is it that this nonsense, through the last two millennia, has become a worldwide cult. It makes no sense, unless the human mind is a lot more pathological than psychiatry has begun to realise. Can we really be so crazy/stupid as to believe this? If there were a deity, this would be an insult to him.

Patient J's Commandment

First I grow myself a garden
Then make two people for it.
There is a snake, also the devil,
Balanced, naturally, by angels.
But trees are my speciality,
My secret nickname is Arborigod.
For the couple I have arranged
A Tree of Temptation, just for me
To see if they will or won't obey
My instructions; I made them free
To eat the fruit of Good and Evil.
My will is absolute, I say, but they
Must be autonomous to do as I say.

THE TREE OF INNOCENCE

There's actually nothing special on it,
Eating from it would have no effect
Upon their knowledge. It is just a way
Of testing their obedience, I need
To know I am supreme, that I rule
In their hearts and minds, a divine will.
But they eat the fruit, and so see sin.

That's it, I say, I am divinely enraged.
I punish everybody, for ever and ever,
I fill the world with everlasting sin. I make
Their children and their children's children
Suffer sickness, madness, death, terror,
And everything horrible till the end of time.
So ask me why I let the Devil tempt them.
I had to, by my will they had to choose,
Not my fault they chose wrong. I'm God.
After all. I must have my way. Otherwise
I might appear too weak. And I'm strong.
My only regret is that my son had to pay
For Adam's arrogance, a sacrifice too far,
But I had to protect my reputation, give
A little, as we say, in heavenly circles.
The masses on earth can be redeemed
By the glorious crucifixion, what an icon!
Yes, indeed, but it makes me wonder if,
Given the sin in human nature, if my lad
Hasn't got too popular, it makes me mad.

Other Edens?

Interestingly, I understand that a cylinder seal, from post-Akkadian Mesopotamia, dated over two millennia *before* the alleged birth of Jesus, has some linkage with the Adam and Eve tale. This seal, called the 'temptation seal', has two figures, male and female, seated on either side of a tree facing each other, holding out their hands for fruit from the tree. Behind them lurks a snake. This could mean that the 'fall' concept dates back to early Babylon. On the other hand, it can be argued that trees and fruit and couples and snakes were pretty common coinage in those times, so no connection with Adam and Eve should be assumed. But this seems naive. Surely the general tendency to think in these terms shows that humankind had been flirting with 'sin', or 'sex', as a supernatural matter in some sense, for at least four thousand years. There seems no reason why it should not have. Stags have been rutting for millions of years.

It implies that the whole Eden story is really based on sexual neurosis and maybe that the entire idea of sin is primarily erotic in origin. Food and killing may have obsessed our distant ancestors, but it is a fair bet that sexual behaviour would have carried the greatest emotional charge, as it still does today. Especially in terms of male guilt, dominance, and ownership of the female, over a range of physical needs, and it might be expected that gods would have been essential extras in the drama.

Gilgamesh

To the extent that historical 'knowledge' can claim any validity at all, the life of Gilgamesh seems to be bordering on 'fact'. It appears that he actually existed, a monarch of the city-state of Uruk, in Mesopotamia, nearly three thousand years B.C. He is purported to have been highly regarded, even adored, by his subjects, for his powers as warrior, builder, and judge. His city was near present-day Baghdad, it seems. How much of this is fact can only be guessed, but the importance of Gilgamesh to the present narrative is in his reputation, described in the wildest hyperbole, for being a great adventurer and sexual athlete. He had a friend, a wild man selected by the gods, Enkidu, who became Gilgamesh's beloved friend and co-adventurer. The story, on a number of tablets, is of a semi-divine being who searches for knowledge, immortality, and, no doubt, erotic conquest. It is perfect material for a modern television fantasy, and no doubt it fed a similar need in Mesopotamia five thousand years ago.

Enkidu, Gilgamesh's bosom friend (after a preliminary bloody battle) is particularly interesting, being a Caliban-like primitive man, covered in hair and living wild with animals. By obscure logic, he is expected to civilise Gilgamesh, having himself a set of sexual experiences designed to civilise him before he gets to Gilgamesh. He dies, leaving Gilgamesh distraught and starting out on a new journey to discover the meaning of life (and death).

As a footnote to these comments, there is also a cameo role for Gilgamesh, in which he cuts down the world tree and deals with Lilith (Babylonian demon Goddess) for the sake of Inanna (Goddess of Sexual Love), a tale that has prototypical relevance to the later story of Eve and the Tree of Knowledge.

Therefore

It seems clear that sin, including original sin, was not a primary concern in Mesopotamia, any more than it was in Judaic thinking two millennia later. Basically, the Christians invented sin, their superfluous contribution to the chaotic knowledge industry. The point is, that around the time that a Jewish subset discovered a new god, as dubious a contribution to knowledge as could be imagined, this idea was being trounced by a new religion of sin. Maybe the whole concept needs a fresh appraisal.

The Seven Deadly Sins

A typical summary of the subject is as follows:

*'The **Capital Vices** or **Cardinal Sins**, is a classification of vices that has been used since early Christian times to educate and instruct Christians concerning fallen humanity's tendency to sin. In the currently recognized version, the sins are usually given as wrath, avarice, sloth, pride, lust, envy, and gluttony. Each is a form of Idolatry-of-Self wherein the subjective reigns over the objective.*

The Catholic Church divides sin into two categories: Venial sins, in which guilt is relatively minor, and the more severe Mortal sins. According to the Catechism of the Catholic Church, a mortal or deadly sin is believed to destroy the life of grace and charity within a person and thus creates the threat of eternal damnation: "Mortal sin, by attacking the vital principle within us - that is, charity - necessitates a new initiative of God's mercy and a conversion of heart which is normally accomplished within the setting of the sacrament of reconciliation."'

What is the possible point of this ideology? All religions use doctrine and rules and ceremonies, of course, but the examination of knowledge is the main focus here, and the remarkable obsession with sin in Christianity does raise intriguing questions about why it became the pivot of knowledge in this complexity of cults.

Why Sin?

I mean, why this word, and what does it really mean? It's generally taken as, say, an immoral act, especially with reference to divine law: That indicates an offence against God and presumably humankind too. But it has a different meaning i.e. the original word, sin, doesn't indicate a wrongdoing so much as to miss, to be absent. It seems to occur in archery, too, where an arrow misses the 'golden centre'.

Wandering through the web, I discovered, for example, that the Hebrew root for the word means to miss and that it can be detected in some English words such as misuse, misconduct, or misunderstand.

The implication is that to miss means not to be there, doing something but not being truly present and that this is the only sin. Conversely, virtue would exist in doing something when fully alert, what George Gurdjieff called self-remembering, Buddha called being mindful, and Krishnamurti called awareness. If this were the 'official' meaning of sin, I would happily adopt it as a useful term.

There is an actual statement on an unidentifiable Facebook page as follows:

'The original Hebrew word for sin is very beautiful. By translating it as sin, Christians have missed the very message of Jesus. The original Hebrew word for sin is so totally different from your idea of sin that it will be a surprise to you.

The root word means forgetfulness; it has nothing to do with what you are doing. The whole thing is whether you are doing it with conscious being or out of unconsciousness. Are you doing it with a self-remembering or have you completely forgotten yourself?'

Statements attributed to 'Osho' expand on this theme:

'Any action of unconsciousness is sin. The action may look virtuous, but it cannot be. You may create a beautiful facade, a character, a certain virtuousness; you may speak the truth, you may avoid lies; you may try to be moral, and so on and so forth. But if all this is coming from unconsciousness, it is all sin.'

Hindus and Moslems have a fairly straightforward approach, in which sin is wrong action, bad behaviour. From the internet, again:

'In Hinduism, the term sin is often used to describe actions that create negative karma by violating moral and ethical codes, which automatically brings negative consequences. This is similar to Abrahamic sin in the sense that it is considered a crime against the laws of God, which is known as (1) Dharma, or moral order, and (2) one's own self, but another term apradha is used for grave offences.'

'Muslims see sin as anything that goes against the commands of Allah. Islam teaches that sin is an act and not a state of being. The Qur'an teaches that "the soul is certainly prone to evil, unless the Lord does bestow His Mercy" and that even the prophets do not absolve themselves of the blame. It is believed that Iblis (Satan) has a significant role in tempting humankind towards sin'.

So the word has an interesting and explicatory background. It is quite simple compared with some terms employed in theology. The word itself seems innocent enough and relatively unburdened with noxious baggage. The problem is, therefore, in the way the Christians have made it a weapon for scourging mankind, without even allowing that human behaviour can be changed and good can come forth freely if we will let it. Making it 'original' is a foul slander, and not allowing humankind to clean up its own act without a Deity's say-so, sets our existence in poisoned concrete.

Absent Sins

In that case, let us take them at their word, for sheer experimental purposes, and examine whether the Christian 'Fathers' have selected the right sins. At least we would then know what we were being damned for committing and be able to decide if we actually cared.

The existing septet are not very convincing nor well considered. Looking at them one by one:

1. **Wrath**. Considering the uncontrollable rage exhibited by the God of Eden who condemned us all to an agonising existence, it is surprising to find this emotion amongst the vices. So God is guilty of one of the deadly sins? Do the Christians really mean that? Or is wrath actually a virtue in a god? To say the least, we have a deep hypocrisy here. I think, in the circumstances, that a new vice is appropriate and one more applicable to godly behaviour: **Cruelty. (Torture and Bullying** are possible alternatives). As for mere anger, well there are situations where it is not inappropriate, but how the anger is 'managed' is very significant.

2. **Avarice.** Looking at the astonishing grandiosity of Catholic churches and especially the Vatican, I wonder where the dedication to simplicity and humility went. How could such a richly embellished regime seriously call a desire for riches sinful? It is no doubt true that striving for wealth in a world containing so much poverty and hunger (and more to come, no doubt) is deeply sinful, unless it is given away. Our own royal family and many aristocrats are as avaricious as can be. Damnation is due to them, accordingly. Is there a sin, however, that looks more toxic than a desire for riches? How about hypocrisy? This must be a dangerous temptation to all pretentious people, whether clerics or marketing managers. So, **Hypocrisy**, then. This could apply to people claiming to be poor, but actually busy accumulating some kind of wealth differentially, i.e. gaining advantage by pretence. Somehow, also, the word **Greed** comes into focus, not in the sense of gluttony, but a more vicious thing altogether, usually with a connotation such as **Power**, a drive to be greater than others.

Sloth. Not a sin at all, in my view. What's wrong with idleness? I am more disturbed by the idea of **activism**, a weakness I'd plead guilty to, as I am not lazy. **Busyness** is the word, meaning useless over-activity. Definitely a sin, I suggest.

Pride. Why was this seen as a sin? It is truly a sin only if it means **self-importance**, or even self-satisfaction. I would accept that these are sins, though they are 'normal' in our culture. More serious is the connotation of **arrogance** or hubris, horrible vices for sure. For all its dissembling, the Catholic religion is swollen with pride of this kind, just as I would accuse it of spiritual busyness.

Lust. A very odd one, in that lust merely denotes strong desire. The Catholic religion is swollen with the lust of religiousness and the desire to proselytise. So this Church wallows in its own sin. But presumably the word is intended as a sexual slur, as if total asexualty, abstinence, is perfection, and nasty sex can only be forgiven if it is over-populating the world. And what about pederasty in this Church? Lust is not a sin, therefore, but **rape, pederasty,** and **pornography** are all certainly sins, if anything is certain in our rather depraved culture. **Overpopulation** is perhaps our worst sin, encouraged by the Catholic Church.

Envy. This seems more of an affliction than a sin. I guess that the church fathers picked on this partly because it links with lust and avarice, as they define these behaviours. I think it would be more creative if the sin relating to envy were behaviours activated by it, such as **Homicide, Theft,** or, say, **Gambling** (as an attempt to get rich quick).

Gluttony. Again, more of a disease than a sin. Our culture is now defined by obesity, but also by assumptions that we should have a lot of everything we want, money, possessions, fame, sex, holidays, self-esteem. Gluttony, maybe better called **Greed,** is truly a very bad behaviour. But it is curious that in a religion obsessed by its god's insistence on *original* sin, the greed for absolute power shown by that god, and its chief clerics, is also its most obvious sin. It can probably be explained by transfer psychology.

As a general proposition, without going through the tedious process of drawing up a new list, it is clear that the seven deadly sins is a creed low in intelligence and usefulness. It should be abandoned altogether, along with the theology fertilising it, and be replaced by a radical schema for improved behaviour of our species, perhaps starting with the Christians. There is big scope for improvement

An Original Mistake

Certainly as far as so-called Christendom is concerned, but perhaps at least implicit in the other Abrahamic paradigms of Judaism and Islam, therefore applying to the mind-set of at least half the human world, there is an assumption that the human creature itself is well-conceived and well-constructed. It is, so to say, 'God's work'. The crux of the story is that humankind, having rather more freedom than it can handle, underperforms relative to the design-criteria, making it a 'fallen being', with an irresistible longing to behave badly.

Buddhists, Taoists, and Atheists, while not subscribing to the weird ideas of the Abrahamics, also tend to the view that humankind needs to live up to its glorious destiny one way or another, in other words, the undoubtedly clever human should shape up and become its full magnificent self.

In all these very diverse notions there is a deep perception that we, the human species, are failing to become what we could become, that is, we are not yet living up to our true potential. In the mind of the scientist, too, is the notion that evolution has taken the trouble to produce its crowning miracle but that it is still only a prototype.

I do not believe a word of any of this. Far from being guilty of some original sin, a wilful disregard of our beautiful destiny, I see human beings as very poorly designed animals in terms of their basic survival-potential, rather as if the amateur process of evolutionary development, in our case, had gone viral regardless of its actual value. It is eerily similar to the story of Dr Frankenstein, in which he, the 'creator', made a sad monster.

In the concept of original sin, who is to blame? Is it God the Frankenstein, deliberately booby-trapping his creation by giving it some free will, or the mindless experimenter, Professor Evolution, or even the poor creature itself, lost in self-regarding solipsism? It is a rhetorical question, as we do not have the knowledge to answer it. But it is a dangerous reality, perhaps the worst that has happened so far in the living world. And if we don't have the wit and will to fix it, and the omens are dismal, then we and our fellow organisms, will just have to suffer.

Four
Revisiting Intelligence

As in the case of the pelican and the proverbial mismatch between its belly capacity and its overdeveloped beak, the human mind has always suffered from the fact that its ambition and expectation far exceed its actual equipment. But whatever the pelican may feel about its dilemma, we humans seem unable to acknowledge that a similar but hugely greater imbalance exists in us. It is still not understood, apparently, that our thinking-equipment falls immensely short of our ambition to know and understand. We are very limited. In our arrogance we assume that we, some day if not immediately, can know all that there is to be known.

Neither theologians nor scientists seem able to grasp that our consciousness, the mysterious non-material essence of our existence, may actually be no more than an evolved function of our biology. There would be disagreement about this, because some, maybe most, people think our mental powers come from somewhere other than our own biological evolution. Ironically, this goes to the heart of the Knowledge-Question.

If the process of evolution is accepted as valid knowledge, then mind is an evolved function. But the thousands of biologists and geneticists would be obliged by the 'facts' of their science to admit that mind (consciousness, awareness, etc) is part of the biological phenotype known as human. In that case, no-one can expect the human mind, in principle, to function any differently from that of any other vertebrate mind, or indeed any mind at all. It has no overriding supremacy whatever. So *everything* it thinks could be as subject to error as are all biological systems.

Suppose, however, that credence is given to the doctrine that consciousness is supernatural, i.e. produced by 'God' or 'The Universe', and therefore additional to living bodies/brains, or even that there is a floating cloud of consciouness, invisible and unmeasurable, which enters our minds and feeds it with knowledge, then it might well be deemed perfect, or absolute, (though not necessarily ideal for human consumption).

In effect, this non-evolutional consciousness would be completely beyond human powers of measurement, and no human could claim to understand the program. On the other hand, we humans have the same problems as any other creature, so we could, if we wished, feel solidarity with life in general, and maybe especially with one another. We are, as it were, all in the same ark. And it is an inherently democratic tub.

Trusting In Knowledge

Our knowledge systems, according to the evolutionary view, have no inbuilt guarantee of ultimate realisation. We are extremely unlikely to 'understand' the universe before we become extinct - as all species do, sooner or later. However, since our dawn, we have recklessly assumed that we are on earth for some purpose and that part of that purpose is to understand, to *know,* everything. We go on assuming that, as the crowning glory of creation/evolution, humankind inherits the right to conceptualise itself and everything around it. This is our crowning folly. Yet, within the limits of our inbuilt insanity, there have been attempts to focus on what we *can* achieve, at least in theory, which is to become happy and well-behaved.

In my book,'Creatures of Power', 2013, I have suggested that we think of progress in different terms from those generally applied in the Western culture, in that we take head-on the challenge of inefficient evolution. It may be granted that, left to itself, evolution has made rather a mess of the human species i.e. it has given us a brilliant brain and left it to us to understand our mental limitations. Consequently, our Tower of Babel style of knowledge leads us into disaster after disaster. I argued, therefore, that we should take hold of the evolutionary process and shake some sense into it. This would emphatically not be any form of eugenics, nor fiddling with the genes, because we could never know enough to make a good job of either.

Guided Evolution

The fact is pretty indisputable that a species does best when it is in tune with its environment. Unfortunately, humankind is rather inept at this process. We seek to change our environment by crude devices that usually turn out for the worst. But there is another way of approaching the environmental challenge. We could do a much better job of adapting to it. This would entail colossal changes in our individual and collective behaviour. Yet we haven't changed much in 50,000 years - bigger and 'better' tools and weapons and devices and methodologies, of course - but our behaviour is terrible in terms of intelligence and loving kindness. I feel sure that the basic error is the way we regard and use knowledge, as if it is a tool of progress. Well it can be, but it works better on means than on ends. It has been a powerful inventor of tools and weapons, the 'means', but is an awful creator of purposes and aims, the 'ends'. Yet we still function as if the ends were more important than the means. This, if the ends are not good, is a recipe for an apocalypse - which is what we are heading into rather rapidly.

The reason for my hostility to all religious belief is that it is a knowledge system of purposes and aims. The knowledge enshrined in these doctrines is presumed to come into the human mind from a superior source and there's no arguing with it. But everyone does argue. We behave as if these doctrines actually mattered in the slightest. We still kill each other for disagreeing. If we could turn around the giant tanker of our absurd belief-structures and concentrate on the quality of the seamanship, then something good might happen. It would not be about going somewhere but would attend to the importance of each moment of the present time and place.

Education, for all its faults, is the best way we have discovered to improve on our behaviour. But it needs to be immensely better in operation and to discard all the shocking nonsense about ambition, competing, winning, and all the other future-oriented diversions. If education could move away from preparing for an unknowable future and focus, instead, upon a better moving moment, maybe we'd have a chance. This would be real guided evolution.

Early Efforts

Are there any historical precedents for guided evolution, i.e. development focused on behaviour and being? Clearly, the appalling theologies of sin, discussed in the previous chapter, point in the opposite direction, in that human behaviour is dismissed as inherently criminal. Before Christianity, aided by Roman Imperialism, pushed the centre of spiritual gravity towards guilt and fantasy, some older philosophies were promising. Stoicism, Epicureanism, Buddhism, Taoism and Confucionism all made intelligent attempts to comprehend existence in order to make it tolerable. There seemed to be a flowering of progressive spiritual movements around 500 BC and obviously included the Judaic ideas as well, though less happily. It is worth looking at the others to see if there were originally ways of being that did not entirely capitulate to god-obsession and its inherently infantile form of distorted knowledge. First there is the interesting case of Zoroastrianism, which, despite its god-obsessiveness, was apparently able to contemplate an evil as well as a good cosmic power and provided a limited spiritual impulse to early attempts to achieve civilised existence.

Zoroastrianism

Unfortunately, the enormous influence of Zoroastrianism included the idea, concreted into a falsely certain knowledge, that the overall creator, Ahura Mazda, (the Great God of Wisdom and Light,) was all good, with no evil originating from him. Animistic and polytheistic religions, for all their crude naivety, had at least the wisdom of recognising that supernatural forces could be malign. But, in the Zoroastrian system, good and evil have distinct and separate sources, with 'evil' trying to destroy the creation of Mazda and 'good' trying to sustain it.

There was some sense in this, as it did recognise the reality of life as a mixture of the agreeable and the disagreeable, as a pot-pourri of pain and pleasure from the human perspective. As knowledge, although it was inherently suspect, it was nevertheless congruent with the apparent facts of nature. But, as religions do, it diversified into a vast fantasy of absolute nonsense, or at least knowledge totally without foundation. Even the language evades comprehension, possibly because language does that when it lacks basic rationality, or when translation and metaphor get entangled.

There was also the probability that, while Zoroastrianism appeared as late as 600 BC, it had already a long history as a very early Iranian religion, perhaps as far back as Gilgamesh. Between the polytheistic culture of 4 or 5 millennia ago and the naming of Zoroastrianism 600 years BC, the religious ferment in the Middle East became formidably complex and potentially disastrous for mankind.

This was the time when perverted knowledge-systems took over human life in a tsunami of sophisticated yet wild thinking. For example, the story was put about that Ahura Mazda was not, either apparently or allegedly, immanent in the world. What does that mean? Is it the first inkling of the existence of 'heaven'? Has God any substance at all? Is God pure consciousness? Is He without any (human) feelings? It is not easy to find answers to these questions. Even if they are thought to matter a jot.

Alleged History

Here is one version of the conventional wisdom, i.e. pseudoknowledge found in current literature: '*Ahura Mazda was represented by the so-called 'Amesha Spentas' (bounteous immortals and divinities) and the host of other 'Yazatas' (gods, goddesses, angels), through whom the works of God are evident to humanity, and through whom worship of Mazda is ultimately directed. The most important texts of the religion are said to have been lost and only the liturgies have survived. The lost portions are known of only through references and brief quotations in the later works, primarily from the 9th to 11th centuries.*

In some form, Zoroastrianism, served as the national or state religion of a significant portion of the Iranian people for centuries. The religion first dwindled when the huge Achaemenid (Persian) Empire was invaded by Alexander the Great, after which it collapsed and disintegrated and it was further gradually marginalized by Islam from the 7th century onwards with the decline of the Sassanid Empire. However, the political power of the pre-Islamic Iranian dynasties gave Zoroastrianism immense prestige in ancient times, and much of its leading doctrine was modified and adopted by other religious systems.'

Hence, the God-idea was, quite quickly, all too firmly implanted in the minds of Middle Eastern humankind. The best that can be said of it is that this ancient cult at least contained the acceptance that the divine was a mixed bag, as it was, for example, in the Greek Olympian dynasty. The conceit that 'God' was good and perfect was already embedded, but He was not all-powerful and His 'works' were liable to damage from the 'evil' source. This uneasy logic has persisted, of course, in the Abrahamic cults in the form of the god/devil theory. On the other hand, the actual notion of two Gods, one good and one bad, was squashed as heretical before it could be developed and analysed theologically or intelligently. And so it has remained for nearly three millennia without being seriously questioned for its sense or its relevance, i.e. a conviction without any foundation except, perhaps, the coincidental human hierarchy beloved of all earthly tribes and their passionate need for power.

Maybe it was an inevitable idea for the early Jews to pick all this up and hand on to Christianity. There was obviously a serious theological muddle around the idea of the perfect god, as Ahura Mazda was regarded. Zoroaster raised the ante considerably by stressing the power of the bad spirit, Angra Mainyu, who opposed Ahura Mazda. What with this polarity, and the spirits and presences considered to aid and abet the adversaries, the scene was set for a supernatural replica of human power-politics, and in a sense, was a justification for terrestrial conflict such as we still suffer today.

Ancient Greece and Egypt are interesting cases. There was no shortage of hard thinking in Greece, and the Olympic dozen gods never quite took over as overwhelming powers, while Egypt seems to have wandered through history resolutely polytheistic, even animistic, and it still seems unsure of itself as a monotheistic state. The Far East went its own way, too, and provides today a welcome antidote to smothering Christianity.

The point being made in this chapter is that religion is a perversion of our human intelligence. If knowledge was ever destined to play a critical role in our species, it should have sloughed off mumbo-jumbo much earlier than now. But it still goes on. We are even adding to the religious freakery. Can we not learn anything from our own absurdity? I am not saying that we shouldn't have sacredness in our lives, quite the opposite; my horror is in the mountains of invention that still dominate all our lives directly or indirectly.

The killer-question, however, is very simple and hard to refute by any knowledge-system. It is common-sense, i.e. obvious. Why do human beings ignore the fact that there are so many different religions and a plethora of different deities? Surely only one of the theologies can be right and only one god can be genuine? Do we assume that most gods and religions are actually false? Does each sect consider itself the only true faith? If so, no wonder we do so much killing of each other. However determined a Catholic might be to tolerate a Muslim, he must be sure that the Muslim is a perfidious heathen. And, of course, the same applies vice versa. There cannot be religious tolerance in a world in which only one god is genuine, surely?

As a more or less neutral observer, I would favour the universal acceptance that religion was just a personal and individual fad. In fact, I think that is quite a good idea. One's religion would have similar importance to a fingerprint, a meaningless bit of identity. And each of us could be content in our private and personal fantasy. Yes?

Stoicism

Although also contaminated, and therefore vitiated, by the concept of an overall great divinity, Stoicism tried a different tack that could and, arguably, should have been better-developed. Humankind had long been habitually attracted by ideas of cosmic significance, which may be all very well left inchoate in an inchoate universe, but the animism arising in our ancient imagination has never died away and in some ways has become more prevalent. We are such *personalisers*, unable to leave anything unnamed and merely fascinating: we just have to know and know that we know. What a burden that is on a half-developed mind, the only thinking apparatus we've got, and how badly it lets us down by pushing us into megalomania, wars, waste, pollution, and ultimately insanity.

Stoics, to some extent, tried to call a halt to this absurd extravaganza. They taught that destructive emotions resulted from errors in judgment, and that a person of 'moral and intellectual perfection,' would not suffer such emotions. Stoics were concerned with the active relationship between cosmic determinism and human freedom, and the belief that it is virtuous to maintain a will that is in accord with nature. Because of this, the Stoics presented their philosophy as a way of life, and they thought that the best indication of an individual's philosophy was not what a person said but how they behaved. From its founding, Stoic doctrine was popular with a following in Greece and throughout the Roman Empire - including the Emperor Marcus Aurelius - until the closing of all pagan philosophy schools in 529 AD by order of the Emperor Justinian I, who perceived their pagan character as offensive to the Christian faith.

If that had not happened, the last two thousand years might have been very different. By elevating human ego into empyrean heights, humanity lost control of its own destiny and created alibis and pretexts for its multitude of crimes (misnamed as sins). Jesus was, in reality, an appalling error of invention (though a common enough trope in the various sacrifice-myths current in the early centuries, e.g. Osiris, Tammuz, Dionysos, Isaac and Adonis) because it shifted responsibility for and control of human behaviour into a kind of celestial nursery with supernatural carers, teachers, doctors, and, indeed, family members. Thus, human beings have never actually grown up, nor become fully awake.

Epicureanism

My all-time favourite non-religion founded by a most remarkable man. Epicurus was a key figure in the Axial Age, the period from 800 BC to 200 BC, during which similar thinking appeared in China, India, Iran, the Near East, and Ancient Greece. He established 'The Garden', his school, in Athens in the third century BC. He worked there for some thirty years until his death. Of the hundreds of his written works little has remained in existence but, fortunately, his philosophy survived in the activity of his followers and other writers. There is enough, for me at any rate, to give a picture of a highly developed and perceptive man. There are two key words in Epicurus's teaching: ataraxia and aponia.

Ataraxia, a form of consciousness, is experienced as freedom from mental agitation. It was strongly emphasised in Greek schools of philosophy, and was practised by Stoics and Sceptics as well as Epicureans, though with slightly different interpretation. *Ataraxia* means NOT being confused, disturbed, agitated, roiled, muddied or darkened; qualities which unfortunately characterize much of our waking consciousness. Ataraxia is often interpreted as passivity and quiet contemplation, but it can also be experienced during activity; this is action which is both internally and externally harmonized. The problem is not passion, however, as passion is a natural phenomenon. It is, rather, the false beliefs which arise from or distort passion. It's the false beliefs that need to be extirpated and then joy may be released into our existence.

As I understand it, the principle here is to live life deliberately free from agitation of any kind. At first sight this may seem impossibly 'glad-gameish', the territory of Mary Poppins perhaps. But I suspect that Epicurus was after much bigger fish than the minnow of 'always seeing the bright side'. I think he was pursuing existential truth, seeing the universe in real terms, and being determined not to enter into false connivance with mad mother nature. He surely knew she was not to be trusted.

Aponia, the other key word, meant that freedom from pain was the greatest physical bliss. Implicitly, however, this put a limit on the concept of happiness. In other words, if freedom from pain was the zenith, then there was no point in looking for anything higher. At the same time the supremacy of happiness was confirmed. This gives a new clarity to the idea of happiness, often an extremely woolly concept. If you are not in pain you are happy. Or, more searchingly, if you do not desire the elimination of a pain, you are happy.

These two words were key but not apparently exclusively so, because friendship was mightily prized in Epicurus's philosophy. He also perceived finiteness in existence as well as an atomic structure of matter. This put limits on human hubris and narcissism: pain and pleasure, by definition, were equivalent to good and evil, respectively. Death was the end of both the body and the soul, thus obviating a multitude of fancies about 'after-life' or 'past lives'. He didn't rate deity too much, either, regarding gods as superfluous to human existence and vice versa. His atomic theory was a recognition of the underlying similarity of all things in the world and an acceptance that individuality was a conceit rather that a foundational fact.

On the matter of his own death, Epicurus was both matter-of-fact and yet sublime. At 72 years of age, in 270 BC, his chronic kidney-stone illness killed him but he wrote to his friend, Idomineneus, the following famous letter:

> *'I have written this letter to you on a happy day to me, which is also the last day of my life. For I have been attacked by a painful inability to urinate, and also dysentery, so violent that nothing can be added to the violence of my sufferings. But the cheerfulness of my mind, which comes from the recollection of all my philosophical contemplation, counterbalances all these afflictions.'*

I suppose that this cast of mind, this 'philosophy', is more or less where I have finished up in my life and in my awareness. Epicureanism, correctly defined, contains everything that makes sense to me and excludes all that doesn't. It is the embodiment of awakeness, it recognises the Void and it focuses on the great continuity of existence. But it might fairly be asked, how does it make life happier and more satisfying?

I find it helpful to visualise Epicurus's School, in his garden, where his small coterie met and examined their existence and its values. His friends were, apparently, hand-picked as personally congenial and his school was the first to admit women without restriction. Slaves were also welcome. Seneca characterised the School's ethos as: 'Stranger, here you will do well to tarry; here our highest good is pleasure'.

Less readily, I respond to the fact that Epicurus found it necessary to operate a hierarchical system in his followers, and had them swear an oath on core tenets. But people do not function too well in complete anarchy, so maybe this was not such a bad idea. We have not solved this problem ourselves, and our 21st century world is riven by exactly the diverse effect of varying opinion that Epicurus tried to control. It is probably an insoluble, even artificial, problem, in that the human mind obviously did not evolve, nor aims teleologically, for tranquillity.

Epicurus was a leader, too, in the development of science and scientific methodology. He insisted that nothing should be believed, except that which was tested through direct observation and logical deduction. As we have seen in the centuries since his time, this is a good principle but easier said than done. His Ethic of Reciprocity did, however, have the laudable aim of minimalising harm to oneself and others as the way to maximize happiness.

As an atomist, Epicurus reasoned that the fundamental constituents of the world were indivisible little bits of matter (atoms, Greek atomos, indivisible) flying through empty space (kenos), and that everything is the result of the atoms colliding, rebounding, and becoming entangled with one another, with no purpose or plan behind their motions.

Looking further at Epicurus's attitude to 'gods', while he was a pioneer in breaking from the god-fearing and god-worshipping tradition common at the time, he blandly allowed that religious activities might be useful as a way of imagining gods as examples of the pleasant life, while avoiding false opinions about gods, such as ascribing qualities that are alien to immortality and blessedness. He seems to have suggested that the gods do not punish the bad and reward the good as the common man believed, but, in reality, did not concern themselves at all with human beings.

Greek Fantasies

In passing, it is worth noting that the intelligent and practical philosophy of Epicurus and of the rather less rational Stoics, co-existed with the foolish cult of Olympian gods and the pure madness of the Eleusinian 'mysteries' that are said to have thrived for two millennia. In the book 'Mystikos' I refer to my own mystical experiences, which occur spontaneously and seem to connect to a similar 'mystery' consciousness as the Eleusinian experience, though without the psychedelic drugs. I have argued that mystical experiences have no essential dependence on, nor even relevance to, theistic religions, though the tendency to be mystical in humans may be pillaged by religious power-seekers.

This is probably the key area in human 'spiritual' consciousness and the all-important concept of Awakeness. As I have said, there is no possibility of the human mind gaining complete, or even reliable, knowledge about the universe, about anything at all in fact. Somehow, we have to manage as best we can, like any other animal, in our environment. It seems that this environment is permeated by consciousness and that rationality and imagination and fantasy are all functions of that consciousness.

The most important practical consideration is in the comparison between individual and collective behaviours. The attempts to make human beings behave collectively have been catastrophic for thousands of years and are not noticeably improving.

We are still as bad as those ancient Greeks in our public life and in our smaller family collectives. It seems to me unlikely that we, as a species, will ever achieve the peaceful, intelligent and helpful ideal of living together. Therefore, we have to accept that we are isolated, mortal, free, and without meaning, as the Existentialists insist, and find individual states of being that are congenial and worthwhile, with the help of similarly motivated friends. In other words, we should follow the precepts of Epicurus. The paradox in my own life of being simultaneously rational *and* emotional, sceptical *and* mystical, has just to be lived through and made as creatively amiable as possible without any absolute knowledge or belief.

Buddhism and Taoism

In principle, the ancient spiritual philosophies of the Orient mirror those of the West. I understand their doctrines better than the Western practices, but I can see the same kind of spectrum, stretching from religions such as, say, Hinduism and Shinto right across to more or less godless spiritual theories, typically Buddhism and Taoism. Confucianism is particularly interesting as it seems to have been a practical code of civilised behaviour, without any religious doctrine or mystical overtones, and which could be called 'Humanism'.

Unfortunately, the rather lacklustre Western Humanism hardly measures up the Eastern models, in which Buddhist, Taoist, and Confucianist teachings and practices were fundamentally secular, ethical, and initially, at least, agreeably free from gods. My personal preference is for Taoism. I find Buddhism tainted by both power and fantasy, though the vast array of different forms does include some wonderfully clear concepts of how a human creature might live and overcome suffering.

As with the early Greek practices, however, the collective does not adequately mirror the individual. I mean that neither Buddhism nor Taoism have, in the thousands of years of operation, perfected human society. They 'work' individually, to a considerable extent, but the mass of humanity goes on behaving badly. And Buddhist communities can be as violent to non-Buddhists as Christians are to Islamic communities or vice-versa. Perhaps the most poignant example of collective religious failure was in the disastrous Crusade campaigns, as in modern ethnic conflicts, where the devotees of one god slaughter the devotees of another god. This is behaviour that does not improve with time. The absence of such improvement makes human survival very questionable, especially when the other global errors are logged in.

Nevertheless, an individual human may find some help in living a worthwhile existence by paying attention to some aspects of philosophies such as that of Epicurus or the psychotherapy inherent in Existentialism. What he cannot get is absolute, or even reliable, knowledge about anything, especially the future. As I shall try to explain in the following chapter, this situation is actually much more satisfactory than it may appear. It does, however, require some radical personal adjustment. More than this, it requires all the intelligence we can muster.

Five
Into The Unknowable

Getting Real

What does reality mean? There is an assumption in the human mind, apparently, that there is somehow, or somewhere, a state which is special and different from ordinary existence: it is where **reality** exists, a place or position in which truth is firmly and undeniably established. Evidently, it is also the environment of knowledge, allegedly, as it would be inconceivable to have knowledge that is unreal, or reality which is false knowledge. Reality, truth, and knowledge form the essential trinity of human consciousness, far superior to, say, father-son-holy ghost, which is not an acceptable trio to vast numbers of people.

Yet these two triple partnerships are hypothetical, mythical, and impractical. The religious trinity is by no means obligatory. Many people manage their lives without it, or its constituents, though I, as a general non-believer, have a sneaking regard for the Holy Spirit. It is something I sometimes think I know in some way, maybe, possibly.

Reality, truth and knowledge are more of a comedy act, three loveable rogues, a trio of tricksters in the human psyche. They belong to the class of words called tropes. They are that most enjoyable of entities known as metaphors. A metaphor is otherwise defined as, say, *'a figure of speech which makes an implicit, implied or hidden comparison between two things or objects that are poles apart from each other but have some characteristics common between them. In other words, a resemblance of two contradictory or different objects is made based on a single or some common characteristics'.*

In this sense, the trio is also an internal metaphor, in that the three words are quite different yet tend to be used to mean the same thing. Is it possible to deconflate this amalgam? Probably not: metaphors are slippery fish. They swim in a fast-moving stream, too, so that they may have passed by in any direction, or may disappear altogether.

The unreliability of truth, knowledge, and reality wouldn't matter if we took them less seriously. But our need for them is overwhelming and so are the consequences of our misplaced faith. Wherever we look, their slipperiness causes dismay and confusion, even warfare and death.

Past Confusion

The metaphors do not wear well over time. How can we possibly know anything for sure about past events? We use photographs, tapes, cctv, written testimony, eye-witness accounts, science, art, poetry, tradition, historicity, anything at all that might tell us what happened, when and how, and why; yet uncertainty still prevails. And the further back we try to peer, the foggier it gets.

The pity of it is that if we weren't desperate for certainty, the past could be entertaining, interesting and even informative in an oblique way. It would be worth something in the same way as art is worth something, or it could intrigue us as games do. But by trying to know for sure, seeking the complete truth, wanting reality, we create trouble for ourselves.

Something can be known about the past. There is a past reality of a sort, truth can be found there, but not in the ways we try to assert. Each of us has a past existence, some life happenings have occurred. We have been affected by them. It is most desirable to surrender to the knowledge that we have lived, and most undesirable to want to convert that knowledge into hard facts.

Genealogy fascinates many people, for example, and there is a need for information about our ancestors. Yet when we delve into the archives, even when we discover unexpected material, what have we actually achieved, apart from emotional effects? It is like the futile attempts to know the 'facts' about Jesus, Mohammed, or Gautama Buddha, though not necessarily so dramatic and world-shattering. Uncertainties and claims about such icons make us go to war with each other, hardly a useful result of semi-knowledge, partial reality, half-truth. And how could we 'know' how a parent felt or thought, except in stray bits of memory or from letters or possessions, inherently open to misinterpretation. At the most intimate level, how could I know how I felt or thought in every minute of yesterday?

The Moving Present

Much is made in spiritual philosophy of the concept of living in the 'now'. It is a seductive idea. Yet it doesn't mean what it says. It is impossible to live in the 'now' as if it were an actual locus, because 'now' never exists in that sense. Therefore, because time is always moving, there can be no knowledge, no truth and no reality because there is nowhere for them to exist. Conversely, as a state of being the 'now' is perhaps all-important. But it isn't important in regard to any particular knowledge, truth or reality, as these phenomena are absent in no time and no place. What does exist is our individual consciousness, or rather everything exists within our consciousness. Thus there is a supreme paradox: knowledge, truth and reality as attitudes or by-products of feeling and thought, may be of little consequence, while consciousness, the moving flow of mind, contains all existence in fleeting fractions of seconds.

It is not only possible, but highly desirable, to live in that flow rather than in the illusory by-products. This is the state of being awake. Admittedly it can be a relief to take a holiday from awakeness and immerse oneself in illusion, but not for long, because illusion is a terrible trap.

Condemned to a Future

If there is any reality it is that the human race has simultaneously a cosmic gift and a cosmic curse. We have the imagination to visualise and be aware of what might be going to happen, but no dependable knowledge of what actually *will* happen. Our history is therefore a compendium of disappointments and surprises. We are also deeply anxious about what might or might not occur and endeavour mightily to control future events despite our ignorance and poor past record of guessing the course of existence.

At the least, we must surrender to being far more ignorant about the future, because it is where each of us must spend the rest of our lives. We should accept that great, albeit suppressed, denied, and sublimated terrors are all out there in front of us. We are all as naked and defenceless as new-born infants and most of us are past the stage when we might hope for the unlimited love and support of a devoted mother. All we have is our own being and that of the other lives around us. We should build on this in our behaviours, and not indulge in illusory expectations.

Being Present

This is the actual 'being in the now' rather than the metaphorical illusion we believe we can attain. The idealistic tropes of truth, knowledge and reality, unattainable as they must be, are replaced by a state of being. How is this done? Basically it is a matter of selfhood plus fear. Our species is hooked on the idea of the self, and we are terrified of anything which may threaten it. But this 'self' is merely a concept and is not a 'thing' at all. It is actually impossible to access your state of being if you are focused on the supposed self. Indeed the 'self' is probably the most destructive element in our belief-system. In a sense, 'self' tends to be the giant in the belief-system of Western humankind. It is a serious pest in the psyche, but it has been hoisted up to the elevated status of ego or superego. 'Self' rules individually and collectively. Dealing with it is complicated by the fact that there is a biological self that requires feeding and protecting, quite naturally, and this gets confused with the imaginary giant dominating the mind.

Being present is the most desirable, even delightful, experience. It is often enabled by compassion or sympathetic laughter or affection for someone or something. It is a kind of surrender to 'what is' and the arts may also be aids in being present. The expression 'lose yourself' is often used for the experience of music, and the word 'sublime' seems appropriate to that experience. Religious music is a very interesting example of sublimity because, although ostensibly directed to the idea of deity, the music itself is very often neutral or abstract and is just very beautiful. Beethoven's Missa Solemnis and Faure's Requiem are good examples of 'sacred' music which transcends the religious context.

Meditation can be a perfect way of being present. But so much meditation is unfortunately self-directed and therefore ineffectual. Meditation should never have an object or a purpose if what is needed is purely being present. Clearing the mind is often a useful approach to pure meditation, although there's much to be said for just allowing thoughts to come and go freely and inconsequentially.

However it is done, this replacement of false attempts to trap the moving moment and opting instead for the state of being present, will transfigure life-experience. The futile efforts to gain knowledge, other than that which is fundamentally present in one's being, can be abandoned and real freedom attained. In those circumstances, the fear of not knowing simply evaporates.

The Perennial Stupidity

This is, in various forms, secular or religious, the database we take as the guide to the future. It is a hybrid of accumulated information and visions in a crystal-ball. It goes by the title of The Perennial Wisdom or Perennial Philosophy. As Wikipedia puts it:

*'The **Perennial Philosophy** (Latin: philosophia perennis), also referred to as **Perennialism**, is a perspective within the philosophy of religion which views each of the world's religious traditions as sharing a single, universal truth on which the foundation of all religious knowledge and doctrine has grown.*

The term philosophia perennis was first used by Agostino Steuco (1497-1548), drawing on the neo-Platonic philosophy of Marsilio Ficino (1433-1499) and Giovanni Pico della Mirandola (1463-94).

In the early 19th century this idea was popularised by the Transcendentalists. By the end of the 19th century it was further popularized by the Theosophical Society*, under the name of "Wisdom-Religion" or "Ancient Wisdom". In the 20th century it was popularized in the English speaking world through Aldous Huxley's book The Perennial Philosophy as well as the strands of thought which culminated in the New Age movement.'

*(Theosophy claims that all religions contain elements of the 'Ancient Wisdom' and that wise men throughout history have held the secret of spiritual power. It asserts that those enlightened by the 'divine' wisdom can access a transcendent spiritual reality through mystical experience).

This encapsulates both the aspirational and the ludicrous elements of the commodity known as knowledge. It is precisely this kind of cultural smugness that puts our existence in such peril. There is, implicitly, a self-congratulatory aura to this archival view of the accumulated, putative, human knowledge-industry.

Also online can be found a list of the contents of this perennial parade of movements:

Hinduism, Buddhism, Jainism, Sikhism, Taoism, Ch'an Buddhism, Hua-Yen Buddhism, Zen Buddhism, Shinto, Tibetan Buddhism, Zoroastrianism, Sufism, Baha'i, Egyptian Mysteries, Hermeticism, Gnosticism, Judaism, Qabbalah, Islam, Greek and Roman Theology, Christianity, Celtic Pantheism, Norse, Zulu, Akan, Minianka, Aztec and Toltec, Maya, Inca, Teton Sioux, Guaymi... and on and on.

Looking at this diversity of 'faith', I am struck by the fact that it is claimed, e.g. by the theosophists, that it is really a unity, with varying 'flavours', and all based on mystical experience. I consider this to be a euphemism at best and a downright lie at worst. Also, the 'knowledge' contained in it is counterfeit, if only in that it is based upon the presumed existence of hundreds of deities.

For a start, mystical experience is by no means necessarily characteristic of these religions, as my own many mystical events have been wonderful yet entirely devoid of gods or godness. In the religions I know best, mysticism is a rather dirty word, too; perhaps because it is a direct experience of the 'absolute and ineffable' without the clergy as middlemen. I experience the mystical as transcendence, bliss, or ecstasy, and often as terror as well, and I am still learning the personal significance of this extraordinary gift. I see no resemblance to the gaggle of religions, though some people might. As for the importance of seeing the perennial wisdom as a unity, it requires close analysis.

Unity or Muddle?

The perennial wisdom, or its more inclusive alternative, the perennial philosophy, is not all that ancient, maybe 4 or 5 thousand years. Its constituent beliefs certainly have a degree of pervasive sameness, but the differences are far greater than the similarities. Rather than being impressed by the unity, I am aghast at the sheer multiplicity of what is clearly human invention. All these modes of knowledge say everything about humankind and absolutely nothing about the mystery of existence. Not that it should be expected otherwise. How could the human mind access the unknowable? By definition, it must be beyond us, if it exists at all.

Is it not that we have focused on another question altogether all these centuries, not really on gods at all, but on our blind terror at our existential predicaments? Haven't the terrors been placed in abeyance, for conscious day-to-day existence, having all been allayed by alleged knowledge or by placebos? If we didn't shelter ourselves from these terrors, if we didn't use the power of denial, we could hardly be naive enough to trust knowledge as an all-purpose safeguard of safety and happiness.

Yet, naive or not, we do trust knowledge and we are in denial regarding the terrors. It is assumed that we already have, or will eventually have, all the necessary knowledge to make human life perfect. If knowledge were not ultimately achievable and absolutely trusworthy, then the terrors would be monsters at our throats. But the actual nature of knowledge, its imperfections, fallacies, and errors, make it useless for saving us from everything, death and all the rest.

In the absence of trustworthy, actual, truthful knowledge in our past, we did the obvious thing: *we made it up.* Far from ditching the idea of an unreliable prop, the collapsible walking-frame, we built an edifice of factual fiction and made it mandatory to believe it absolutely. The vast number of contradictions, paradoxes, and quarrels that have always characterised knowledge, failed to make us adjust to a more mature view of existence. We are, astonishingly, still praising one god or another, as if there could be no doubt of their existence.

Just as astounding is the way we fall for changes in scientific fashions. Seduced by the false comfort of 'evidence' and the total reliance on mathematics, we accept that there was a steady state universe, that it is now a big bang universe, or maybe many universes, and maybe no big bang after all. We trust that cancer or heart disease or even mortality itself will one day be cured by research yet to happen. We believe one week that we should take that medicine or avoid this food, only to hear the opposite a few days later. Not all science is so fickle, of course, but it is essential to understand that the mind can only make probabilities and that facts are imaginary fossils.

The Knowledge Market

It is still with us, this childlike faith in the gigantic bunch of knowledge systems, or selected pieces, chosen at random and changed only by fashion and new fictions. It used to be that the perennial wisdom, or some other elixir of the imagination, had a charismatic hold upon us primarily due to the authority behind it. Aristotle, Plato, Abraham, Thomas Aquinas, and all those other seers, magicians, thinkers, spiritual leaders, logicians and philosophers, made a net in which all of us have been more or less caught like a shoal of herring. We have also taken our orders from kings, dictators, writers, statesmen, and lawyers, who tell us, still, what we must do. There are also the revolutionaries and anarchists who tell us a different story. None of these has any authority for what they claim to be the truth. It is all in their heads and therefore in ours. This wisdom, or this rag-bag of wisdoms plural, rules our lives as has happened for millennia. Of course, there is diversity. The pillar of knowledge is a tower of Babel. Most people, brainwashed as they are, have still to choose between different beliefs and traditions. They are liable to kill one another for these differences.

The New Messiahs

For a few centuries, like a straggling cavalry, purveyors of a superior form of wisdom have tried to change our lives and our minds. These are not just searchers and finders, they also claim to *prove* that they are right. Not that they are the first to claim perfect knowledge, but they are the first to show what actually and demonstrably *is* perfect knowledge. They have gained charisma that even archbishops have come to envy. The dread phrase 'Scientists have discovered...', strikes fear into every gnostic heart. It's not unlike papal infallibility used to be. At the core, science has been charged with rescuing us from the unknown.

Yet it has failed to establish anything but conventions, however exquisitely wrought by experiments and mathematics. This point needs detailed and careful examination. I am a scientist by training and experience. I do sincerely trust science as a way of thinking that is far ahead of mere imagination and not in the same skull-space as fantasies of the supernatural. Yet I don't trust science any further than I could throw it. Why? Because it is limited by the restrictions in the human brain/mind which, fantasies apart, was not ever designed or evolved to discover the non-existent snark known as 'the truth'. But just because it produces evidence and repeatability of events, important as they are, it cannot be a touchstone for the elusive spirit that is erroneously imagined as absolute truth.

The big problem with science is that it is advertised as the path to truth in an age that has put religion into a sacred box-room of desirable heirlooms. We, as metaphorically two-headed chimeras, are also extraordinarily prepared to believe simultaneously in religion *and* in science, on the slender basis that they are *different kinds* of knowledge. Well, I can subscribe to scientific and religious concepts as well as the next chimaera, but I don't regard them as different kinds of knowledge. My only absolute belief is that we should not fall into the trap of believing we can choose the kind of knowledge to believe in. We do not have that awesome power. The reason for my one belief is that I do not accept that we could have the superior mental function required to distinguish between faiths, sciences or religions. They are all dubious and we aren't beyond the law of due doubt by claiming ability to judge events within it.

Egoic Anxiety

It is a difficult point for an egoic species. We humans cannot bear to be ignorant. But we are. There is no area of existence in which we can absolutely and safely claim perfect knowledge. I am aware that many people do claim it, but their authority rests with an unknown divinity, which is itself subject to some doubt. Putting it another way, knowledge, as a function of living, is on a long and complicated continuity and no-one knows how to divide it up.

Think of the massive range of the mammals and ask yourself where the divisions should be. I warrant that you cannot even decide on what would be an acceptable division in any *absolute* sense. In fact, all species, by definition, are unique (otherwise we couldn't call them species). So, to form a view of what it means to be human, you might refer to our ability with language and tools, and say that the most important division is between human and non-human. But they are our criteria. Had we chosen a different species, there would be different criteria. Therefore, any knowledge system which depends on being human must perforce differ from all other knowledge-systems, whether animal, vegetable, or mineral. The knowledge-system of the element carbon, for example, allows it to adopt several different identities, such as diamond, graphite, buckminsterfullerene, etc. Unicellular Protozoans carry out all the functions of life by using their one and only cell, compared with our trillions. What would be their view of the meaning of life compared with ours? How different were the world-views of the various hominids? How does the salmon know where to go for spawning? Couldn't we develop more respect for the knowledge we don't possess and surrender to the reality that most knowledge will remain beyond us?

Taxonomy is Taxing

The absurdity of identity-knowledge springs from the open or denied tendency of humankind to regard the whole of nature as its stamping-ground. We feel the need to identify and name all our fellow living organisms. That is a convenient way of telling each other what we see or hear around us. It is a sort of basic useful knowledge, like a telephone book. But it is extremely limited as existential knowledge. We classify scientifically, nowadays, but not necessarily all that accurately. The point is that to name a plant or creature is the smallest possible piece of knowledge that could exist, and it may be wrong. Errors pop up everywhere, such as in the long failure to classify the Fungi as animals, plants, or something else. We humans like to classify, and it is certainly useful to have names for 'different' things, but much Taxonomy is almost as non-scientific as Astrology or Phrenology.

Take another look at humans. Have you reliable information on the umpteen species who are extinct? Do you actually think all humans to be the same animal? Don't the different 'races' of humankind look a bit different, collectively? Do we not vary greatly in height or intelligence or hairiness? Are we not simply a small continuum, more or less seamlessly part of a much bigger mammalian continuum? Do you really care, either way? Does it matter to you whether you are a Pygmy or a Masai, an Aborigine or a Semite, a Welshman or a

Norwegian? If it does, you are lost in a Sargasso Sea of useless information.

There is, of course, some genuine need for knowledge, but it is like a lie-detector: It tells us what is a lie, what is a possible lie, or what is a useful lie, but it can never tell us the truth. Like the Void, truth is always with us but cannot be pinned down. It is the greatest chimaera of all. We may ask, is it even true that truth exists? To be consistent, the answer must be no. We must all settle for the lesser state of approximate *probability*, although it is still guesswork, because it is the one useful feature of science.

Does the Future Matter?

It is a matter of choice. Though the human mind suffers the burden of future awareness, perhaps uniquely, perhaps not, it is not obligatory to find it painful. In fact, it is often pleasurable to anticipate coming events. That is not obligatory either. One way of 'living in the now', if we really want to despite the physical impossibility of freezing the moment, the best stratagem is to ignore the future.

As in meditation, or in listening to sublime music, or in being *present* with another person or in your own psyche, it is feasible to unhitch the focus from the unknowable world yet to happen. Any of us can take a holiday from anxiety or anticipation. Mostly, we do not choose to do it, because we suffer fear or desire. However, the future actually is unknowable, even if we think we are making it happen, so trying to have it before it is available is really dysfunctional behaviour.

Yet all our instincts and most of our education push us into that dysfunction. We are taught to live in the future. It is where we must all live. We can't change the past, as the saying goes, therefore we have to concentrate on the coming days or years, unknowable though they are.

In a sense it is a harmful set-up. We are lambs for the slaughter or lions for the feast.

Consider, on the other hand, how you feel when watching a film or a play, or perhaps listening to a conversation or a stand-up comedian, does in not happen that you find in yourself a different consciousness, one in which you are the observer rather than the actor? It can happen on a country walk. Or in a deep conversation. Or in the act of love. Instead of being an observer, then, you are a part of a continuum. Not dissimilar from being part of an audience. You can be simultaneously involved and observant. It is part of your inheritance as a human being. To some extent, it must also be the experience of most intelligent creatures.

These platitudes contain more sense than we realise, in that they show how much we don't need knowledge of the future to be happy. At their more elevated level, these considerations are similar to the idea of mindfulness in Buddhism, which can be extremely approximately described as the experience of full attention, with a direct quality of perception, and not being diverted by emotions or beliefs. The future can be dealt with in a similar mode, in the sense that we meet it as it arrives, with composure, and arrange for it to be met by moderate interest. We do not need to indulge in panic or desire, though we do need to be mindful of basic responsibilities to ourselves and others.

Such a state of being is both natural and learnable. Unfortunately we tend to teach and learn the opposite mind-sets. Mindfulness does not require great knowledge - except of how to be mindful - and the future cannot be waylaid by preconceived certainty. So entering the unknowable, which means merely living moment by moment, is not so fear-ridden as we pretend it to be. Fear exists, of course, as does love or joy, but it is fruitless and foolish to enter the future with great expectations or great apprehension. To enter the unknowable future it may also help not to carry excessive assumptions about the basic facts of existence. The accumulated knowledge of the past has little to offer us in facing the life ahead except as an infinite list of catastrophes and errors, which could at least make us wary of the whole knowledge-gamble.

Six
The Poisoned Chalice

Big-Knowledge

Our species is so enamoured with knowledge, or the idea of it, that we fall easily under its spell. It is as if we are all putative London taxi drivers who must study for four years and pass a test to be allowed to drive customers around the city. Many of us take degrees or the equivalent to become adept in some discipline or other. You can be educated into the profession of anything, from acting, painting, singing, or surgery, to teaching, policing, writing, or undertaking, so that we are well-acquainted with the social uses of knowledge. However, to find new and better ways of doing anything, the old knowledge has to be challenged and replaced with new knowledge.

Then, again, some knowledge is sub-optimal, perhaps for a long time, in that it is causing harm. There is a long list of evil-doers whose knowledge is harmful in some way. Assassins, poisoners, drug-dealers, cutpurses, abortionists, gamekeepers, whalers, tree-fellers, sharpshooters, evangelists, forgers, embezzlers, and many other 'trades' can use their undeniable knowledge to perpetrate foul deeds.

These forms of knowledge are not, however the main problem nor the most toxic. They are 'everyday' kinds of knowing, 'know-how' knowledge, and are directly connected to tasks, projects, and various kinds of work, some legitimate, some criminal.

Humankind cannot exist without this kind of knowledge, preferably used benignly. This facilitative knowledge is not generally the kind that leads us into disaster. It is similar to tools and weapons, indeed it usually *is* tools and weapons, and has made big differences to life on this planet, some good, some bad. I do not exonerate any knowledge from culpability, as, for example, pesticides, drugs, and intensive farming. So quite small bits of knowledge can have huge effects. But the kind that matters most, **'Big Knowledge'**, it can be called, is that which rules our minds and our lives, past and future.

Forms of Big-Knowledge

The categories are well-known, though not perhaps generally recognised as harmful. The point of this narrative is, of course, that they actually are harmful. I have already referred to the perennial wisdom, certainly Big-Knowledge and certainly harmful, as I hope I have demonstrated. Religion, all religion, belongs in this category, and I will return to this problem frequently in subsequent chapters. For different reasons, science is Big-Knowledge and is always liable to cause harm. I have touched on this previously. The next offender is philosophy, and that must be admitted even though this book could be accused of being philosophical in tone and content. It is a special problem for me, because bits of philosophy have made a great difference to my life. But I have to be very selective, and separating good thinking from bad thinking is inherently challenging. Maybe philosophy is the worst offender in the stakes of Big-Knowledge, because it puts itself forward as rational, something that religion cannot do however hard it tries. And, unlike science, philosophy does not submit itself to physical proof. It takes the intellectual high ground and speaks in foggy language so that most people don't know quite what it is saying. That is very dangerous for our species with its tendency to grasp at straws of apparent safety.

On the whole, I absolve all the creative arts from culpability as Big-Knowledge (unless they are in the service of one of the others, religious art being particularly bad because it makes the religious knowledge-system seem so charismatic). I am inclined to say that politics is a very offensive form of Big Knowledge, though I am unsure if it is even knowledge let alone Big-Knowledge. On the other hand, how huge is the damage wrought by politics upon our species and our world? If it is translated into power, which is generally true, then it certainly looms big, and maybe it is knowledge too, since swathes of people are caught in its lethal embrace by clever talk and near-genius inventions of the imagination. It uses the arts to manipulate our minds, which is unfortunate, but this is balanced by the arts being effective in satirising the absurdity of politicians.

This leaves me with global business, whereby the tyrants of our species cheat and incite their way into all our lives, surviving, and usually profiting, by the simple fact that we all have to eat, drink and live in shelter of some kind. Their Big-Knowledge is grotesque and grotesquely huge. It is primarily exploitative knowledge, usually regardless of the suffering it inflicts on the world. It knows how to trap us in our own desires and fears. Basically, big business runs, and ruins, the world even more than the other kinds of Big-Knowledge.

This list of Big-Knowledge culprits could be modified or extended, but sufficient has been said to show how we are controlled and manipulated by false promises, backed up by vast power. Here we still are, numerically gigantic but collectively powerless to face the future with confidence of spirit; all we have is a fragile faith in the leaders who draw up manifestos made of pie-crust.

The Fear Horizon

The past is over; our focus must be on the future, opaque though it is. How do the categories of Big-Knowledge fit into this cosmic void? As it is, they seem to be irreplaceable, immovable, obstacles to any possible solution to the terrifying possibilities ahead. The **perennial wisdom** still hangs heavily over us, growing heavier day by day as new foolishness is added to the mass that already exists. **Religion** still breaks us upon its monstrous wheel, with little sign of giving way to secular sanity. **Science** is burgeoning and getting less pure with every monetary inducement. **Philosophy** sails serenely on like a colossal cruise ship going nowhere in particular but full of its own importance. **Politics**, the arch-Machiavelli, ties its knots and sets its land-mines, leaning heavily towards the mountain of **global business**, where it derives and exercises its elephantine mass. Finally, how are we, as mere people, to disarm and control the huge armies of **global capitalism** and **global commerce?**

How can we begin to free ourselves from these seven monsters of presumption? The answer must be to exercise greater scepticism in each of them, and systematically to demolish the icons of Big-Knowledge in favour of a new sanity and a new awakeness. A few examples follow, starting with the folly of religion.

The God of Hypocrisy

The Romans had an important god, called Janus, before Emperor Constantine made them have a replacement. Janus was two-faced. He looked backwards and forwards. January is his month. We also use his name, nowadays, to describe someone who cannot be trusted. Big-Knowledge is also Janus-faced and it, too, purports to control our past and our future as did Janus the god, and it certainly aspires to godlike status.

It is significant that the Romans put their past and future in the hands of a god, a very important deity when the world was still Pagan. Did the Romans actually believe that their transition from past to future was being managed for them by a heavenly magician? It is most likely, given that billions of people today believe the same, just the gods being different ones from Janus. It seems that the Romans took on the Catholic Trinity with the same trust that they had shown towards Janus. It could be argued that they were rather two-faced in the matter of chosen deities.

Anyway, Janus is interesting because of this particular talent he was supposed to have had as a time-lord. He was considered to be the guardian of 'the gates of heaven'. I have read some grandiose accounts of his power, such as his:-

'Mastership over time, the beginning of the world, religion and the gods themselves, as well as access to Heaven and to other gods. He symbolized change and transitions such as the progress of future to past, and was worshipped at the harvest and planting times, at marriages, deaths and other beginnings.'

It beggars belief that such a cosmic phenomenon could have been dethroned on the instructions of a petty mortal, a mere emperor. But he shrewdly called upon a mass of bishops to make the decision (nominally as to which Christianity to adopt), and he let the Pagans go on with their myths while directing the Christians which of their myths should become the established wisdom. The whole charade ought to have put off the human race from religion for ever. No such luck, all that happened was a continuation of god-intoxication, while merely changing the fashion and the brand of alcohol. If Janus had been real, would he not have exacted revenge? How could such a mega-god simply fade away, without a whimper or a plague or two?

Is it not profoundly hypocritical to have so many gods? Do we really believe in any of them? Taking the Christian god, for example, do we really believe he made the universe and rules everything in it? If so, where does the Holy Spirit and the Christ, Jesus, fit in? Are there actually three gods, not just one? Or are we hedging our bets? Do we feel safer with three gods, or thirty, or three thousand?

Why is it not clear to all humans that the idea of a god is no more than wishful thinking? I think I know the answer, but I don't particularly like it. I suspect that religion is actually a form of gambling. It seems to have all the symptoms of that disease. The idolatry, the sacrificing, the hysterical excitement, the 'sure and certain hope' of winning, the certainty that we will be 'saved', all point to a protection-racket of immense proportions.

We are, after all, very frightened creatures, however much we deny it. We need reassurance of some kind and will act extravagantly to get it. We even take risks in order to feel safe. That's the madness of a betting man. It is not difficult to identify the religious mafia. The demeanour of priests may be saintly, but underneath they are using us for the support of their masters. Of course, the similarity can be stretched too far. But sometimes hyperbole is needed to expose an uncomfortable reality.

Does it Work?

I would ask this question about all the Big-Knowledge systems. If they don't actually make our lives happier, or safer, or more purposeful, why do we bother with them? It is claimed that religious people are happier than unbelievers. If that is true it is a plus point for religion. But is it true? I don't know. I am an unbeliever and I know believers and I don't see much difference in our happiness. On the other hand there are many features of religion that scare me. The power of dogma and the rule of doctrine make my blood run cold. I am actually afraid of religion. The killer-question is whether there is anything in religion that strikes me as positive or beautiful, and my answer is quite negative. I don't think there's much truth in it, either. On the whole therefore, I think people are foolish to have religious belief. But that is largely because I really don't think it works, except as a placebo, a false remedy for misery or a false stimulus for euphoria.

Would I ban religion if I could? No, I don't have that kind of certainty. I would, however, love to decree that it becomes an absolutely private and personal matter. There would be no churches, no religious services, no collective worship, and no clerics. With luck, we might have no more religious wars. But I guess the prisons would be full of spiritual exhibitionists. Humankind is obviously not yet ready to grow up. The future, therefore, will continue to be endangered by religious mania. It is one of the worst outlooks to contemplate.

The Dream of Destiny

This is not quite a problem of religious Big-Knowledge, but its close. I perceive it as a very broad picture of Big-Knowledge, a mixture of religion, perennial wisdom, philosophy, and even science (as psychology). I see much of human entrapment reflected in the quite insidious phenomenon of stereotyping as it ramifies overtly or covertly throughout the collective psyche. The outstanding example is the theory of archetypes but it is only one of several ways of glamorising individual specialness. It may also be a negative process, as in branding certain racial or tribal qualities as inherently undesirable, as has happened with Jews and Australian Aborigines.

After a lot of consideration of the merit of the idea, even when it appears to be positive, I conclude that it is wrong and dangerous. It either aggrandises or demeans the subject. Its harm is subtle. It is a seductive idea because it makes the human psyche seem almost magical. Indeed it may be a branch of magic, in a way, and is certainly a foolish aggrandisement or degradation of the human condition. It is, therefore, a useful example of Big-Knowledge run riot. It has tentacles in every direction, particularly in the murky region of determinism. After all, destiny is a dream that lurks in the mind of every aspiring human, the sense of fame or wealth or importance as a birth right. We also read doom into the being of others, if not ourselves, as a febrile superstition.

Therefore, apart from religion per se, the destiny concept, in its many manifestations, is a prime example of harmful Big-Knowledge and warrants extensive consideration, especially as its dangers are not as obvious as those of science and philosophy, being less centre-stage than these more overt knowledge problems. The biggest hazard of the destiny-cults is the assumption of determinism.

Theories of Inevitability.

As the future must be wholly unpredictable, this brand of Big-Knowledge is absurd. Yet it thrives. It is even manipulated, as in the ubiquitous attempt by parents to make their children successful to compensate for their own sense of failure. It may be laudable, but is it not also a burden for the child? However, the idea of fate is the worst effect of this kind of pseudoknowledge.

Just imagine being told that you have absolutely no control over whom and what you are. The semi-scientific Enneagram methodology is a whole system of typing that, for all its merits, leans in the direction of prediction. As already mentioned, so does the idea of the archetypes. Genetics especially in one of its less scrupulous varieties, is not so far different, either. Does the human template really exist? Is it even probable? It is certainly a key feature of the perennial wisdom and maybe is still alive and well in our scientific culture.

It also connects with the various religious forms of determinism. The Roman Catholic version, with different levels of post-mortem punishment and degradation, depending on the sin/virtue balance pre-mortem, is an astonishing assault upon personal autonomy. Worse still are some of the methods of reducing the sin-debt. But Lutherism and Calvinism went a stage further in the depravity of power, the pre- and post-mortem fate of every human was deemed to be totally fixed by the divine dictator, and there was nothing any of us could do to mitigate the misery. Only the clergy stood a chance of a good eternity. As they were, obviously, special.

Of all the deterministic systems, the theory of archetypes is the most insidious, because it bears the imprint of the great Carl Jung. His immense body of work has an enduring impact on the global culture and he is seen as an authority on the mind in all its devious glory. As he invented the collective unconscious, a semi-religious idea of the human race being in effect a single mind, so also did he invent archetypes as the machinery of that racial connection. This being the case, apparently, I will take archetypes as the exemplar of determinism, a big kind of Big-Knowledge.

Archetype as Determinant

Using Jung's ruminations as the basis, the entirely metaphorical idea of the archetype was converted into a literal map of the human psyche. The authority for this seems to be the stories, symbols and dreams, and the products of artists and the musings of priests, as well as mythology and even popular entertainment. This must be an outstanding example of circular thinking: that because something crops up here, there and everywhere, it must be deeply significant. A case for Occam's razor if ever there was one. Because there is a pattern, however vague and diverse, the temptation is to use it to explain human development and behaviour. In fact, it is merely a pattern, a picture of the human creature at work and play; it proves nothing. It is not, in my opinion, adequate evidence for creating a system.

It is even worked up into a program describing and implicitly predicting social success or failure, or the level of well-being of individuals under the influence of any of the archetypes. This is exactly how knowledge is claimed to exist; from a presumptuous and pretentious reading of happenstance. Jung's descriptions are not trivial, but neither are they definitive. What they are is pseudoknowledge, the commodity that tends to rule and distort our lives, and make living in the future an absurdity. It is worth examining typical archetypes to see this in practice.

This snake oil often comes in twelve bottles, though it may be seven, or four, or several hundred bottles, depending on the mood of the classifier. As Jung seems to have favoured a round dozen, in three groups of four, I have followed that arrangement to try to find some solid basis for the whole idea. It appears that the three categories are: Ego, Soul and Self.

These are questionable for a start. The history of our species could be written and rewritten according to different concepts of identity. The three icons are not compatible or equivalent :-

Ego is a moveable feast: is it the mature manifestation of adult personhood, or is it a pathological parasite in one's being? Are we glad to have an ego, or ashamed, or merely resigned to it? Certain mystics and gurus put massive effort into ego-reduction. Children, in whom ego may be said to have hardly grown yet, are often the most egoic creatures on the planet.

Soul is conjectural and just as muddled as ego. It is generally regarded as good compared with bad ego, and is used as a metaphor for sensitivity or the even vaguer spirituality. It forms a sad and mournful complex in some people, often compared with the liveliness of spirit. Whereas most people can accept the eradication of ego by the process of death, there is a large following for ideas of soul immortality.

Self is a nest of snake-oils, a metaphor as absurd as the idea of self itself. I have written at some length about 'self' and suffice it to say that I regard the concept as both repellent and preposterous. As several of my books, including 'Freedom River', have claimed, only the biological self that we share with all conscious creatures, has any actual validity. The vast madness of the imaginative self in humankind is largely illusion or delinquency, while the so-called higher self is as delusional and as delightful as any other form of mysticism.

The three types are usually subdivided as follows:

Ego Types

    1. Innocent dreamer: naive, mystical, utopian, hopeful, traditional, saintly

    2. Everyman: OK neighbour, good fellow, realist, orphan, needs to belong.

    3. Soldier: strong but arrogant, needs to fight, crusader, winner, chivalrous knight.

    4. Carer: saintly, altruistic, generous, parent, helper, supporter, martyr, victim.

    (Are these really egoic? The opposite, surely. But there is a pattern that is strongly other-focused. Maybe these are types that the majority like. Good 'soap' material?)

Soul Types

    1. Seeker. Needs to escape, be free, challenge, assert uniqueness, travel, be true.

    2. Rebel. Rule-breaker, revolutionary, wild man, misfit, iconoclast, radical, outlaw.

3. Lover. Needs intimacy, to attract, a partner, friend, spouse, sensuality, to belong.

4. Creator. Writer, artist, innovator, inventor, needs to have and realise visions.

(A vast range, though with soul-flavour, yet it is too heterogeneous to have much value as a guide to personal growth. The archetype idea stretched to breaking point.)

Self Types

1. Fool. Live it up, be funny, be a trickster, a joker, comedian, terrified of boredom.

2. Sage. Truth-addicted, needs knowledge, academic, thinker, teacher, philosopher

3. Magician. Shaman, healer, witch-doctor, visionary, catalyst, clairvoyant.

4. King. Power-addicted, controller, leader, role model, manager, aristocrat, ruler.

(These, if anything, are much more egoic than the first four. And these types are generally unattractive beings, in their solipsism at least. Hence the most archetypal?)

The wide range of characteristics of each of the twelve archetypes gives cause for further doubt. They are also inconsistent within the archetypes, though an approximate relationship is discernible. The whole arrangement is strikingly amateur, and evidently lacks a solid basis of research. It has the quality of an anecdote rather than a science (but that is not unusual in psychology).

How did Jung explain his fantasy? He apparently believed that archetypes are actual models of people, behaviours or personalities and that as the psyche is composed of three components, the ego, the personal unconscious and the collective unconscious, these three engines are co-operating in creating the world view of archetypes, maybe even *are* the archetypes. However clever this may seem, the fact remains that human consciousness would actually be *making* the archetypes. They have no separate existence from the human mind. While that may seem obvious, how easy it is to forget it.

Jung got around this incestuous system by claiming that the collective unconscious serves as a kind of psychological inheritance and that it contains all the knowledge of our species. But that still means that we have made the archetypes just as the brothers Grimm made up fairy tales. Furthermore, is it not excessive inflation to claim, as Jung and others have, that the archetypes exist in the collective unconscious as if there is actual certainty that *it* exists? Like the archetypes, the collective unconscious is a neater and superior concept than gods or God, but only because it doesn't add the extra fantasy of a 'spy in the sky'. (Or, terrible thought, perhaps it does.) It is even more of an inflation to say that archetypes are 'innate, universal and hereditary', or that 'they are not acquired by learning and that they organise our experience of the world'.

'All the most powerful ideas in history go back to archetypes', said Jung. He might just as well, and more accurately, have said that that the archetypes were distilled, as concepts, *from* the most powerful ideas in history. Whenever there is a clear chicken-and-egg formula, like this, we can be fairly confident that we are being bamboozled. It is mumbo-jumbo to say, as he did, that the central material of religions, philosophy, science, and ethics are merely variants of the magical archetypes. His coup de grace is that the job of consciousness is to turn the external world into a visible reality. Another chicken-and-egg proposition.

This is what pseudoknowledge does. It takes a seminal idea, which merely means a concept with potential to become bigger and more developed, and turns it into an irrefutable law or doctrine. Like the papal decrees, bringing out certainties like the necessityof celibacy, the anathema against contraception, the redemption of sins (defined by the church), all of which could just as justifiably be called symptoms of collective insanity.

Another Determinism?

I am reminded of the Enneagram system, a useful and ingenious way of explaining how human creatures create their individual personalities. There are two issues in Enneagram work that illustrate the pseudoknowlege error so embedded in archetype theory. First, intentionally, there is exposure of the falsity of the human personality, actually much like the archetype. It is convincingly demonstrated that our so-called personalities are mere contrivances invented in extreme youth to manage what the infant perceives as reality. They are, originally, working hypotheses, strategies for survival or success. Unfortunately, but predictably, there is a tendency in all of us to take our personality seriously, as a kind of absolute given. It is not, of course, but just try changing it! The human personality is an ultimate con-trick, including the poor sucker who carts the personality around as if it were genuine or real.

Second, as if the inertia of self-labelling wasn't bad enough, unless real work is done to unravel the skein, there is another deep-seated mind-set in the Enneagram, whereby it is believed that we each have a divine essence, a pure original dedication or drive, that is usurped by the personality-process and yet is the only way back to a original reality. I am not saying that this is necessarily incorrect, but it is surely yet another piece of pseudoknowledge in itself. There is absolutely no hard evidence for the existence of this essence, even though any of us can sense the possibility of an unknown something operating in the depth of our being.

Mundane Big-Knowledge

Politics and big business are certainly Big-Knowledge, but how do they suborn the future? The clue is that they rely upon strategies and plans and manifestos. Indeed, these all too human enterprises are heavily dependent upon creative gambling. The starting-point of all politics and all business is the situation analysis, which simultaneously assesses the present and foresees the likely future; and there follows an examination of chance, in the form of opportunities or threats, i.e. the future environment. I am describing the more rational and conscious political and business practice. There will also be those who just do what first comes into their heads and hope replaces planning. There is little known about the relative effectiveness of the two approaches.

There is also the scientific method known as risk analysis. It is sensible theory, except that risk is inherently a forward projection, so it means gambling on risk. It is a sad paradox that in the areas where risk is greatest, politics and big business tend to make the worst decisions. Nothing shows this more dramatically than the most heinous of political practices, warfare.

Future Violence

This is a function of all the forms of Big-Knowledge added together, as religion and perennial wisdom, science, and even philosophy, are all involved in setting the scene for making war. Though the future is unknowable, a few things are very highly probable. War is one of them. But only to the extent that war is virtually bound to be a major phenomenon in human future. The kind, the size, the degree, and the amount of killing, are all unknowable. All that we can be quite sure about is that some kind of war will happen and probably several at the same time. Why would this be? It's not just that we humans have been warring for tens of thousands of years. It is inconceivable that peace would break out globally: it does not fit with human nature. Like sex and god, war seems hard-wired into our brains. The reason is ultimately mysterious but there is a possible explanation in our evolutionary story.

All sentient creatures are acutely aware of their environment. Most creatures' have fear and aggression built into their psyches. Survival-need is automatically implicated in everything the animal does. In the human psyche, there is also a strong concept of past and future, which immensely enhances the survival-imperative. The most certain way of beating an enemy is obviously to eliminate him. So the survival-imperative has killing encoded in it. This is not a sin, but merely part of every creature's survival kit.

In the case of mankind, however, killing has been extravagantly fostered by all the Big-Knowledge factors. Originally quite a weak animal, the human prototype had few options for increasing his survival. Killing a sabre-toothed tiger or a mastodon with one's puny bare hands was so high-risk as to be confined to suicide attacks. But with spears, bow and arrows, co-operative tracking and collective assault, man's chances were improved. That logic is deep in our minds today and will be there for the future unless drastic brain-washing is endured by us all.

Then came the other Big-Knowledge options into the primitive human brain. Early on, humans sought safety and support from magic and the supernatural, usually enacted by shamans, and later on, prophets and priests. Kings were invented as totemic or actual figures of power allied to the supernatural gods and spirits. Bloodthirsty sacrifices became popular as powerful inducements to the gods.

Then came politics, basically schemes whereby powerful people were manipulated and weak people exploited. It seems as if a great behavioural snowball was being created by necessity combined with greed. Religion and politics uneasily joined forces, and formed a noxious glue holding the great ball together. Similarly, earthly and heavenly powers were amalgamated and forced upon the underclass to make them servants of the overclass. The time-bomb was ready to command the minds and bodies of all men.

This ridiculous subjugation of human will has come very freshly into my awareness because the purveyors of history have been busily televising their (somewhat too well-known) confections. Again and again, extras dressed up in armour or chain-mail beat hell out of one another, stabbing, gouging, decapitating, strangling, fracturing, until the blood-sodden grass is strewn with bodies Yes, we get the message: fighting is vile, painful and not really very valiant. Except that there is some lord, baron, or monarch, and nowadays, politician, who has been able to persuade the common man to do this horrible thing just for the glory/safety of the realm. I see the pathetic creatures in their finery, the queens and the kings and the princes and the nobles, and I think, how on earth could anyone die for them? As for the gods, well it is even more nonsensical. But, hearth and home and life-partner, that's another matter. I would die for them. We all have our price.

Future Profligacy

So, war it is, then, perhaps until humans cease to exist. But what of the unknowable effects of the lords of commerce and trade? Already, they are halfway to destroying the planet. And they are manipulating our everyday stupidity and greed so as to use what is left of our precious earth before it becomes an inert desert. It may already be too late to halt this rapacity. Big business and global finance are now so complex and riddled with corruption that it is impossible to imagine a future in which it doesn't get worse. I was watching a young man on TV recently, an investigator trying to expose the ways in which consumerism is being whipped up to a frenzy, and every time he cornered a person who was obviously screwing the world, out poured a gush of technical logic. There was 'no problem', 'all great businesses were entirely ethical', 'only the customer mattered', and such bilge flowed on and on.

I find it hard to write this, so appalling is corporate behaviour, and so helpless and even stupid are we, the so-called public. The future can't be any better, however little we know about the perfidy to come - we know so little, anyway, about the perfidy already with us. It is futile to list the crimes being committed, because the criminals are really in charge. The masters of big business, banking, and global communication, just the people who should be leading our species into moral greatness and civilised practice, are usually the ones indulging themselves with a lavish lifestyle, and even invite us to be admirers at their feast. They become celebrities, the foulest of useless adjectives, and we are gullible enough to admire, or even worse, emulate them.

I would prefer to be saying how glad I am that we have such able people to manage the machinery of our practical lives. I think I once was, long ago. Now I know better and I do not enjoy the simple, homespun knowledge, which says to me, 'most of these people are actually no good'. I mean ethically no good, as it is often the case that they are good at what they do. But that is not fool proof, as the recent global financial collapse showed. There is no reason to look to the future with confidence. It is an unknowable of awful proportions.

The Leaders We Deserve

Politicians seem to be innately Janus-faced. I have met a few of them, and was impressed by the fact that I couldn't conceive of trusting any of them. Here is the super-irony of human life: those who seek the power to lead us show us a benign, even utopian view of existence, a life they want us all to have, yet they practice skulduggery as a trade, upon each other and upon all of us. In these last few years of my life I have seen politicians fall from grace, largely by their own cupidity and mendacity. I suppose this is a good sign, but what does it mean in terms of this Big-Knowledge? Is it ourselves we should blame for having such mountebanks as our leaders? Is it because we are also mountebanks, living false lives, being greedy, malevolent, and egotistical? Perhaps, but I find in the people I know best, and even some on brief acquaintance, a sweetness of spirit that shines out of them, even if they also have basic human pettiness.

There is, in our nature, a jewel of goodness that is often hidden or maybe is sometimes counterfeit. That goodness is the only quality I can think of as a saving grace in the unknowable years to come. If only it could be developed as our chief characteristic. It would be a gigantic educational task for all of us. But it would offset the unknowable. Working together to make the most of our potential goodness is something we could do without any increase in knowledge, but rather by a casting aside of all the past certainties. They have failed. Why not try something entirely new?

One thing is sure, each of us would need to become a leader, the leader of awake beingness that is potentially within every one of us. We each have this inner talent and we do not really need external authorities to tell us what to do and how to live our lives.

Seven
Changing The Rules

Bad Knowledge, Bad Rules

Life is short. There's a lot wrong, especially in the area of Big-Knowledge. But so what? Does all this matter? Does so-called Big-Knowledge really obstruct us in living a good life?

These questions arise from a fatigued sensibility. It is tiring and tiresome to worry, especially as the state of things seems to be inexorably awful. Of course the future is unknown, so why fuss about it? Life isn't so bad for most of us. Why not just follow the rules and keep plodding on? Nothing we can do will make any difference, anyway.

I ask myself these questions and they are the questions I hear from most people when they have made their complaints about life and failed to see any way out for themselves. It is tempting, and understandable, to give up and, in effect, to surrender to the greater powers that govern us. We keep on grumbling and, when asked, will often articulate cynicism or rage, but basically we submit to the regime in which we find ourselves. Some people, sometimes, act rebelliously, and the rest of us look on with mixed feelings. It is hard to be a rebel and remain a decent person, it seems, and we recoil from what we secretly would like to join. Consequently, we accidentally condone what we abhor. As Edmund Burke said, amongst all his many pronouncements, *'The only thing necessary for the triumph of evil is for good men to do nothing.'* (And he is often said to be the father of modern Conservatism!)

Burke was a politician, clever with words, and superficially wise and generous of spirit. But he was a politician. He was working the public to achieve his objectives, whatever he might say about their rights and needs. In the famous quote he implies that there is a general tendency towards evil in the world and that good men must stand up and oppose it, which is an almost Manichean mind-set. The alternative is that evil and good are part of a complex nature and not always easy to distinguish. But politicians have to simplify, it seems, which is why politics is a bad Big-Knowledge.

The Rebel Within

My own approach is that it is, indeed, important to oppose the manifold errors of thought and action that emanate from Big-Knowledge. But another dose of Big-Knowledge is liable to make matters worse - which is why politics so often fails to achieve true reform. Rather than invent new and worse systems and try to impose them upon the public domain, I would favour individual stroppiness, though not necessarily the ill-tempered variety. It need not be externally expressed, either, but can be effective held within as a bulwark against invasive bullshit.

At the same time there is something to be said about civilisation, by which I mean the creation of a benign and creative human environment. Socrates seems to have got the balance about right, as did Epicurus and the Buddha, but the process is essentially individual. To be sure, it is desirable that people should behave in a civilised manner to one another, but this is never, in my view, achieved by the agents of Big-Knowledge. Religions, governments, monarchs, and institutional educators or lawyers, do not achieve civilisation by their *professional* efforts, but often the reverse. As individuals, their behaviour can be inspirational to others, which is often the best they can do.

As humankind has been behaving en masse, however, the result is typically chaos and bloodshed, in a world made by us with the declared intention of making it a civilised environment. (If that actually were our intention.) I, for one, do not wish to be governed by nonsense, which is generally the substance of Big-Knowledge. It is, I admit, often impossible to be sure of the difference between sense and nonsense. It is also why it is so crucial never to presume to have truly functional knowledge, nor even approximations to some truth or other. We are still, basically, wild animals in an impenetrable jungle or an endless desert.

Civilisation is a fantasy, albeit a desirable one in principle. But we, as a species, have so far failed to create a durable and desirable civilisation. We have only been trying to do it for a mere hundred thousand years. And we have tried to do it partly by technology, i.e. tools, and partly by rules, i.e. social tools. Tools can only ever be validated by their usefulness. This must, I suggest be true of rules. What, after all, is the point of a rule that doesn't enhance civilisation? If civilisation means the happiness and wellbeing of the greater proportion of living beings, then we certainly don't have it. Inequality in virtually every sense is the rule that actually governs life on this planet. Is this a good rule?

The Competitive Spirit

Human behaviour is basically competitive, and it is also basically co-operative. The Janus-face, again, describes our fundamental drives. The two impulses may balance one another in some individuals or situations, or they may oppose one another, even cancel out each other. This is a primary cause of human unpredictability. But we shouldn't be surprised by our behaviour, because all sentient creatures have the same duality. Selective pressure is an evolutionary force, but it is imposed from without, and a species that is unable to compete will become extinct. An individual creature must compete or die, and the competition will be both within its species and with other species.

In our case, typically, we become very self-conscious about competition, turning it into a social fetish. Our appalling wars, and the ruthless exploitation of people and resources, are examples of excessively competitive behaviour. Alternatively, we preach non-competitiveness, but not necessarily with sincere intent. We like to teach our children to compete, as if they were not naturally full of the inclination to do so. We become jealous when we come against superior ability in another, or we may try to emulate it.

It is hardly surprising, considering the wide variety of competitive behaviours, that we have tried to put some limits on the chaos. Given the unpredictability of human behaviour, the limiting of competitive pressures is done with variable sense and effectiveness. It is a psychological minefield. I recognise that this minefield is also in each human psyche in the form of the egoic self. Each of us needs to be protected from the egoic self of others and also from one's own. But, as a general rule, we nurture the egoic self and are rather proud of it.

Human life is full of rules, largely to protect existence from excessively competitive behaviour. It would be funny if it were not so appallingly tragic that we have even put rules into the practice of warfare, the irony being that it is the actual object of war to kill and damage. We are also ambivalent about our warriors: we don't like to think of our soldiers, sailors and airmen as trained assassins, but that is necessarily what they are. We pride ourselves that they obey rules of combat and we punish them if they disobey. A marginally less gruesome example is how we recoil from the competitive necessity in education. There is a ferment of emotion about fairness. Do we love or hate public schools, where the rich pay for superior education of their children? So-called selection, as in passing tests to get to a grammar school, is a big bone of contention, yet we all want our children to excel.

It's as if we want competition as much as we condemn it, and we love it as much as we hate it. It reminds me of the three poisons in Buddhism, which are hate, greed and delusion. The antidotes are love, moderation and enlightenment. If you mix the six together you've got competition. Whereas the Buddhist aims to convert the poisons to their opposites, which requires a deep inner conversion for each person, the occidental mind turns to its old favourite, the rulebook. It's a moot point which approach works best. But, in practice, there also seem to be a lot of rules in Buddhism for achieving the deep inner conversion. It would be wonderful if our rules could have the same effect.

Who Decides The Rules?

How do we know what is a good rule and what is a bad one? So far, it has always been a minority decision, even in so-called democracies. Often it is the decision of one person such as a king, a great warrior, or a cleric. Or it may come from an aristocratic or tribal clique. Other animals have rules dictated by evolutionary selection: also approximate and imperfect. For non-human animals, the proof of a rule is in survival. A good rule tends to protect the species from extinction; a bad rule hastens its demise. It is more or less the same for the individual creature. But the human animal is unique, and its rules are often lethal. Or at least they are unfavourable to species' survival or individual wellbeing. As with other animals, there is some discrepancy between rules that are good for the species and rules that are good for the individual. Nature is far from perfect. But in the case of humankind, nature is chaotic.

Think of the rules governing war, rules which oblige us to fight each other en masse. Human beings fight each other so bitterly and stupidly that there is no sense either in the process or even in the outcome.

The misery implicit in war is not entirely due to rules, of course, but there is an inculcated code that insists that there is abstract nobility in decapitating or disembowelling a fellow human.

Animals tend to have rules against such absurdity, reserving killing for animals of different species. In the case of man, there is ambiguity about who is the other species. So not only do the rules demand that we massacre each other, but they are muddled as to whom we should massacre. Here the rules of patriotism or nationalism are invoked. The simplest version of this is the ancient native injunction: 'If you meet someone on the jungle path who you do not recognise, kill him.'

'Go forth and multiply' is another insane rule, now that there are too many of us. Similarly, the Hippocratic obsession with prolonging individual lives is counterintuitive, especially for an individual ready to die. But doctors and lawyers and priests are driven by rules that belong to another place and another time.

At the other end of our life-span there is an extraordinary attempt to make rules to ensure a human birth regardless of practicality or foetal abnormality. How a species can sanctify this at the same time as killing and mutilating its own individuals in warfare is beyond comprehension.

These few examples should suffice to show how rules are often inefficient or downright crass, the result of using Big-Knowledge, or applying theories bearing no relationship to reality. The source of this madness is usually the mistaken assumption that we can know something for certain, or that we have special knowledge or prescience of a future that is impossible to anticipate. How has this happened?

Challenging The Rules

Somewhere along the course of human history, probably at a number of different times and places, a set of rules became deeply entrenched in the collective psyche of humankind. They were not necessarily consistent from one tribe to another, nor were they always consciously expressed and understood. These rules may, or may not, have reflected the human phenotype as we now describe it, or human nature as it is also identified. This natural humanness is also questionable, as it seems more variable and unpredictable than might be expected of truly inherited behaviour. The old antinomy of nature versus nurture is still relevant in our collective wisdom, i.e., as I have said, in most cases it is impossible to be sure of the alleged knowledge.

Although I am confident of my opinion about the plethora of human mistakes that is passed off as if true reality, I know that to question the status quo is inherently risky, and that strongly voiced arguments are easily characterised as didactic and dictatorial. It is important that the critic or rebel present the argument without seeming to know better. For it to be thought that the rebel against Big-Knowledge presumes to know a truth inaccessible to others, is to accuse him of committing the very error he is rebelling against.

The objective is to reduce the overall burden of Big-Knowledge rather than increase it.

My greatest wish is that there might be much greater freedom from doctrines, dogmas and rules. I would like us to stop murdering each other on the battlefields of race, religion and greed. A lot more love and a lot less hatred would be good.

Rather than adding to the burden of knowledge, I plead for cheerful scepticism?

Occam's Razor

Perhaps this is the nearest I would wish to get to a general rule. It is at least worth serious consideration because it is an honest attempt to oppose the madness inherent in most Big-Knowledge. Who and what is Occam? Wikipedia says:

> **Occam's razor** *(also written as* **Ockham's razor** *and in Latin lex parsimoniae) is a principle of parsimony, economy, or succinctness used in problem-solving devised by William of Ockham (c. 1287-1347). It states that among competing hypotheses, the one with the fewest assumptions should be selected. Other, more complicated solutions may ultimately prove correct, but - in the absence of certainty - the fewer assumptions that are made, the better.*

There are paradoxes galore in this William, not the least of which was the fact that he was a Franciscan friar who was in considerable trouble for alleged heresy. The theology is not important for my purpose, especially the theology rampaging around seven centuries ago. But more relevant to me is the fact that Occam's razor is accused of unfairly condemning supernatural explanations. William was, of course, a super-naturalist by persuasion and occupation, and this seems to me the main paradox. He was simultaneously part of the Big-Knowledge cabal *and* an opponent of it. It is not easy to attain complete clarity in these matters, and the inherent lack of clarity in existence is precisely what I wish to emphasise. In the universal absence of clarity, I would adopt Occam's razor, i.e. keep it as simple as reasonably possible.

The razor is not absolute, which is a critical distinction from Big-Knowledge. Though himself an absolutist in theological terms (I assume he believed that God existed) he was a relativist in secular matters (possibly in some aspects of Papal diktats as well), so the simplest assumption only stood until a better simple assumption appeared, particularly when new evidence became available.

I could say, however, that far from being a paradox, i.e. living within an uncomfortable mixture of theism and logic, William of Occam was actually having his cake and eating it, or, to choose a more complimentary metaphor, was seeing the wood *and* the trees. Rules, by Occam logic, should be precisely fashioned to fit the simplest essence of a problem, but they would also have to be flexible enough to be adjustable to changes in the problem. In effect, the razor should remain sharp and also be able to distinguish between flesh and hair of different kinds.

The Good Arboriculturist

It can be quite hard to see the surplus trees in the wood of knowledge. It could be the whole forest. Or just the odd oak. Similarly, it is often impossible to be sure that it is the human collective or, alternatively, the human individual, that most needs corrective restraint. It may require explanatory handbooks to guide the reformer. Some actions will always need to be controlled by specific instructions or legal limits. But that doesn't excuse the intense manufacture, on a near-industrial scale, of mighty encyclopaedias of Big-Knowledge that no one person can ever read and understand let alone obey.

Discernment is essential. We need to decide just how much knowledge we really need and how much uncertainty we can stand? How many rules make a person happy? And are rebels and sceptics a help or a hindrance in the evolution of awareness? The questions need to be answered over and over again.

Human society and our environment are not well understood by the makers of rules. The complex and interconnected nature of people and their communities is usually simplified far beyond Occamist limits to find ways of controlling them, while the resulting rules are stupendously draconian. It is as if the arboriculturalist knows little of trees and nothing of natural interaction. We are likely to lose the rainforests and our place on the planet by a bad management, whether of people or of forests.

I suppose that we must start with people and trust that if they became more awake and aware, the care of the forests would improve. It is unlikely to happen the other way round.

Good and Bad Rules

Broadly and very approximately, there seem to be two kinds of rule.

First there are the rules, sometimes called codes, of conduct, that are agreed collectively and followed because they are useful, even essential, for a safe, interesting, and happy life for all members of the society, ranging from the family group to the largest communities. These rules are fairly free from dogma and doctrine. They are, as it were, utilitarian, except that, in some sense, spiritual or ethical behaviour may also be part of the agreement. Definitions and specifications are detailed and essential, and there will be checking and updating to ensure the rules remain fair and relevant. These rules may be subject to serious conversations, cheerful dinner-party banter, and even or especially shouting-matches. We all need these codes and we are damned well determined to ensure that they operate properly and fairly. In desperation, we may even go to volunteer experts to help us sort ourselves out, and that is a powerful way of endorsing the sensible practice of having such codes.

Second, there are the rules that seem designed to protect or promote sectional interests, which are a good idea if designed to protect disadvantaged minorities, typically vulnerable women or children, but a bad idea if they are coercive and doctrinaire, imposed on everyone indiscriminately by self-interested controllers. These latter commandments are the rules that cause most trouble, because a section of the community tends always to be elevated or victimised by special interests. Another reason for dismantling them is that they may be proselytising a viewpoint or belief-system that cannot be analysed or validated, i.e. they are false Big-Knowledge.

Any rule can be subject to criticism for its divisive potential, but sectional rules actually invite criticism. Currently there is concern about a number of such rules. Terrible practices such as Female Genital Mutilation, demanded by tradition and custom, or the deliberate indoctrination of children into one or other religion, do not have the general approval that should be the *sine qua non* of civilisation. Sharia Law may be acceptable in an Islamic country but has dubious relevance in a secular or non-Islamic society. The idealisation of democracy is liable to confuse or disrupt a society used to tribal rule, while dictatorship or constitutional monarchy is anomalous in a free society. Forcing young men to become soldiers is offensive to the ideal of personal choice. Forms and degrees of punishment for crimes range from humane to pathological. There is a long list of rules that contravene the concept of a free and fair life, and many of these rules were imposed upon our species before we can remember why and wherefore they exist.

Gods and monarchs are particularly difficult to fit into a good category of rules. Yet religion and autocracy are practised everywhere, often without question. How can this be? How has it happened that so much of our existence is overlorded by privileged sectionalism? For some unexplained reason, there is great media attention in the UK towards present and past royals. There must be an innate, or inculcated, mind-set in Britons that leads them to very nearly worship a king, a queen, a prince, or any other scion of the Tree of Exclusive Existence. At least we no longer suffer the mass psychosis that operates in North Korea, or that so recently ravaging China, but the world still harbours power-drunk mountebanks masquerading as saviours or great leaders.

Fom such sources we have been bequeathed a gigantic burden of rules that are really unjustified by any first category criteria, i.e. they do not enhance the general well-being, but often and violently the reverse. And the sectional interests governing most rules are deeply-buried landfill material, a noxious and dangerous waste. The Ten Commandments or the Seven Deady Sins, and most of the so-called Holy Scriptures, do not connect valuably with the general human condition, nor reflect real issues in this modern world that we have laboured so hard to ruin.

Culling the Rules?

It is at least interesting, even if the opposite of reassuring, to observe what should be the most active and effective rule-cleansing activity available to humankind: the parliamentary process. But how is it in practice? The British parliament, with its long and often turbulent history, has made a very large number of rules in its time. Yet it is hard to judge whether the process has been good, bad, or too mixed to be sure which. Great issues such as female suffrage or employment of children, and especially the vileness of the slave trade, have left scars on the collective conscience, and it was far too long before corrective legislation eventually happened. Then there are the hangovers from even worse times, such as the second chamber of non-elected notables, and the persistence of royals and aristocracy who have more power than is admitted (e.g. the queen's elderly son's attempts to have his ideas enshrined in law or practice).

The system is fatally flawed, too, by the very electoral system that is intended to protect democratic rule. Politicians notoriously pander to the populace before elections and change their stance if elected. We, the people, have abundant evidence of lies and corrupt practices. There can be no doubt that power matters more in politics than honesty, and that sheer greed is often a primary motive. Yet we are arguably one of the best parliamentary democracies.

The great issues of governance - education, defence/security, health, jurisprudence, demography, and, dare I say it, happiness of the people - these are endlessly debated and frequently reformed, but the results are lacklustre, confusing, or destructive. In questions of morality, conscience, egalitarianism, there is immense confusion, and endless argument. When it comes to using force, whether internally on our own citizens, or externally in war or military intervention, it often seems to be the smallest possible cabal of ministers who make the decisions, not always transparently, but often with chaotic results. And in our case, in the UK, there is the added neurosis of being partly governed by foreigners in Brussels, something that the British seem to dislike intensely (even if it is good for them).

The Unassailable Collective

From time to time, every few years in Britain, we have an election and even if our country is then realigned it is still an almost mediaeval dictatorship not significantly different from the one it succeeds. In between, the people are frequently on the streets in protest marches, or workers are on strike, and the police finish up fighting us, their employers. There are sectional interests at play, sometimes racial, sometimes religious, and even the toffs have been known to demonstrate against restrictions to their beloved blood-sports. The undemocratic Anglican alliance, that of state and church, adds another factitious factor, and currently we have a weird debate about Britain's identity as a Christian Country: this involves much moral gerrymandering, and the added insult to our intellects of our prime minister hectoring us to be more Christian. I think that this might actually be illegal and if not, it should be.

It isn't merely unassailable, the collective is also untrustworthy. Britain is, in its sedate way, a dangerous country, although I accept that there is a long list of more dangerous places to live in this unfortunate world. The search for civilisation is hard and even dangerous, despite looking in all the right directions, with the best of intentions. What, then, does a person do for peace and serenity and a modest degree of fulfilment? How are rules so bad when they are so necessary? What can be trusted?

Move Your Goalposts

It may be the time for rebellion, personal rebellion, preferably not law-breaking as that could lead to worsening life circumstances, but rebellion against the rules that make life dull, restricted, and arduous. It is probably not so much the external rules that matter most anyway, but those that have entered into, or been created in, the psyche, poisoning its creativity and crushing its vitality. These internal goalposts are usually the most restricting, least useful, quite insignificant to the external world, and hardest to move. For these reasons the internal rules are the ideal targets for progressive rebellion.

Some system such as the Enneagram or humanistic psychology can help the process. On the whole, however, it is best to avoid ritualised enlightenment, as offered by even the least doctrinal religion or spiritual philosophy. The Enneagram, for all its merits, suffers from a doctrinal mind-set and is heavily influenced by the notions of sin and redemption: there is even the divine reference-point, usually characterised as essence. For myself, I have found Existential work most useful, as well as some Taoist modes, and, especially, the whole mystery of the so-called Void or Emptiness. In my experience, the demon king in the Play of Personal Life is the Self, the element that seems to command us to be as we think we should be. In fact, the required rebellion is probably mostly against the Rules of the Self.

As I explained in the book, 'Freedom River - The Infinite Beginning', the very idea of the unitary self is completely absurd. As a conservative estimate, the average human being is made up of trillions of separate living units, diploid and haploid body cells of the type-species plus parasites, lodgers, and permanent residents. Each of these living units is an individual, a cell or a 'self', so that to call the overall conglomeration of thousands of millions *the* self is totally preposterous. This error, widespread, even global, in our species, is a supremely serious and foolish mistake. It is a mistake for humankind in general, probably uncorrectable because of our limited awareness, but also a mistake for us as individuals. This, therefore, is where the rebellion should begin.

Trojan Horse-Sense

Fortunately for anyone seeking respite from the delusion of selfhood, there is an inbuilt opportunity for shifting the goalposts. It is the nervous system; the communication network that keeps a semblance of order in the multicellular, infinitely complex, horde of constituent cells of animals such as the human. Typical of the vertebrates, though by no means exclusive to them, evolutionary development over millions of years has so far invented consciousness, or at least its minimal relative, sentience. The ability to think and feel, which is the human way of describing the process of its own subjectivity, does seem to work fairly well in keeping the fantastic and diverse complex of cells in a coherent state. There is no way of knowing how this has come about, nor why it should have happened at all, and such is the nature of the mind, there must be doubt as to whether it actually exists. My sentience and my consciousness seem to be real enough, but only because my sentience and consciousness work in that way. Even this, rather basic, awareness is inherently suspect and perhaps a collective and individual delusion of my kind. The vast field of philosophy and science that constitutes human knowledge, like the more primitive arena of religious ideology, may be utterly nonsensical, and none of us can be sure that this is not the case.

Out of this interesting fermentation that we describe as thought, arose the ancient and persistent mind-set called 'self'. This label seemed to fit the reflexive experience of being a coherent state of conscious and biological activity in human animals, and was extended to apply to some degree to non-human animals as well. This seemed quite reasonable, at least as a working hypothesis. It was never, of course, a plain fact. If one does nothing beyond exposing the pseudoknowledge involved in the great confidence-trick called the self, there will be much moving of goalposts and a weakening or elimination of many of the worst rules imposed upon the individual psyche.

My own assault upon the self-citadel began about a decade after I began to work on *awareness* and *being* as more important than the usual round of beliefs and doings. The book 'Ways of Being', first published in 2010 under the title of 'Mystikosmos', gives an extended account of my battle with the fixations of selfhood. In some ways, the self is the repository of all that is onerous and destructive in the internal rules that seem so important until we see through them.

The fight goes on. These self-rules are entrenched, much of them hidden in the unconscious mind, and they infest the collective as well as the individual psyche. The so-called ego is the most obvious manifestation of self-mania, and much work is done by some people in an attempt to tame the ego and make themselves less obnoxious. In general, this doesn't work well, because the ego-taming is merely a sop to the self and a process still trapped in the rule-nexus. You have to go deeper and further than the popinjay ego. By all means give the ego a serious drubbing, but be prepared for a bigger struggle when facing the self. At this stage of the book, it will suffice to explain one aspect of self that is particularly virulent, and leave wider discussion until subsequent chapters. All I want to do at this stage is to illustrate the harmful nature of self-induced rules. It is apparently an innate need for human animals, and who knows what other creatures, to have a complex idea called self-esteem. What is it?

I Am Good

Ask a friend how he is and nowadays he does not reply 'I'm OK, thanks', or 'Pretty well, considering', but he utters the strange phrase, 'Oh, I'm good, thanks'. I am not suggesting that this is highly significant, but rather that it is ironic to declare in terms that could be confused with virtue. It merely symbolises, for me, the importance each of us is liable to attach to the health or success or congeniality of the complex organism standing in our shoes; or the opposite states, if we feel miserable. There is, in the multicellular matrix called 'me', a duty to do well or to be well or to seem well. It is, however, dangerous to tell the truth because we may then be pitied for our wretchedness or pilloried for our self-satisfaction and unfairly good luck.

In other words, the rule is to manage our image so as to optimise our self-esteem. The rule is, to be blunt, to tell a tissue of lies. Or to obfuscate by claiming the truth of something that could not stand up to drastic investigation. Our self-image is like an internal god, or a hoary archetype; so much so, indeed, that the primary and deepest archetype is usually publicised as the self, which says a lot about the Jungian ego. The fabrication of selfhood, something that is innocent enough at the biological level, is in the vainglories that are made or achieved in its name, whereupon it is no longer the basic, biological being, but an imagination-game, a flight of endless fantasy.

Eight
I Am God

The Crime of Self-Importance

The work to be done is to explore the falsity of the central archetype, this self we have created in our imagination, and to expose the fantasy, thereby to edge into reality. (Or *leap* into reality if you subscribe to the notion of instant enlightenment.) Just as the false self is the most reprehensible aspect of the human psyche, the worst danger of the false self, as the rampant ego, is its self-importance.

Given the highly sentient nature of the individual human mind, and its capacity for fantasy and exaggeration, it is understandable that a human creature's consciousness of itself will be gigantic. It, the human creature, is, however, a conglomeration, a massive miscellany of microscopic bits and pieces, several trillion of them, and thousands of different kinds. Its fantasy of oneness is just not realistic. It may suit our individual pride to conceive of the individual person as a unique unity, but this fiction does not stand up to critical analysis.

I am not asserting that we are empty of selfness, far from it. Our egoic or self-based behaviour demonstrates how determined we are, biologically and imaginatively, to hold a position in our environment, to survive and act purposively and successfully. The issue is that we fudge our complexity and variability. As a metaphor, the Buddhist 'oceanic' quality of selfness is very persuasive. Like the sea, my self is a moving, changing entity of great complexity.

I may be like a sea, but I am not like a sea-god. The philosophy of self is of relatively little interest or importance, like the self itself, but ideas about one's personal self can distort an entire life That is important. Also important is the extent to which each of us claims to be important. And especially important is the way we activate or use our supposed importance.

It could be fairly claimed that each of us cannot possibly assess our own importance. That is for others to do. You may say that that is only worldly importance and that your importance is as a spirit or a soul. Then it is something beyond mere day-to-day interactions, whereas the self-importance I wish to demolish is that which makes a person feel superior (or perhaps inferior) to others as a result of some imaginary and largely secret personal qualities.

Once again we come across the distinction between behaviour and belief. Self-importance is a belief-system, and as such is entirely a fantasy. It will affect behaviour, necessarily, usually by increasing personal obnoxiousness, but it isn't behaviour *per se*. If we concentrate on our behaviour, we can evaluate its significance largely by how we impact on the world around us. Is it good behaviour or bad behaviour, regardless of how we think of ourselves? There are no excuses. It is just the way we behave.

The world does however appear more complex when we focus on our behaviour rather than on how wonderful we are. We have to take notice of how other people react to us. Perhaps we begin to see a more subtle world, as the detail comes into focus. This is part of the process of coming awake as, inevitably, to be self-important is the very core of asleepness.

A Sensory Analogy

I was asked to write a poem about the five senses. I have always felt revulsion at the crudity of this concept. How could a multi-multi-cellular creature possibly be confined to five ways of experiencing the world? Again, we are faced with over-simplification in the interests of unified significance. It is true that there are five basic ways of experiencing the outer world but that is not the same as saying we have five senses. What is a sense, after all? How do all these cells and lodger-organisms operate in terms of experiencing their world?

For a start, every one of the millions of bacteria that are part of 'my' body, have some awareness of their environment. That is millions of awarenesses. Then there are the millions of cells which carry 'my' genes, each of which is in some way aware of its environment in 'my' body. 'I', the 'me' that I identify as 'myself', am actually a vast and diverse colony of living organisms each with its individual sense of being.

After a bit of research, I realised that the number of sense-organs in a human body were also in the millions, not just a quintet of superordinate functions, sight, hearing, touch, taste, and smell. I wrote the poem as a homage to this vastness. Below are the first two verses of the poem, to make the point that while it may be accurate enough to think in terms of five major areas of sentience, each of those areas involves a vast array of secondary characters, each of which is sensing, and sending messages to the central nervous complex.

The verses also refer to a deeper mystery, i.e. how does mind, or consciousness, fit in with these immense legions of sensory units? It reminds me of an acupuncturist friend who, when I questioned the absence of the brain in his ancient charts, blithely said the brain was not involved in acupuncture. Really? That needed some careful thought.

I concluded that neither acupuncture nor acupuncturists could be expected to function too well without brain-activity. Conversely, the amount of sensory data being processed by the actual human brain is phenomenally huge.

Who, if anybody, or any brain, is rethinking the Big-Knowledge delusions of complementary medicine?

THE SENSES

Aristotle's Dragon Children:
The Famous Five

Here there be dragons of multiple meanings.
In this vast sea of consciousness they do breed.
At first there were only five, Aristotle's children:
Dragons of his mighty mind. A mind, supreme
In opinion of itself, with a quintet of scaly senses.
They saw, they heard, they felt, they smelt, they tasted,
And thus he conquered for two thousand years and more.
While consciousness drags its feet, an endless mystery.
But yet, imagine a mind without the senses, as blank
As a lifeless sea, or a laptop lacking a whiff of software.
Could consciousness exist without a jot of input data?
Is there an overwhelming question going begging?
Does mind actually exist except in our imagination?
We either downgrade thinking or upgrade sensing:
We can't have our consciousness-cake and eat it.
There's more. It's time to catch the bus of neuroscience.

Look and Listen Closely:
Eyes and Ears Multiplied

The five old dragons don't give credit for all that we can do:
At least a dozen further senses swim in our internal sea.
There are the Sensors, witty little beasts enabling a sense to be,
They tune in to one specific sensation, a sense within a sense.
In each eye there lie millions of sensors, the rods and the cones.

One hundred and twenty million rods pick up rays of light and
Seven million cones, in three varieties, selectively see colour.
A myriad of senses in each window of the soul, yet there's more,
Before listening to the ear - here, as every student knows, a trinity
Performs: first the gathering of sound to the drum, second to the forge;
The hammer, the anvil and the stirrup gather up vibrations, and third:
To the coiled cochlea and its vibrating hairs, which feed the nerve
That feeds the brain. But, 'miracles never cease', there is another
Sensor yet inside the box, fixed upon the gravitational field, keeping
Constant check on orientation, letting you and me keep balance
In an uncertain world, a sense of stability, where we might fail and
fall.

How Am I Important?

Objectively speaking, the human body-mass is a very big multicellular miscellany. But is that somehow actually important? A sperm whale is even bigger, but does that make it many times more important than a human. Its brain is over five times the size of mine or yours but it has a gigantic body to manage. The male sperm whale is 50 feet long and weighs 40,000 kilograms. For an animal several hundred times human size, how important is the sperm whale's self? Maybe it is too intelligent to bother to have a self. A paramecium animal is so small (length measured in thousandths of an inch) that it needs to be seen with a magnifying glass, and is only a single cell, but does that make it a creature of virtually no importance? Perhaps paramecium needs a gigantic self-importance to compensate for its lack of size? No, of course not? That would be a scandalous solecism? It is intriguing, then, that we humans think we are so important? Why is the human self, in particular, such a grand affair? Why do we give it such great importance?

A Popular Delusion

Our psychiatric sciences are in a difficult quandary. Diagnosis of pathological states must imply some concept of what is normal, and psychiatry has the task of finding how to identify the abnormal and how to moderate its severity. That must be extremely difficult, if not just impossible. What, for instance, does an atheistic psychiatrist make of a religious patient? Or, if you like, vice versa. The mind-set of a Catholic or a Muslim has to seem very strange indeed to a rationalist; and again, vice versa. A Buddhist, faced with the usual egotistical demeanour of a Western entrepreneur, must surely feel the shock of alienation. How is delusion identified in these confrontations?

I perceive that the human species as a whole must be delusional in terms of its idea of the self and its importance. I do regard humankind as pathological in this matter. I see it as a very serious mental disease, especially in a life-form that is so intelligent, and so powerful as it develops its weapons technology. Therefore, other than the modest level of selfhood we share with other creatures, I regard the colossal absorption with our individual person, and our focus on its importance, as a collective psychosis.

If blame is the right word, I consider the main culprits in this pathology to be the Big-Knowledge religions, primarily Judaism and Christianity. Christianity is outstandingly the worst because of its absurd claim that we all suffer from original sin, and the ridiculous fiction of the Garden of Eden. The self-psychosis is diminished in certain spiritual philosophies, such as Tao, Buddhism and Epicureanism. But the global situation is dominated by the self-importance delusion. Unfortunately, science and philosophy are Big-Knowledge ventures that exacerbate rather than reduce the sickness. Politics and business are, virtually by definition, self-importance delusions in the extreme.

Universe in the Skull

In another poem, I look at the egotism lodged in the human mind, or brain, or total being, or wherever we keep it. There is considerable ambivalence and some chaos in the psyche, but overall the multitude of thoughts and feelings seems to insist that what is in our heads is of cosmic importance. This would be oddly true if we accepted that our notions of the universe were confined to our minds. The universe would then be a construct of the human mind, which would necessarily cause us to feel significant. However, and whether or not, the universe actually is, it is surely the case that its nature depends on the observer. Or, more, accurately perhaps, the universe looks different to different observers, even of the same species and in different stages of the observer's development. It is as if the universe exists (uniquely) in the sensory apparatus of each living thing.

Bigbrain

Bigbrain longs for knowledge of
Itself. Otherwise assumes the worst,
And best, of its own imagination:
True, pending truth, till knowledge comes.
Believes there must be thoughts
That bless the thinker and
Understanding that can elevate
The understanding head.
Bigbrain allows no possibility
Unworthy of a cosmic crochet-needle;
Turning up patterns in the dusty attic,
Searching for significant items, left idle
But useful, somehow, given time
To work it out, where it fits, there

In Bigbrain's attic, the truth appears to lie,
And if not truth, maybe beauty. Virtue?
The reward is knowledge. Even bad news
Has its price, or do I mean its own reward?

My World

I have more or less settled for the view that the universe is in our heads, and that the human head is the origin of the universe as we claim to know it. This is a hypertrophy of our consciousness, which forbids us from realising that the so-called universe may not exist, or if it does, might bear no resemblance to our (variable) view of it. Our minds are the mother and father of the cosmos as we perceive it. We have no doubt whatsoever that we are far and away the most important animals on this little corner of the supposed universe. We look for other kinds of life on other planets, but our racial insanity could only be intensified if we discovered real competition.

Of course, I don't *know* that the universe is a figment of human imagination; it is just a probability, based on certain undeniable biological 'facts'. It is pretty certain that different species have different concepts of the cosmos. It seems self-evident that a killer whale, for example, would experience the world differently from an earthworm. The senses and the nervous system impose limits and extensions on any creature's picture of existence. The plants would add another unknowable mass of perceptions. In this way, at least, there is a multitude of universes.

Staying with the human capacity for ideation, it should be obvious that we, as individuals, also have different concepts of the cosmos. Ask anybody and you will find that you will disagree in some way. Then, we can vary our individual perception, almost at will. I remember doing meditative exercises which involved extending our mental picture from the immediate room out into the farthest reaches of the world and beyond. We used to call it out-of-body-experience, and we imagined a silver thread to follow when we wanted to come back. It was easy, the only snag being that some of us were certain that we had actually gone somewhere else while others thought no such thing could possibly happen.

My point here is not whether humans can leave their bodies and go psychic walkabout. Why would that be such an issue for an animal that can produce delusions on demand? The actual issue is the extent to which each of us *feels* or *thinks* that we can envisage the infinite, whether it is the Big Bang, God, or little people at the bottom of the garden. And, more questionable still, whether we can have any knowledge of, or effect upon, the future. Here lies true madness, if only in the shape of megalomania.

Pathological Grandiosity

It seems that we, as infants, were naturally and necessarily megalomaniac. That is the impression I get from psychological literature. If true, this means that we come into the world with inbuilt grandiosity. We are, as infants, weak and inept, unable to function by ourselves. Yet we feel all-important, perhaps even all-powerful. This immense contradiction, between how we are and how we feel, is supposedly ironed out in the process of growing up. That would appear to be a natural development so that the individual can function out in the world. It is how other animals seem to do it.

In the non-human infant, the parent is programmed to withdraw progressively and, within a relatively short time, offspring and parent separate completely. Or, as in some species, there is a family or tribe in which the young animal eventually takes its place as an adult. So, in the human animal, how does this function?

Clearly it does, to some extent, with some human tribes having coming-of-age rituals to assist or promote the onset of responsible maturity in the young person. Yet infantile behaviour persists in human beings, often to an extreme degree. It is as if we have exceptional difficulty in growing out of our infantile grandiosity. I notice youngsters as they come out of school early in the afternoon, and they are obviously very far from maturity. But it is not much different when adults meet and behave as social creatures. I compare the play of fox cubs with human adults at play, and the similarity is unnerving.

No other species of mammal, except some fellow primates, shows such infantile behaviour in the adult phase. Maybe there is some play, but mostly the adult animal is seriously engaged on being grown up. If it has time for it, there will be a sleep in the sun. But racing about a playing field and screaming at competitors is, at most, an aberrant practice of monkeys. So are we more monkey than human in our love of infantile behaviour? Our mania for competition is largely infantile behaviour extended far beyond its natural time-span. It is generally not merely condoned but energetically promoted. It can be regarded as the luxury of an advanced species or, conversely, the failure of the normal development process in an animal type that is actually degenerate. The question is, why has it happened, however it may be judged?

The Naked Emperor

Hans Anderson told this good story. We can each be duped into foolishness by an effective swindler. The emperor parades before his people stark naked because he has been persuaded that he is wearing invisible clothes that enable him to see the flaws in his subjects. Driven by the need for superiority he becomes a figure of fun. Such is the stuff of grandiosity.

In the case of humankind as a whole, we are all emperors in our heads. That is how our heads have evolved. We might think the human head is the crown of creation, but it is merely the structure that happens to be upon our neck. It is a factory of megalomania. Our heads make us mad. We are convinced that we are emperors, each and all of us - though, of course, some more than others.

In a sense, this does not matter. Evolution is a hard-bitten master. It is a process that has no feelings. It has caused the Emperor Penguin to have a life of frozen horror, it has caused the Emperor Man to have a life of infantile madness. Who is there to care? Man is expendable, as is the ice-bound penguin. The biosphere needs flies and bacteria and photosynthesis, but it does not need man. We are a superfluous species, biologically and environmentally. But only nature itself, the blind and indifferent progenitor of all life, can put us in our place. If nature has made a mistake in making man it will correct its error by unmaking us.

Who cares? Well, I do, for a start. And I know a few other humans who care, too. It is not so much an affection for our species as such, for it is not very attractive as it is. But we think humankind might have more to offer and more potential than it has allowed itself to develop. It could become a remarkable part of nature. We even suppose that our species could degrandiose itself if it really wanted to. But I, for one unimportant human molecule, do not rate our chances at all. Our big-brain fetish shows no sign of letting up. We get worse, if anything.

Shrinking the Self

All efforts to reform our species must fail unless we unravel the skein of selfhood. Until we recognise our unimportance we cannot begin to civilise our species. Our minds are fixed upon our absolute magnificence, so the world collapses around (and because of) us while we continue to search for more ways to exploit our power.

I have written at some length on the subject of awakeness, the open door of the psyche through which we encounter a deeper reality than the merely biological field. Unfortunately, the undoubted capacity of the human mind to find and accept truths, however relative and provisional, is stymied by the human need for aggrandisement. Therefore our discovered 'truths' are typically slanted towards ourselves. It is the knee-jerk reaction of the enquiring psyche. Somehow, as individuals, we must learn how to interrupt the reflex. If we could do that collectively it would be a miracle.

How can a person do it and what benefit ensues? I think it has to be a developing habit, a continuing audit of what one thinks, feels and does. We have had a sort of grounding in this at school, at home, in church or in some service or other. A very poor grounding, it must be said, because the proposed disciplines have been aimed at different targets. However, by identifying and choosing more appropriate targets even those inefficient methods could become useful in trimming the worst excesses of self-importance.

Outfacing The Monster

The monster is the god in the human head, the (usually) unspoken assertion that each of us is God, the self, projected into lordship of the universe as we see it. A lot of us are atheists, which is a rather promising sign. Unfortunately, god-obsession still seems to proliferate, often with encouragement from people who ought to be more responsible. The question is not so much whether God exists or not, but how long the human race and the suffering biosphere can survive the God's influence in the human psyche. It is not really a god at all, of course, but a massive projection of the human ego out onto an innocent universe. God and Self are the same human delusion.

God is really a fabricated excuse for not being responsible for everything we do and everything we are. It, the manufactured deity, is made responsible for what we do and supposedly gratifies or punishes us for wrongdoing. It is the most powerful and elevated form of the ultimate rescuer and its main purpose is to protect us from fear, especially of death, but also from the hard work of living an awake and responsible existence.

In a sense, I would have a lot of sympathy for God, if there were such a being, because of the way He (It, Her, Them) is made a scapegoat for our lack of moral fibre, our lack of skilful will, our lack of compassion, and the way we nurture the three poisons of lust, hate, and delusion. As I have already mentioned, the Christian juggling trick whereby the unfortunate deity is made into an ogre of selfish, maniacal, spite, is very shocking and shows just how perfidious we can be.

I admit that there may be people who experience God as a kind of super-nature, a neutral, sublime entity that does no wrong and does no good either, but just absolutely *is*. Indeed, the superb Baruch Spinoza provided the civilised world with the ultimate resolution of the God-problem by saying God and Nature were the same thing. The only snag with this is that nature is pretty foul in many ways. And there is, of course, neither fairness nor kindness in the heedless universe. Unless you count the strange capacity of humanity to show love and gentleness along with its other attributes. But that's not confined to humans, as anyone who has received the blessing of love from a cat or dog can testify.

Therefore, the least each of us can do is to live in an awake manner and try to avoid the many temptations to be an egomaniac, particularly the complex religious trap in which a supposed creator of everything is modelled on, or by, the perverted human mind. Big-Knowledge is the ultimate monster, and it should be outfaced if we are to achieve our potential instead of wasting it as we have for millennia. At least we can attempt it individually. That would probably count for something.

The next chapter explores the feasibility of challenging our collective egomania, and of refuting the massive Big-Knowledge forces from the past which threaten to continue to dominate and ruin us in the unknown future.

Nine
The Cleansing

In the previous book, 'Freedom River - The Infinite Beginning ', I concluded with a confession of my own need to make radical changes in my state of being, so that I might become more awake, or more real. It is encapsulated in the following quotation:

'Radical Choices'

Bearing in mind that I, we, face an unknown ending, and that we have much less knowledge than we pretend to have, choosing radical alternatives should be done in a spirit of humility as far as possible. I wish not to be grandiose in my assumptions. There is far too much grandiosity in humankind, along with a significant degree of wretchedness. So, at my age and stage of life, I will be cautious. Yet I do favour as much radicalism as I can manage. In a way, it is what I live for. I have tried to define it, and now I would like to itemise some radical opportunities, including those I have already tried to take and implement.'

I then itemised the areas of my behaviours, the negative content of my personality, where the radical changes seemed most necessary. I considered that I was still too competitive and dogmatic, while also feeling under duress internally and externally and being too desolate in my emotions and opinions. I vowed to work on these four radical opportunities.

The result so far is a greater comprehension of the deeper problems that express themselves as competition, dogma, duress and despair, these four pillars of my negative personality. They must also be, to some extent, the expression of my self-importance, or my ego, or maybe just my particular set of self-delusions. There is probably no simple one-to-one connection between the four qualities I selected for radical action and the constitution of my personal egomania. However, as I explore my own emotional chemistry I do find that radical change is occurring, and I suspect that there may be wider implications for my contemporaries.

From self-analysis, I categorise five main forms of my self-importance, or egomania, that connect to the four components of the negative personality. At times, there is crossing-over or blending of the two sets, thereby giving further evidence of how Big-Knowledge and self-importance work together to poison one's existence. What follows is an exploration of the scope for trimming the hypertrophied self and, possibly, the resulting freeing from aspects of negative personality.

Slimming The Self.

1. Mirror-Image. Narcissus fell in love with his own reflection. The story goes that he didn't realise it was merely a mirror-image not an actual being. You might think that anyone as stupid as that was better dead. Anyway such was Narcissus's disappointment, even grief, at not being able to 'have' himself, that he did die, by his own hand. As a metaphor, this myth has great poignancy. We are often astonished by the suicide of young, bright people whom we might consider to be on the verge of flowering into powerful adulthood. What is it that drives them to lethal despair? It could be that the Narcissus myth is all too accurate. Perhaps the beautiful young realise their external qualities are of little worth compared with their inner yearning for purpose and meaning. Or, like my second sister, they may be so terrified of death that they feel they must bring it forward and thereby save themselves from further fear.

To a degree, there is Narcissism in all of us. And it is not necessary for one to be beautiful for the bad magic to work. It is enough to be obsessed. The point is that it shows us our degree of self-importance, if we care to see it, and may free us up to do some demolition-work. I might question my own Narcissism as follows:

'You are vain and you are vulnerable to your vanity. It will control you if you do not control it. Think why you are so dazzled by yourself? What is the benefit to you of all this self-idolatry? I, the real person trapped in your false image, get nothing but pain from your fixation. In fact, nothing matters except the simple processes of living and being. You are able to live discreetly, if you want to. Your exhibitionism is embarrassing to me, your true self. I think you are making a fool of you, also of me. I really don't mind how beautiful or ordinary or ugly you are in your mirror.'

Some, all, or none, of this kind of inner dialogue might bring on a degree of self-honesty. It is impossible to know what might work. All I can do is try. Whatever happens, as I edge closer to the truth, it is at least possible that I comprehend my own absurdity. It requires vigilance, too, for Narcissism does not survive ruthless observation. Like the mythical Greek, either my self-love dies or I do.

There is great danger in neo-new-age insistence on self-love. It may seem innocent enough to say, as gurus do, 'You can't love others until you love yourself'. But it is dangerous nonsense. It makes love into a commodity, as in, 'until you have enough love for yourself there won't be enough left over for anyone else.' This dictum in fact promotes Narcissism. It also seems to feed on the malign concept of original sin, the need for forgiveness, for example, being convinced there is love for you in the universe.

Sure enough, it is necessary for me to be in a *state of* love, but that is not the same as *having* love or *giving* love. Love is a behaviour, or an emotional potentiality of behaviour. It is entirely mysterious, naturally. I just have to be ready for it to happen and when it does, not try to commandeer it for my own purposes. To expect it for oneself, or to proclaim it for someone else, is artful self-importance. For the first, why should I be so special as to warrant it? For the second, actions speak louder than words.

2. God-Intoxication

Here the problem is identification with a supposed super-self, typically gigantic but invisible, and beyond the limits of ordinary reality. It might seem that such a fixation would reduce, not increase, self-importance. After all, you the worshipper are infinitely miniscule compared with the great universal deity. How could you be so mad as to assume that you have any significance at all? You are a mere molecule. Unless, of course, you regard the supreme power of the universe as your papa, or a kindly aunt, in which case you are hopelessly and insanely infantile.

Unfortunately, the human mind doesn't really work as logically as that. Remember that reflected glory may be better than no glory at all. This is all too obvious at the mundane level, especially as we are in the throttling grip of a celebrity-culture, in which even the mere birth of a royal baby may have large sections of the populace in paroxysms of excitement.

As an Atheist and anti-royalist, perhaps I assume that I am free from God-intoxication. Well, I'd be wrong in that assumption. My form of it might be the most lethal of all. Following my own rationale, I consider the whole God-fantasy to be a projection of the gigantic human ego out of the microscopic human person and into the limitless external space. I deliberately avoid this manoeuvre yet I am willing to bet that my sense of personal significance is as big as a pope's unrecognised megalomania.

If it is, as I suspect, *the* human disease, then I will have a superhuman task in curing it in myself. But I don't accept that it's impossible. Surely it can be challenged at least? But I have difficulty in imagining a corrective inner dialogue for a literal God-believer. It seems like wilfully presenting myself as a lunatic. But if I imagine a God-stricken friend I might try the following:

'Which of the thousands of gods have you chosen to be your celestial overlord? The "One God", you say? And which one is that? What do I mean? Well, leaving aside the thousands of tribal, local and historical, spirits, demi-gods, river-gods, volcano-gods, fertility-goddesses, Osiris, Isis, Tammuz, Odin, Wotan, all those Egyptian and Indian people- and animal-gods, not to mention Yaweh, Allah, Jehovah... No, I am not being frivolous, nor sarcastic, I just want to know which is the One God you purport to give all your love and trust. Who? Or whom? Why? Because it seems that you don't so much recognise God as make him in your own image, as he is supposed to do for you.

'Nonsense, he exists, he is real, he is everywhere. You are just blind and obstinate.'

'Well, we might both be that, certainly. But why are you so specific in your God-identity? And how have you chosen one rather than another? Why not just see nature as remarkable and mysterious and wonderful and beautiful and terrible?

'But that is how I see God.'

'So it's just a name, then? We are both lost in mystery and wonder?

'Er. Um. I wouldn't go that far. I need my particular faith.'

For an Atheist, it is a different dialogue, perhaps even more difficult because there is the belief that God has been extirpated so there's no case to answer? Wrong: the old monster has just gone underground. I will have to chase him through the psychic catacombs. Those, like me, who have seen through the confidence trick of faith in a deity, have still a rampaging ego-self, fear-laden, to assuage. If I cannot hang my self-importance on the God hat stand I have to find somewhere else for it. Chances are that I will choose my own glorious specialness, or that of my family, or tribe, or country, on which to elevate my personal monument.

How do I not do that? Mock humility is a favourite ploy for the ungodly as much as the godly. 'It's only me', we announce at the door or on the phone, and then spread our ego-marmalade thickly on every available slice of toast. With the greatest of humility. No-one must know the guilty secret of our unique wonderfulness.

If I awake from this sweetest of sickly dreams, I will be too shocked to believe what I have been doing. But, with patience and surrender to reality, I may be able to accept the truth about myself. I find I can live with, even celebrate, that it is *actually* only me, but in the sense of being part of a colossal continuum of consciousness, at best, or basic sentience, at worst. It is hard to be a micron in an infinite Gaussian curve, but it is also an immense relief once I accept that I am free of that damned self-importance.

3. Ambition

It is quite futile for me to try to remember how and when I first became ambitious. At a guess, it was probably around the age of ten or twelve. Grammar school was a forcing house for the seedling of my desire to achieve. Before then, I was a boy who played marbles, rode bikes, coarse-fished, shot with bows-and-arrows, catapults and peashooters, and read adventure-books.

Then my world changed, or I did, and I began to have goals and standards and tried to be the best I could be at anything and everything. That condition steadily worsened, until I reached exhaustion point in my late middle age and my world deteriorated into drabness, despite the beautiful things in my home and environment. Power and importance had been my driving forces and I gradually realised that they were false gods. A new life was then open to me, and I have tried to become awake and secure in my being, without power or importance.

I have recently addressed this process in writing books that mean everything to me and very little to anyone else. To some significant extent, this has been a fundamental part of my new way of living. Instead of the self-gratification of achievement, my energy has transferred to the inner dialogue, in which I question all my assumptions. I still enjoy it if someone nods agreement to my thoughts. Why should I lose that small pleasure? But I would strongly advise writing the inner dialogue. It would probably help anyone who seriously wishes to challenge the given mandates of ambition.

I have just written a poem about the process I have lived through. It is as follows:

A Day Dawned
A day dawned golden, when I knew I was a river, not a road.
As when a child I had dreamed and lived a country stream,
Before my youth set out upon a path bearing the futile load
Of mere ambition, leaping banks, crossing bridges, eyes agleam.
Not a road then, nor following a path, except the ways to hills
And down again, through valleys, to have the company of brooks
Was to be within the water, the water within me, such childhood

MICHAEL SCOTT

Required and was given in and of the nature in which I wild-lived.

Once lost, my river-self drowned in dryness, as if a soul parched,
Full-human in my hubris, travelling upon the earth, my river-being
Trapped in aridity of canals, dead water, or locked in traffic jams;
I was now man, a maker of blank miracles, no longer inner-seeing.
Not that I knew myself lost. The beacons blazed bold promises,
I was on the road to everywhere, clear in the achievement-brochure
There were no dragons, no minotaur's raged, I ached with destiny.
And the river I had been was dammed, blasted, silted, and abandoned.

How, then, has this golden vision shone through, anew, on this day?
It has been thirty summers and thirty winters, to make the void and
Then make it full, a sweet space, for my stream-self to flow again,
For bridges and manufactured waterways to fall and fail, the roads
And rails to pit and break, the green of travel wither, the high life
To lie low, a generation, to joyous catastrophe: the bells rang loud
In my creaking skull, they slowly made me wake. I knew them,
Though not their meaning, and the understanding came near late.

To live a river is to stand, still, in time, yet move molecularly, enigma
Unknown to life as road, which lies low and lets the world go by,
A busy nonentity, as was I, before I became a stream again. Moving
As a rivulet or brook, I stay within my world and it moves with me
I am a continuity within continuity, everything is congruent with all.
Nothing has changed, everything has changed, I am a rural beck again,
I harbour little fishes and water crowfoot, kingcups on my shoulders,
A kingfisher shines bright above me; I watch the tadpoles grow feet.

4. Charisma

Charisma is a certain quality of an individual personality by virtue of which he is set apart from ordinary men and treated as endowed with supernatural, superhuman, or at least specifically exceptional powers or qualities. These are such as are not accessible to the ordinary person, but are regarded as of divine origin or as exemplary, and on the basis of them the individual concerned is treated as a leader. (Max Weber, German sociologist in the 1920's.)

This is heady and imaginative, but how true is it, and how meritorious or useful? By Weber's definition, I suppose Adolf Hitler would be a charismatic leader. And by the same token, one of the greatest British leaders, Clement Atlee would have scored nil points. Hitler destroyed everything he touched and left a legacy of loathing and depravity, Atlee quietly puffed on his pipe and laconically led the British to a degree of post-war recovery.

I am tempted to put charisma in the category of diseased selfhood, or more pointedly to say that, confronted by a charismatic person, I would run for cover. Yet we feast, as a race, upon the flesh of charismatics. We do not confront them, denounce them, or put them in a ducking-stool. Or perhaps we do, when they fail to deliver on their promises or display mental instability. It reminds me of the great art of shamanism, in which a possessed person was either a demi-god to his tribe or a figure of fun or detestation.

On the whole, I think charismatic people are untrustworthy, though less for themselves, perhaps, than for the gullibility of everyman. If we look deeply and honestly into ourselves, we may perceive an aching desire to shine. We want admiration; we'd like to be adored. This is not about talent or brilliance or genius. It is about wanting to glow in the dark. It is a hunger for admiration.

Now why do I want to be admired? Is this not a skewed competitiveness? Is it not the ravenous self-looking for a banquet? If so, why do I need the applause of others to feel good within myself? Is this not a similar infantilism to that of the god-seeker? The self-fault here is in the giving away of one's own integrity. There is everything possible wrong with depending upon others for my self-esteem, and even worse is the need for self-esteem as a vital process. Why can't I just let myself be and concentrate my efforts on real work like being in a loving space with others and making the world as beautiful as possible? The vaunted self is just not worth the trouble. Self-love and self-hatred are the faces of Janus, they are both unsustainable poses, neither is genuine. They are toxic effluents from a rotten state of being.

5. Rescue and Redemption

I am beginning to comprehend why Christianity seems to me to be the very worst of the plethora of religions. For reasons I have fully explained elsewhere, I regard all religions with abhorrence. But most of the many Christianities stand out as particularly ugly and dangerous. The human self-mania is at screaming pitch in this awful global plague.

The overweening human self is at the core of the Christian disaster - disaster because of the misery and backwardness it has wrought, despite some generous intentions of some practitioners of the cult. In its general tenor, apart from its abominable proselytising of itself to people all and sundry, it may seem no worse than any other occult practice; it may seem merely a fondness for the supernatural. If that were all, I would probably dislike it no more than Hinduism or Islam. But I do dislike it specially. And even though all religion is ego-self tainted, the contamination is at its worst in Christianity.

In terms of the error of self-importance, how could anything be worse? The premise is that a major god, allegedly The God of All, has made the universe, maybe *is* the universe. This god is no worse than any other, and certainly not a fiercer and sillier deity than its Jewish precursor, Jaweh or whatever. No, it is his half-son that is the problem. There are son-issues in the other religions, and famously in the vile tale of Isaac's near demise at the hand of his father as directed by their monomaniac god. The Abrahamic gods seem to have had a predilection for filicide.

Fathers and sons do have a problem. Regardless of imaginary goings-on in celestial hyperspace, there is plenty of trouble down here. Maybe mothers and daughters have their problems too, this is not exclusive territory. But the Christian myth parallels so much horror in human affairs. I am sure that I expected my father to love me and be interested in me for myself (not his projection of himself onto me, if he did that). But, as I grew up, he distanced himself from me. It seemed like dislike. I became afraid of him. Then, when I had left childhood behind, he suddenly became rather friendly and, much later, almost seemed to develop an affection for me.

I have been interested in the work done by people like Robert Bly, which has generally indicated that many men suffer seriously from perceived faults in their fathers or from faults their fathers seem to have found in them. For all his obvious faults and my own, I miss him, though he died over three decades ago. There seems to be a missed opportunity, too, though I could not imagine what we could ever have done for each other.

So when I consider rescue and redemption, I feel these words as having special resonance for me. If it is not too fanciful, I sense that my father and I had failed to put them into our lives, especially in relation to each other. Perhaps this is what we could have done for each other. Anyway these thoughts lead me to question whether the daemon of self-importance is what fathers and sons most need to deal with for their full development. It is, it seems to me, the special gift of father to son and son to father, to rescue each other from self-importance and redeem the errors they have made in terms of behaviours such as jealousy, competition, bullying, petulance, and haughtiness.

The human self-ideology lying behind the Christian fantasy interests and offends me. Why would the human mind expect, wish, or fantasise, that the Great God would kill his own son to enable humankind to forgive itself for breaking the Great God's rules? What is it about our particular species that expects the Lord of the Universe to make a terrible sacrifice on our behalf? Who do we think we are?

That is the real issue. Our own grandiosity. We have made a religion out of our sheer, gargantuan, self-importance. I almost feel sorry for the mythical celestial father and son caught up in the love-affair of humankind with itself. Doesn't it demonstrate dramatically and terribly how vastly the human mind overrates itself and its position in the immense continuity of nature? Is this not why we behave with such patronising disdain for our fellow living beings? Is it not the basic premise from which we calculate we can do anything we like to everything else?

These are surely crimes that are unforgivable. Shouldn't meditating on them help us to moderate our arrogance just a little? Whether or not we become better people will depend on how far we can go in taking responsibility for ourselves rather than piling all our pathology upon an innocent celestial icon, real or imagined.

The Mindself Conspiracy

Somehow, useful as it might be, the self-trimming process by mere shrinkage, as in the examples above, doesn't seem to go deep enough into human motivation. It is too much a palliative. A mere placebo, perhaps. It doesn't address the major problem, which is probably that we have great intelligence but yet not great enough. Big brained we may be, but it seems to me that primate evolution was not working on intelligence as much as technology: tool making, in fact. Many animals make or use tools. We might even say that plants use tools, in the form of pollen, perfume, fruit, seeds, and underground reservoirs. Being static, they probably have to be tool making to survive at all. Animals, who evolved later than plants, feed on plants and other animals, using locomotion to find and consume their food or prey. There is less need for tools of the kind plants needed merely to survive.

Of course, animals do use generative organs and products to spread their kind. In that sense, gonads are tools. But it is relatively unusual for an animal species to use tools for finding and eating food. In general, tool making and intelligence seem to be the critical link in animals such as apes, especially hominids. Putting it another way, intelligence is implicit in the making and using of tools. Or there are social strategies that require intelligence, as in the hunting by packs, prides or pods. It is an extra step in the manipulation of the environment. It goes beyond mere serendipity.

It is not known whether non-human animals are self-regarding in the various ways that humans are. But it may be an accidental product of intelligence, the highly developed tool making mind, to become self-conscious. Pride, or imagination, or, indeed, self-importance, may have been inevitable consequences of the development of the tool-making skills. Who knows how and why they coincide? But they seem to.

In any case, we are proud of our inventiveness and our power over less intelligent life-forms. Ant colonies may have the technology to farm aphids, and we might claim that that was a mere evolutionary blip, compared with the vast industry of the human species, which we might regard as a, if not the, defining feature of humankind. We feel godlike in our power, and it is a small, if stupid, step to assume that we are gods, or are descended from gods, or are on our way to becoming gods. We nod, metaphorically, at the heavens and think, conspiratorially, 'That's where we are going. If in no other way, it will be by resurrection and ascension after death. We have the myth to prove it.'

Doomed to Greatness

Look at the way royals and ecclesiastics and war-makers dress. One of my favourite comic images is the heir to the British throne dressed up in military finery. One day he will be an admiral, the next a field marshal, and the next a marshal of the air force. He will be bowed down by medals and gold braid, the rings of rank on his sleeve run from wrist to elbow. It is as if he has never heard Gilbert and Sullivan.

Archbishops and cardinals come in all shapes and sizes but they all dress like fashion models in a science fiction film. They are like overblown actors looking for fans. And, of course, they find them. We all like a good spectacle.

Dressing up is a human craze; and seems harmless enough. Except that it isn't. It is make-believe. It is falsehood, in the same way that the human personality is shot through with mendacity. I remember my parents, poor people, dressing up in their Sunday Clothes to go for a walk: showing off, bless their hearts. I certainly caught the bug early on. I loved to pretend I was a cowboy and I adored my choirboy outfit. Even the hideous scout-cub uniform, bilious green, with badges of dubious achievement and yellow circles on every surface, even that was somehow exciting. What is all that about, I ask?

Each of us is dyed-in-the-wool special, isn't it that? Is not that the great illusion we would die to defend? Perhaps we just can't accept that it is an illusion. Maybe we are patronising toward Walter Mitty, but isn't he in all of us? Recognised, it is a sad and foolish reality. But unrecognised it is a time-bomb in every mind. Absolutely no-one is really important, not as a general reference. One person might be important to another, but that's about as far as it goes. Fame is absurd. It makes fools of us all. But who actually acts as if that were true? Our actual doom is merely the end of our existence, our pretended doom is sublime, our terminal mendacity.

Ten
Blissful Unknowing

Complexly denied though it is, our fear is probably the absolute root of human distress. The fear in humankind can be described in many ways and categorised variously, but it seems generally certain that the top fear is of death.

The absurd inflation of the self might appear to an impartial observer to be quite enough of a burden for the human race to bear. But there's more. Thanks to existentialist analysis. It is, of course, closely connected with the self, ego, or personality and consists of an immense concentration upon *fear*. This also joins up with the Big-Knowledge projected into an unknown future, where the fear waits for us. As we are justifiably afraid of the future (experience of the past being quite enough to scare anyone), we simultaneously pay close attention to it but also deny the fear. This may seem a bizarre thing to do, but existential analysis (and, frankly, common sense, if you really think about it) demonstrates the many psychological conjuring tricks we perform so as to avoid facing the fear actually overwhelming us.

There are other serious fears, of course, though generally subordinate to the big one. We are also afraid, for example, of being isolated, collectively and individually alone in the universe, a fact that we also deny, preferring to think that we are mysteriously connected to some universal consciousness or other (a wilful misunderstanding of the reality that we are, indeed, connected to everything in nature but not in a nice, chummy, way). We are even, perversely, scared of freedom when it comes to practising it, because it means we have to take full responsibility for ourselves. The meaningless nature of existence is also a nagging misery to most of us; and we are really very afraid of being without a cosmic purpose. But our mortality frightens us the most.

Being an intelligent, conscious species we can't help being aware of these horrors. A great deal of our so-called knowledge consists of arguments and devices for neutralising the fears. The biggest divide, perhaps, in the way we deal with the fears is between the religious and the secular. It isn't only supernatural fantasies that are used, however, because a wide range of phenomena (e.g. hero-worship, nationalism or tribalism, ancestor-worship, sport, the arts, romance, humour, and even war) are used to keep terror at bay, often achieving the opposite of what is intended.

The Anatomy of Denial

This is an extremely interesting phenomenon. It cannot be even slightly understood without taking into account the vast amount of the human mind that behaves *unconsciously*. I observe in my contemporaries a reluctance to acknowledge the extent to which they are motivated by mental energies that are beyond their knowledge or control. The nearest most people get to this awareness is the idea of a person being mad or temporarily disconnected from rationality. This is probably our root denial. How can we accept that we are, say, 80% unaware of what we think? I feel sure that my acquaintances do not really accept this, because they persist in expressing opinions or judgements that they seem to believe have been fully thought out, which is not possible if the existence and nature of the unconscious mind is as claimed by psychologists.

As I have said, knowledge is a most imperfect thing, and the fact that most of our mind is a closed book is obviously a matter of opinion. Still, there's a lot more evidence of the existence of the unconscious mind (and its lack of accessibility) than of many other widespread notions. One of the earlier, and generally accepted, ideas of unconscious activity was focused on the 'shadow', a part of the submerged mind which contains thoughts and feelings we have discarded from the conscious level, like unwanted material thrown overboard. There are other personifications of unconscious activity, such as the aforementioned 'trickster' or the 'internal predator' (a self-destructive daemon), and they are supposed to block or expose errors being made at the conscious level. They are thought to be particularly averse to the conscious trick of denying unwanted material.

Another unconscious form, called the 'sub-personality', is said to exist in each of us as part of a group of metaphorical individuals. It is surprisingly easy to access this little inner tribe, as if it is actually there waiting to be activated. I have done the exercise occasionally and have been interested to discover my hidden constituents. As they are not usually present and active, it might be reasonable to assume that these sub-selves are themselves denied a recognised existence. One thing is certain, these supposed unconscious entities do embody the emotions and speculations that are repressed at the conscious level. Dreams, too, are often quite inexplicable unless credence is given to the unconscious activities and complexes that dreams imply. So are some of our accidents or mistakes, which may prompt us not to forget our true vulnerability (or not to over-egg our actual problems). Jung's so-called archetypes seem to me to be nothing but personifications of unconscious fears and desires, in which form they can be useful reference-points (rather than bizarre semi-godlets).

Denial of Mortality

A good starting point might be the work of Ernest Becker, who died at the age of 49 in 1973, the sad loss for the human species of a *rara avis*, a unique and special human indeed. 'The Denial of Death' was his posthumous book, published in 1974, which won a Pulitzer

Prize. This extended quote from Wikipedia will suffice as an explanation of Becker's book:

*The basic premise of **The Denial of Death** is that human civilization is ultimately an elaborate, symbolic defence mechanism against the knowledge of our mortality, which in turn acts as the emotional and intellectual response to our basic survival mechanism. Becker argues that a basic duality in human life exists between the physical world of objects and a symbolic world of human meaning. Thus, since humanity has a dualistic nature consisting of a physical self and a symbolic self, we are able to transcend the dilemma of mortality through heroism, a concept involving our symbolic halves. By embarking on what Becker refers to as an "immortality project" (or causa sui), in which a person creates or becomes part of something which they feel will last forever, the person feels they have "become" heroic and, henceforth, part of something eternal; something that will never die, compared to their physical body that will one day die. This, in turn, gives the person the feeling that their life has meaning, a purpose, significance in the grand scheme of things.*

From this premise, mental illness is most insightfully extrapolated as a bogging down in one's hero system(s). When someone is experiencing depression, their causa sui (or heroism project) is failing, and they are being consistently reminded of their mortality and insignificance as a result. Schizophrenia is a step further than depression in which one's causa sui is falling apart, making it impossible to engender sufficient defense mechanisms against their mortality; henceforth, the schizophrenic has to create their own reality or "world" in which they are better heroes. Becker argues that the conflict between immortality projects which contradict each other (particularly in religion) is the wellspring for the destruction and misery in our world caused by wars, bigotry, genocide, racism, nationalism, and so forth, since an immortality project which contradicts others indirectly suggests that the others are wrong.

Another theme running throughout the book is that humanity's traditional "hero-systems" i.e. religion, are no longer convincing in the age of reason; science is attempting to solve the problem of humanity, something that Becker feels it can never do. The book states that we need new convincing "illusions" that enable us to feel heroic in the grand scheme of things, i.e. immortal. Becker, however, does not provide any definitive answer, mainly because he believes that there is no perfect solution. Instead, he hopes that gradual realization of humanity's innate motivations, namely death, can help to bring about a better world.

Another product of Ernest Becker's thinking-process, or intuition, or whatever he was using, is this:

The lion's share of the evil which forms the narrative of human history stems directly from the unconscious and uncritical allegiance to the symbolic meaning systems which the various cultures and societies have developed.

Human beings gain their sense of safety and worth by blindly following the internalized modes of power and authority which were presented by parents, family, social group and nation during the socialization process.

Rather than becoming a centre of rational free choice, the individual blindly fights to protect those internalized models of power on which his life has come to depend.

Praise to the Rebel

Ernest Becker was a fearless and disruptive rebel. If it is foolishness to pretend to knowledge, as our species is wont to do, how dangerous it is to challenge knowledge as if it were mere tinsel on a Christmas tree? A rebel runs multiple risks, apart from his own loss of comfortable nostrums. He will be attacked, denounced, vilified, ignored, sacked, and ridiculed. That is inevitable, given the nature of his targets. There is also the unavoidable problem of his straying into knowledge territory himself, thereby to be seen as joining the foolish scrum of pretence and the society of esteem-merchants.

If Becker has any of these faults, it doesn't matter very much. The important thing is that he has laid bare the skeleton in the closet of our species. For all our brilliance and power, it takes the chutzpa of a rebel to point a finger at our great disgrace. I reserve my thoughts on Becker's apparent certainty that we, as a species, are unique in having a divine eternity of some kind, as that must be pseudoknowledge, but I am grateful to have on record such a clarion statement of the size of our terror, and our egotism, and our astonishing capacity to superimpose hysterical denial upon the one basic truth of our existence.

His book has been available for forty years. Yet I have come across it by accident. There are people who know about it and who promote it, but it does not have a high profile. Books that tell us the truth are not widely read, when that truth is that we are mortal, vulnerable and nowhere near as important as we like to think we are. For Becker, the heroising of ourselves is a key factor. That is as may be, and it fits the absurdity of the archetype as master-plan. Humanity has a high built-in resistance to common-sense, an oxymoron to treasure.

My other source of clear mind is Existentialist radicalism, whereby the fact is accepted that we have no unique knowledge of the supposed secrets of a divine cosmos and that we are entirely responsible for our own lives. This realisation has been around for a long time, even thousands of years, if we count Buddhism in its original pure form, and the philosophy of Epicurus and Socrates.

Yet death continues to bother us so much that we cannot bear to think about it as a personal reality and an absolute finality, especially the latter. Some people say that death itself is no threat, though they have anxiety about the process of dying. I go further and express my rage that I cannot have a nice, quick death on the NHS because the Archbishop of Canterbury, for one, wouldn't like it. I may also talk brashly about how welcome death would be to me right now, but I have some reason to suspect that that is a form of denial. In fact, it may be that, at the unconscious level, my death scares me witless.

The Labyrinth of Unreason

A labyrinth, if you are on a single circuitous track, or a maze, if you are on a complex of turnings and choices, are useful metaphors regarding death. The confusion is self-inflicted, arising from the need for clarity, or knowledge, concerning the essentially unknowable. The maze is particularly relevant when self-deception is at work. As I have suggested, we operate at different levels of consciousness, perhaps denying death at one level and claiming knowledge of it at another. The labyrinth is apt in another way, it shows us that the way out is the same as the way in. This is especially useful for those of us who think we are on a journey of discovery, travelling from one space/state to another. As there are no choices, the path merely twists and turns, doubling on itself, apparently going in a new direction but ultimately taking us to where we began, we may come to appreciate that we have been fooling ourselves all along.

My own, rather typical, evasion of reality takes me to the place of surrender, where I am convinced that a quick, painless and immediate extinction would be the ideal. Yet I am sure that this is at best only a half-solution to the problem of age, illness, or ennui. My basic conviction at the rational level is that coming awake, and being fully present in life, are the essential aims of a wise person. These two mind-sets are in conflict, if considered contemporaneously. You can't seriously want to be dead at the same time as wanting to be fully awake. But I think I do, in different psychic compartments.

Thus, denial of death might be no more than a failure of communication between different departments of consciousness. There must be tension between the two, somewhere in the system, and it could lead to unpleasant results. But this is mere speculation, with the merit, nevertheless, of making us wary about our certainties.

My companion in the maze is, of course, fear, and mainly fear of extinction. In effect, I am plodding around the twists, the turns, and facing the divisions, in the false hope of finding the way forward or out. This is, implicitly, denial of my mortality. If I am more of a know-all I will be trudging around the labyrinth, thinking of how glad I will be when I get to the end, an end which is astoundingly my beginning.

Our much-vaunted reason fails us when we need it most. In logic-mode I can see the absurdity of labyrinths and mazes, but that is when I have switched into control-gear, when I think that I know what I see, and won't be bamboozled. But this is just another mind-fetish, another tool in the box.

It becomes useless under certain stress conditions. I may know I am giving way to fear, yet fear rules inexorably once it takes root. Then I finish up trotting around the tortuous pathways again, fearing I will run into the Minotaur.

The Importance of Being Important

There's this other Face of Fear, particularly the Ultimate Deathmask, the Loss of Importance. Death is perceived as the end of meaning, i.e. the end of our individual meaning in the world, which is what we have spent our life pursuing. Death, in prospect, makes each of us feel unbearably trivial. More terrible still, it makes us wonder if there is any meaning in the universe, as it can do without us so easily. This is double-think. Logic may inform us that the universe has no meaning anyway and that our importance was a delusion. But in the maze, or on the rack, we feel hugely significant however much we whisper, 'It's only me'. Then, again, we become rebellious, maybe towards the Necromancer, God, who is supposed to talk to us dead or alive, or towards the entire human species for failing to acknowledge us. Parents, in another phase, become the villains, they who had to be obeyed and who failed to make us feel worthy, and who often died before we could really get at them. Listen to yourself on the telephone and count the number of different standpoints in your mind or in your speech. Chances are that you shuffled quite a pack of options to find the right one. A lot of it is about keeping your end up, an unfelicitous phrase that speaks so much truth.

In a weak moment of apparent self-aggrandisement, Wilfred Owen wrote, *'O what made fatuous sunbeams toil/ To break earth's sleep at all?'* Why, he seems to ask, are we created, only to find that we are temporary, subject to termination without an explanation or redress? We expect something better. We have been led to believe that being human is important, so how can it be that we are so easily discarded? We *know* that we are special creations, don't we? Isn't that the basis of our contract with existence? Whether a God or a tribal elder or our own dear mother, there are authoritative sources from which our specialness is deduced by each of us. We have been told that we are significant, unique, precious, even sacred, so it is unthinkable that we should so easily be snuffed out, is it not?

An Odious Comparison

To understand the rather curious assumption that we are so very important, and the even odder idea that death is an error in our case, we must surely take into account all the other creatures. Animals are different, I am told. They do not, allegedly, know that they are going to die. We human animals are unique, it is said, because we do know that we are going to die.

This is obviously pseudoknowledge, i.e. it cannot be known what another animal thinks, if it is unable to give us that information. I remember being told very recently by a friend, a scientist who makes some claim to spirituality, that animals are definitely not aware that they will die one day. I confess that I laughed at him. I told him that he could not possibly know such a thing. I think I said that it was a racist remark.

Well, here we are, *Homo sapiens sapiens,* allegedly terrified of dying but allegedly in denial about it. I am trying hard to come to terms with this conundrum as I sit in my chair prodding my laptop computer. The next room is a conservatory in which there lies a Burmese variety of *Felis domesticus,* who has just begun his third year of life. I see that he is flat on his back in his bed, licking his front paws, apparently lost in a summer idyll. He has just had his lunch.

He does not lack self-importance, as far as I can tell. He is a martinet about his food. He exercises regularly. He sleeps long hours. He uses my lap in the evenings as a secondary couch. I have absolutely no idea what, or what not, he thinks or feels about his own death. But I can see that it is unlikely that he is in denial of the fear of it. He is a fast reactor to danger, that's for sure, but nothing much seems to scare him. On the face of it, my scientist-friend may be stating the obvious.

Before this one, there was another cat, a bushy-tailed Siamese, a rescue-survivor, who lived happily with us for ten years. One day, my wife said to me, 'I think he is dying'. As time proved, he was, but it took several months. I watched him lose his strength. His voice became weaker. He gave up eating. He asked for comfort and got plenty of it. The poor, weak, emaciated creature gave us so much love and we were suffering with him. At the end, the cat received his euthanasia injection and as I held him against my shoulder he purred before he became unconscious.

What do I make of that, apart from my own grief? It seems inconceivable that he had no knowledge of his approaching demise. I remember my father's distress when his twenty-one year old cat disappeared to die under a nearby hedge. We both felt there was premonition active there at some level of the cat's consciousness. It is possible to see animals such as elephants standing transfixed in the presence of a dying creature of their own kind. It is all too easy, as my scientist-friend demonstrates, to assume what we can't actually know.

A Reverse Odious Comparison

This pre-mortem awareness that seems so unique to human beings, rather than a sign of our superiority might actually be the trait that makes us inferior to other animals. If the fuss and bother is added up, it's a huge burden to know we will die. Whether we acknowledge it or deny it, there's a lot of energy being wasted on something we can't alter very much. It is also something that stops us living in the moment and therefore robs us of true awakeness. In evolutionary terms, it is hard to see the genetic merit of an awareness of death as one's ultimate destination. It may be the opposite, especially now we have become so numerous. For all our other strengths, this awareness of mortality could be our greatest flaw. And if it is true that we are neurotically denying death, then that makes it even worse, because in that case we are not using our extra knowledge to give us a survival-advantage. The vast and questionable expenditure on medical attempts to keep people alive also shows how this one quality of the human mind perverts our ability to live and die naturally.

Cosmic or Comic

The ideas of Ernest Becker are paralleled by the work of Existential psychologists, such as Irvin Yalom, and we are fortunate to have their guidance in our labyrinthine affair with death. Yet I am reminded of those old adverts for dried potato, in which aliens in their space-craft were shown falling about in laughter at the human obsession with peeling grubby potato tubers instead of living normal lives with the real thing, i.e. potato processed and powdered industrially.

Whether denying or bemoaning death, we are a sorry species to be so fixated. I am an old man and not long for this world, and part of my consciousness is delighted to be near the end of the long struggle of life. There's another part, if 'part' is the right word, which is scared and angry. The death of people I love is horrible to imagine or to experience. Yet another part of my consciousness is irritated by my emotional focus. And if the Beckers and Yaloms are right, I make quite a mess of my life trying to cope with these death-focused elements within myself.

One thing seems clear to me, however, which is that the degree to which I indulge in self-importance exactly mirrors my outrage about death. My wonderful self is insulted, raped and degraded by the nasty facts of death. Now that really is comical.

If They Really Don't Know.

I confess that I am not a vegetarian. Nearly, but not quite. Besides, I love plants, as living beings, so why choose to devour them if animals don't know they will be killed by nature or by humankind (the same thing, almost)? But it's not that simple, anyway. On the same day I read an article worrying if meat is good for us or maybe it gives us heart trouble and cancer, and then another article, in the same newspaper, agonising about the fact that billions of animals are killed every year to feed us, the mega-predatorial human race.

What a species we are! Our attitudes to our fellow animals are not merely diverse. Those of us who claim to have perceptions of morality should tear their hair and cover themselves in hot ashes. Humankind may think about morality, indeed kill in its name, but we are most emphatically an immoral and amoral species, either lacking any ethics at all or having them and trampling them underfoot.

Think, if you will, of sentient creatures, all kinds of them, mammals, birds, or fish, as they face death en route to the human stomach. Can you imagine billions? Of course, dear old Mother Nature would kill them anyway, so why worry that we get our share? It doesn't matter what we do to them, we can say it's perfectly natural. In which case, why would you blanch at someone eating your pet dog or cat? Why would you fuss about animals becoming extinct? Why do you prefer not to watch videos of slaughterhouses or factory farming? Are you one of those prudes who are sickened by bullfighting, hare-coursing, badger-baiting, cock-fighting, and, yes, foxhunting? I am, and I find it hard to look at cattle or sheep being herded to their death.

At the least, the consequence of thinking about the deaths of animals must be that we, as a species, are in a state of disgrace. It is one of those matters that must be close to us, considering the life and sensitivity of feeling and thinking fellow creatures. It isn't just our own deaths we deny. We also turn away from the facts of mass killing perpetrated by ourselves. If there is any balance in this equation it is that we are almost as bad in our willingness to kill fellow humans, given the appropriate excuses.

Carousel of Terror

Not a merry-go-round at all, but an insidious circle of pain, a dance of fear, this life of ours, with five 'stations' on a continuous turntable. These stops, aspects of the human condition, seem ineluctable unless we resort to fantasy. They are as follows:

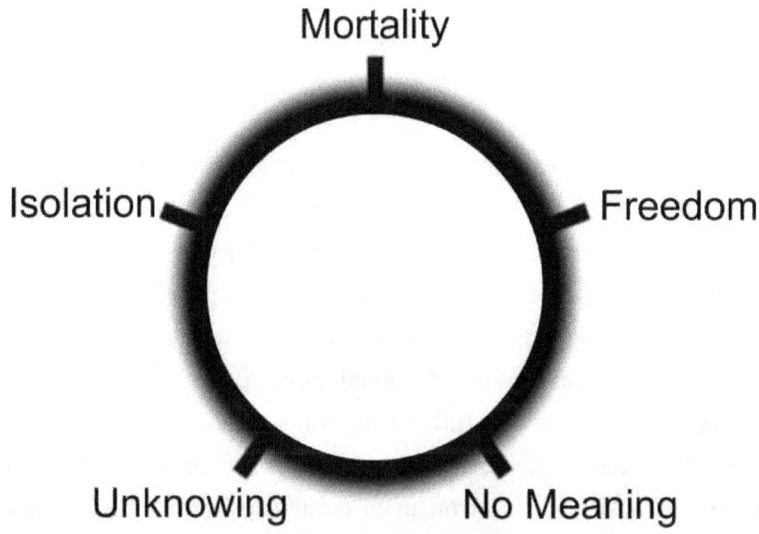

This quintet is not definitive. Anyone can identify types and nature of fears. It's the principle that matter. This principle seems to be written into the inner constitution of the human psyche: the five or so fears are assumed to be unique to the human mind, with secondary, offhand, acceptance that other sentient creatures are also susceptible to fears, of course, but not at our elevated level of comprehension. This arrogance is repeated in our attitude to other humans. We make similar comparisons, consciously or unconsciously, about different human types, though we may make a big play about not calling them different races, or not being disrespectful in the word we use for certain individuals that have abnormalities of some kind.

Denial is, therefore, a primary feature of human thinking. Its opposite and reciprocal feature is fantasy. In denying what we know and fear we invent fantasy escape-clauses. We find ways of evading the fear of each type in the carousel. It is, as has been pointed out already, the substance of human imagination and, in turn, the foundation of our vaunted and infinitely variable civilisation.

Writing a few years after Ernest Becker's death, the psychologist Irwin Yalom produced his masterpiece, 'Existential Psychotherapy', which incorporates the concept of denial of the great fears. He takes denial of death as a primary error, which then spreads into the other four fears and becomes the denial of them too. For Yalom, this process is the main engine of mental disease. He writes mainly for clinicians, yet he speaks a truth for us all if we care to pay attention.

Another version of the waywardness of the human mind involves the idea of basic design-error, even though, or more likely *because*, the designer is a *blind watchmaker*, to use that ingenious metaphor, as reworked by Richard Dawkins. In this idea, it is perfectly reasonable to see human thinking as always and unavoidably flawed: it is merely a chance product of evolution. Our mind is an accident waiting to happen. Its short life may soon be over. Or, to be positive, it may be a mutation that could rule the planet for millennia. Bacteria and insects are long-term chance dominators of this world, so why not humankind? Could humankind become as successful and so durable as grass and forest? It would be quite natural, though not at all certain.

Eleven
Zibaldone

Giacomo Leopardi
This 19th century Italian is described by Wikipedia as follows:

The Zibaldone contains the poetic and existential itinerary of Leopardi himself; it is a miscellany of philosophical annotations, schemes, entire compositions, moral reflections, judgements, small idylls, erudite discussions and impressions. Leopardi, even while remaining outside of the circles of philosophical debate of his century, was able to elaborate an extremely innovative and provocative vision of the world. It is not much of a stretch to define Leopardi as the father of what would eventually come to be called nihilism.

Schopenhauer, in mentioning the great minds of all ages who opposed optimism and expressed their knowledge of the world's misery, wrote:

'But no one has treated this subject so thoroughly and exhaustively as Leopardi in our own day. He is entirely imbued and penetrated with it; everywhere his theme is the mockery and wretchedness of this existence. He presents it on every page of his works, yet in such a multiplicity of forms and applications, with such a wealth of imagery, that he never wearies us, but, on the contrary, has a diverting and stimulating effect.'

My interest in Leopardi and his 4,500 page notebook (zibaldone means hotchpotch), which this unfortunate man wrote in his early adult life (he only lived 39 years), is the alleged 'nihilism', his supreme anti-optimism. Such an attitude was perhaps not the most acceptable view of human existence in 19th Century Europe, especially in Italy, but is perhaps only slightly less abhorred in our 21st Century, where religion and science and learning are highly prized, together or separately, by most people.

As it is claimed to be nihilism - or *if* it is nihilism - to think and write like Leopardi, the word needs careful attention. It is not how I would have described him, anyway, preferring, as I do, the adjective *realism* for his world-view. But I can see how he must irritate anyone who nurtures a sense of self-importance coupled with some form of faith that the world has meaning and will somehow emerge from the shadow into which we have thrown it.

Chambers Dictionary is straightforward, as usual;

'**nihilism**; *belief in nothing; denial of all reality, or of all objective truth (philos); extreme scepticism; nothingness.'*

The internet is also quite clear, if rather diverse, e.g.

1. 'Philosophy that suggests the negation of one or more reputedly meaningful aspects of life.'

2. 'Belief that all values are baseless and that nothing can be known or communicated.'

3. 'Total rejection of established laws and institutions.'

4. 'Belief that traditional morals, ideas, beliefs, etc., have no worth or value.'

Many thinkers and writers have put forward nihilistic ideas, often wrapped up as satire. Voltaire's 'Candide', for instance, ridicules the comfort zone of a Leibnitz. Swift was another satirical demolisher of cosy illusions. It is arguable, at least, that Socrates was an early nihilist in his rejection of sloppy thinking. And what about William of Ockham, a severe, thinking, Franciscan whom the Pope detested for his sharp criticisms?

It seems to me that the boot has been put on the wrong foot: it is they who peddle fantasies who should be upbraided, not the searchers after some kind of true reality. In the case of Leopardi, I think we may have an example of a realist too far; he pushed the human mind into a corner and wouldn't let it escape. He wrote fine poetry, but that didn't help him. He tried to make friends but he was too much for most people, or not enough, from their perspective. He was sickly and rather ugly. He had a hunched back. Why would anyone want to know him, this odd, unattractive, gadfly of a man? The easy thing would be to push him aside as a miserable, negative, creature, an 18th century party-pooper. But some people loved him, obviously, and some still do, like the people who have laboured to bring 'Zibaldone' into the fine English version now available to all.

Leopardi Was Wrong(ed)

Not as wrong as his critics, by any means, but his error was strangely similar to that of his detractors. He did not see the whole truth, while they failed to understand a tenth of it. While Leopardi was looking desperately for a real reason to appreciate existence, his critics persuaded themselves that their false reasons were true.

Knowledge and rational analysis were anathema to Leopardi, Christianity being particularly reviled by him for its empty, erroneous, reasoning. He wanted a natural, innate, reality, but failed to find it, except occasionally and briefly in his poetry. Most people made do with souped-up placebos, as they still do. The question is, what could he have done if he had known what was available to him? His magnificent autodidactism failed him. There was no-one to help him. Or if they existed, he did not know how to find them. The irony is that in the present time, so war-torn, greedy, and dangerous, there is a new awareness that could have been just what Leopardi needed. It is hardly likely that many of his contemporaries would have cottoned on, just as most people even today stick to the unhealthy fantasies.

The first and worst wrong done to Leopardi was the rule of his father, who intended that young Giacomo should become a stalwart and proselytising Christian. He obtained a vast array of books for his son to read, and the boy became a linguist as a result. He was a prodigy of learning. One of his projects, directed by his father, was to expose the errors of Paganism. Giacomo's mother made matters worse by her rigid, cold, nature and her fixity of Christian faith by which she believed literally in all the miracles and promises.

As it happened, none of this actually suited the boy who, while not openly rebellious, gradually veered into both atheism and resistance to deterministic rationalism. His search for meaning and substance in the natural world led him to his so-called nihilism and he was therefore wronged all over again. This second error was that his education had not included anything about the concepts of the non-Christian spiritual philosophies. Had he understood more about the Buddhist Void or the Taoist Emptiness, he might have found his way to a happier state of being. The narrow focus on Christianity that was forced upon him at an early age seems to have persisted as a thinking-block, or a habit of adversarial logic, which deprived him of the chance to find a different reality.

Giacomo Was Right

He was more of an existentialist than a nihilist. The distinction is crucial. If nihilism denies and rejects, existentialism accepts human responsibility for itself. It varies, but the best existentialism is that which frees us to make our own purpose and create our own being. While nihilism looks at nature and finds it repugnant, existentialism sees life as it is, even perfect in itself without human judgementalism.

Existentialism leaves room for transcendence, which would have suited Giacomo perfectly had he known of the potential within him and any other human to surrender to reality and make a good life regardless of nature's sublime bloodiness. Aside from religion, there are mystical experiences that, while having no obvious origin or purpose, make for a different state of consciousness than usual. The experience can be small or cosmic, sublime or terrifying, but this kind of consciousness does exist. In my own book, 'Mystikos', I have described a few of the many mystical experiences that have happened to me. They most definitely have not been formulated by me into any belief-system. How and why should they be? But they have brought radiance to my existence. Similarly, the opening of Gautama's awareness during his long meditation, brought to him an extraordinary state of being, which has in turn, influenced millions of people (even if they do not experience quite his level of mindfulness).

Fortunately for Giacomo Leopardi, he was an accomplished and imaginative poet. This enabled him to evade the monstrous fixatory power of ordinary words and phrases. It was a way of escaping from the false rationality of his parents' religion. One of his poems, 'L'Infinito' says what was unsayable in his analytical notebook. A small section of the poem expresses the mystical otherness that he so needed in his life, and which is the polar opposite of a knowledge-system,

> *But sitting here and gazing,*
> *I can see*
> *beyond, in my mind's eye*
> *unending spaces,*
> *and superhuman silences, and*
> *depthless calm,*

> *till what I feel*
> *is almost fear. And when I hear*
> *the wind stir in these branches*
> *I begin*
> *comparing that endless stillness*
> *with this noise:*
> *and the eternal comes to mind...*

He may not be quite lost in the experience, but he seems to be moving in the right direction. One of the interesting phrases in the poem is, *'till what I feel is almost fear';* and although this is a translation, and may not quite capture the nuance intended by the poet, it is significant if he actually meant fear as we know it in English. I could compare this with the comment of the spiritual teacher, Adyashanti:

'If we would only see that all limitations are self-imposed and chosen out of fear, we would leap at once into the arms of grace, no matter how fierce that embrace might be.'

I might speculate that Leopardi was within reach of a profound truth that would have changed his life for the better, had he been able to leap over it into the arms of love, which I take to be Adyashanti's meaning. Human life tends to function upon an axis that reaches from fear across to love and back again. This is a bridge between two worlds, or two kinds of consciousness, or states of being. What do I mean by this? To explain, I need to push the boundaries of meaning of both words.

A Mother's Love?

Leopardi's frightful mother provides a useful start. She illustrates how Christianity has lost the plot as regards love, and just as accidentally exposes the fragile foundation of that religion's concept of fear-control (I assume the woman in the following piece was modelled on his mother if not actually her). Here is an exerpt from his notes on the subject:

'I once knew very well the mother of a family who was... unswerving in her Christian faith and in the practice of her religion. She... felt no sympathy for parents who lost their children in infancy but positively and sincerely envied them, because such infants had flown safe and sound straight to paradise, and had freed their parents from the inconvenience of supporting them.'

This seems central to Leopardi's own love-starvation. It also relates to the abominable practice of burning people of different faith to purify them (in hell?) as if a generous gesture to those misguided persons. And we still kill each other for religious reasons. The question, as always, is: 'What is love'?

Do we, possibly, deny love in a similar way to our denial of fear? Or, a more searching question, do we misidentify love and think we know it when we don't. This would be all of a piece with our general incompetence in the area of presumed knowledge. It could be that we assert confidently, 'Oh, yes, I know exactly what scares me and I know exactly who (and how) I love and who (and how) others love me.' This assertion strikes me, when I hear it in its many forms, as mainly poppycock. The literature I have quoted shows how nonsensical is our awareness of the big fears, clearly delineating our stratagems and ruses for side-lining our fear of death, isolation, and so on. But where is the information relating to our misidentification or denial of love? Do we know it all? Is love an open book?

A Blank Space?

Psychology doesn't seem to have much room for love. I believe that the acceptable euphemism is 'attachment' as in:

> ***'Attachment theory*** *describes the dynamics of long-term relationships between humans. However, 'attachment theory is not formulated as a general theory of relationships. It addresses only a specific facet' (Waters et al. 2005: 81): how human beings respond within relationships when hurt, separated from loved ones, or perceiving a threat.' (Wikipedia)*

More provocatively, the famous (or infamous) Harry Harlow, who did extensive and controversial behavioural work with young monkeys in the 1950's, while being prepared to annoy the psychological establishment by using the word 'love' instead of the acceptable 'attachment', was reliably quoted as saying,

> *'The only thing I care about is whether a monkey will turn out a property I can publish. I don't have any love for them. Never have. I don't really like animals. I despise cats. I hate dogs. How could you like monkeys?'*

The ancient Greeks didn't hesitate to explore the semantic fog around love. They even identified different sorts of love. Agape means spiritual or unconditional love, Eros is physical or romantic or it may refer to the beautiful. Platonic was taken to signify intense love without physical attraction. Philia refers to love of friends, family and virtue. Storge is a cool sort of love, referring to offspring and it may be demoted to mere tolerance. The Greek models have been heavily borrowed by religions and literature ever since they first appeared two or three millennia ago.

Nowadays, in the West, *love* is an omnibus word ranging from the deepest passion to the most trivial whim. It abounds in aphorisms and popular songs such as *Love makes the world go round* to *All you need is love* to *Love is my reason for living*. In New Age and related movements, love is a buzz-word, closely followed by spiritual, and in many cases the two words are taken as synonymous.

There are other uses of the word that are fraught with confusion and danger. For example, a British patriotic song, created in 1921, from a poem by Sir Cecil Spring Rice and set to music by Gustav Holst:

> *I vow to thee, my country, all earthly things above,*
> *Entire and whole and perfect, the service of my love;*
> *The love that asks no question, the love that stands the test,*
> *That lays upon the altar the dearest and the best;*
> *The love that never falters, the love that pays the price,*
> *The love that makes undaunted the final sacrifice.*

A beautiful tune, admittedly, and a joy to sing, but the sentiments chill me to the bone. They muddle patriotism and godliness in the way that drives us witless. The idea of loving one's country is extremely odd, too, because of the total lack of clarity about the supposed object. Does it mean the land, or the vegetation, or the animals, or the population, or the aristocracy, or the buildings, or the government, or maybe merely one's tribe? It is after all, an invitation to martyrdom: you'd have thought more care would go into an incitement to die for love.

Then there is this even more abhorrent idea of dying for love of a deity. Killing or dying in some god's (or monarch's or pharaoh's or dictator's) name has been widely and intensively practised throughout the world for tens of thousands of years. How is it possible for an intelligent creature to offer up its life for love of a Hitler or a Stalin? Are there really people in England today who actually love Queen Elizabeth II?

I suppose that these are really another variety of love altogether. I am tempted to dub it fantasy love, because it obviously belongs to mysterious recesses of the human mind. There is another possibility, harking back to Existentialism, which is the idea of an ultimate saviour or specialness as a means of denying fundamental fears. However bizarre it may be, the notion of a suicide bomber dying in the name and love of a cause/divinity fits perfectly well with the imagined grace of transcendence. So maybe a kinder name would be transcendent love?

A Crowded Space?

Taking all these kinds of love together, one thing is clear, the word is virtually meaningless because of its preposterous overuse. Fear may be denied, suppressed and misconceived, but there is no problem in knowing quite precisely what the word means. Adyashanti and his followers know exactly what he means by fear, even if they are less clear about the method of leaping beyond it. But what does this brilliant young guru mean by the word love? He makes a pretty good effort:

'You're transparent. You are empty. It just goes through you and beyond. Through you and beyond. It's only when you hold yourself in

a particular way that it feels too much. You are holding an idea of your personal boundary, your edge, and of course you can't contain it. Love was never meant to be contained.'

Of course; this is the transcendent form, not that of grandiose sacrifice-scenarios. In a sense, Adyashanti is saying the same thing about love as he was saying about fear, i.e. that it cannot be contained. Fear is contained falsely in denial postures, while love is contained within rigid personal boundaries.

For me, therefore, the problem enshrined in 'Zibaldone' is my old friendly enemy, self-importance. I am too important to myself to suffer fear, so begone fear. I am too self-important to be hurt by love, so put it in a locked casket and let it out on a sunny day.

Unzipping Leopardi

Another guru, another day, told me that sooner or later I had to throw open the door and let the monster come in to my living-room. He said it to ninety others at the same time. I am now saying it to the long-dead Leopardi, whose ghost must surely be at my side as I write this.

'Giacomo, dear friend, you did so well. But you left yourself no way out. Your wonderful clarity showed you awful truths. But your wounds would not let you embrace love and fear as two old friends. The universe is in your aching head, I know it. But it is your personal universe. Do not spoil your cosmos by clutching at love and screaming at fear. Do not care so much. You don't deserve it.'

I then realise that there is another metaphorical presence on my other side. I am not really here, except as a shadowy middleman, the two men on either side of me are the ones who need to meet, because they are the same person, in two incarnations separated by nearly 200 years.

Adyashanti has put in an appearance yet again. Like Giacomo he lives a life devoted to truth. Unlike Giacoma he seems to have found it and teaches it to the world, or whatever part of the world that will listen to him. His birth name is Steven Gray, and his Sanskrit name means primordial peace. He considers that love is actually truth, and that truth is actually love. In his own way, Giacoma thought the same. He devoted his short life to finding the truth, which was a futile attempt to find love (considering that he was actually finding it with every truth and not recognising it as such). Truth, by and large, is the opposite of knowledge and poor Leopardi had swallowed the cultural lie that they were the same thing. Awakeness is, as I have said, the process that matters and it is a profound experience of discovering and demolishing the lies infesting so-called knowledge in its grandiose form.

I will slip away and leave Giacomo and Steven to talk to each other, at last.

Where Am I Now?

I have just been vouchsafed an AFGO, an acrostic which means, 'Another Effing Growth Opportunity' in the sophisticated language of advanced transpersonal psychology. If I had thought, as I probably had, that I was really quite awake, thinking now about those two men, on either side of me, and about Ram Dass and Richard Moss, earlier gurus in my search for reality, has shifted my focus drastically. Or perhaps it is my own day to day experience that has again jolted me into a new phase.

The subtle trap of Big-Knowledge is the way it hoodwinks its followers into thinking they have discovered the treasure which had enticed them into the search. In fact, at best, I suspect that we merely reach another milestone, which makes us temporarily satisfied that we are at last in Nirvana. It is easy to see this in the case of Leopardi, because he died unhappy and dissatisfied with his lack of achievement, a sure sign of incomplete awakeness. Adyashanti, on the other hand, does give the impression that he has achieved his goal. Partly he does this by assuring us that goals are inherently illusory. So he is content with his process and accepts the total mystery of everything-and-nothing, the non-place where he lives.

I thought my other great guides were like that too. But I had met them, as I had not met Leopardi, obviously, and nor have I personally encountered Adyashanti. Now, thinking about Richard Moss and Ram Dass, twenty years after attending their workshops/retreats, I can see how naive I was to suppose that they had already found the truth. And the two men I knew best, whom I shall not name, yet loved as my supreme idols at one time had, by the time they died, become more like I am at this moment. In other words, they were still unfinished business at the end of their lives. I think they knew it. But they didn't let on to me if they did. Similarly, I am sure that I deny my incompleteness as much as I deny everything else. The principal shortfall, my chronic denial, is in the areas of fear and love. Where else would it be?

I think myself an expert on death-denial. I go on about it at considerable length. I have explored all the stratagems, and exposed the foolishness of the human attitudes to mortality. Good for me, I say. But I am a many-layered cake of consciousness and I can see, now, some very dubious recipes and flavours down the layers. As Giacomo said about Christianity, it is mere intellectual posturing if it does not embrace the deep truths of nature. All religions do it, so it doesn't much matter which god you choose. He referred to his prodigal and prodigious intuition as his source of judgement of human foolishness. But I fail to see any element in human awareness that has that infallible precision.

As such, my awakeness is at best a half-baked prototype. It is probably better than no awakeness at all, but I cannot be sure even of that. To my chagrin, therefore I recognise that I am far more similar to Giacomo Leopardi than I am to Adyashanti. I am as it were up the proverbial creek without a paddle. While I do not suggest that this shameful realisation invalidates the rest of this book, or its predecessor, 'The River of Freedom', I think it is more honest to fly my flag somewhere to the middle of its pole.

This mixture of metaphors means something else, this time to my advantage. One way or another, all spiritual philosophies tend to aggrandise the human mind. This universal contagion leads to frustration as and when any one of us recognises our clay feet. I remember feeling uncomfortable when first listening to the tapes of Adyashanti holding a satsang. He was superb, as one might expect, but there was also an inevitable sense of superiority about him, his control of the event, his mastery over it. I know he has moved on from his Zen days, but Zen also has this almost harsh attitude to human stupidity. And why not be harsh towards stupidity? Well, how do we know for certain that someone is really stupid - or really awake, for that matter?

Something is missing.

I mean personally: I mean something is missing in my comprehension. But I begin to glimpse what it might be. I think that I have already hinted at it, but now it looms much more significantly. I am referring to our racial lack of humility. It is not merely that we look down on other life-forms as intrinsically inferior to the human, though that is bad enough. But it is also the quite unjustified assumption that the human mind can understand the cosmos and its workings.

It is not good enough to confess that we still have a lot to do before we will know everything. Surely the point is that we have absolutely no way of knowing that *any* of our knowledge is true or real. All we have is a nervous system with a very big ganglion at the top, not all that different from the mind of a cuttlefish or a chimpanzee, and we presume that the human brain or mind has the ultimate lien on the truth on any matter. Our knowledge depends upon our nervous system in much the same way as the honey-bee's knowledge depends upon *its* nervous system. So which is actually truest? If they are equally true, then bang goes our assessment of our own species.

You might almost say that if Adyashanti is right to say that love and truth are the same thing, then we have to love all life forms because they each possess a truth, if not *the* truth. That may be a theory too far for our grandiose self-importance, but we might at least test it out within our own fraught species. How would it be if we acknowledged that no one person's truth was any truer than any other person's truth? Such enlightenment would break all our existing systems, because civilisation is based upon a hierarchy of authority. Maybe we must have rules, but why should they be anything other than those that we all initiate and support? It might be argued that in such anarchy nothing would ever get done. Is that true? It is a critical question for each of us and all of us.

Twelve
An Accident Waiting To Happen

Human Hubris

As a new species, not yet a million years old, are we not seriously error-prone? We are interesting, admittedly, at least to ourselves, but our judgement seems too flawed for a rising star. That first big mistake, to invent gods and expect too much of them, has been followed by another, perhaps even sillier, to invent evolution and expect too much of that. Third, worst of the three, may be our worship at the altar of consciousness.

I have been looking at recent accounts of the subject, now that people, specifically science people, are beginning to get excited about it. Consciousness is the human Achilles tendon, the bit of us that both defines us and lets us down. Everything else about us seems measurable and has substance, energy, size, or sensory validation. But, like the love of god, or soul, there have, as yet, been no data about our most important personal possession, the one that is claimed to define us, the one that allegedly makes us human.

You don't even have to be awake to be conscious, if dreams are anything to go by. Nor do you have to be intelligent, or sober, or educated, or happy, to be conscious. It's like swimming, which is impossible without water, or breathing, which requires air. Neurobiology is trying to comprehend the phenomenon, but it is hard, even impossible, to develop an hypothesis for testing.

The problem, as it appears to me, is that science, like religion and philosophy in earlier decades and centuries, still takes it for granted that the world of nature, including humankind, is somehow valid in a cosmic sense, as in the foolish phrase, Laws of Nature used by scientists to add gravitas to their theories. What, precisely, is a law of nature? It seems to me to be Big-Knowledge at its maddest, this assumption that the universe is governed by a set of irrefutable laws. The replacement of, say, the laws laid down by Newton by different laws identified by Einstein is glossed over, and the laws of quantum physics still hang about waiting to be squeezed into the jigsaw. The human assumption is that the universe makes sense, and, hence that the evolution of consciousness has a profound, if complex and hidden, wisdom.

A Slight Scepticism

In my search for a sane assessment of consciousness, I have been heartened by at least one person who seems to share some of my doubt regarding evolution as a fool-proof process (I have already paid my tribute to Richard Dawkins in my 'Creatures of Power', although I fear that his faith in rationality may undermine this wisdom). I suspect that most geneticists would toe the line that the world is governed by unthinking genes, as well it may be. But they don't seem too happy to step over that line and see evolution as a reckless and essentially pointless play of physical chemistry.

On the other hand, maybe David Barash just might be veering in that direction. He is a prolific author of interesting books with titles including: 'Homo Mysterious: Evolutionary Puzzles of Human Nature', 'Marmots: Social Behaviour and Ecology', and 'Payback: Why We Retaliate, Redirect Aggression, and Take Revenge'.

There is also a particularly enticing one, 'Buddhist Biology: Ancient Eastern Wisdom Meets Western Science', which sets all my Big-Knowledge allergies jumping. I am also an atheist Buddhist, in the sense that this philosophy of being, as I would name it when it is free from gods and gobbledygook, has important elements of awakeness in it. Yet the Big-Knowledge problem remains and is at the heart of my scepticism about the human vision of nature as a sort of kingdom with a system we can understand and applaud.

To take nature, or the universe, or life, as seriously and appreciatively as that, is actually endorsing the basic reliability of human thought. We thereby take it for granted that both the world of nature and our own minds are trilling upon the same hymn-sheet. Using the word perfect as an assessment of intrinsic value, we seem to believe, as a species, that both the universe and our perception of it are perfectly perfect. It seems not to occur to us that the human mind could be a faulty faculty, one that could never get to any kind of truth because it is not capable of defining or discovering that which it imagines could be true.

Uneasy Lies the Head

Of all the features of life, it has at last come to pass that consciousness is named as the crown on the head of Desmond Morris's 'Naked Ape'. Or so it might have been declaimed in a Viking saga, had the Scandinavian privateers been more deeply philosophical. The imaginary hierarchy of living organisms, in human opinion, is a gigantic mountain with King Homo Sap at the top and his emblem of ultimate power is supposed to be his superior consciousness.

I regard this as preposterous. I am with Professor Barash in the view that, in his words,

'Most likely, consciousness ranges across a spectrum rather than being a special state that only humans experience.'

Although I would go much further. So much further in fact as to redefine the very meaning of the word evolution. First, it seems to me that *every* living organism is, by definition, conscious. I accept that this requires that definition to be clear. By conscious, I mean: aware of and responding to one's (the organism's) surroundings.

Every living thing, from lofty redwood to tiny bacterium, must be aware of and responsive to its surroundings. Otherwise it would be dead. Even seeds and spores, apparently lifeless, are alive and will burst into active life as their circumstances become suitable for growth.

This responsiveness to external environment, which I define as being conscious, can also apply to non-living systems. Indeed, organic chemistry deals with substances that change in response to external stimuli, as in the simple case of sugar crystals becoming liquid in the presence of water. But the connection is even more omnipresent in that everything in the universe seems changeable in appropriate circumstances and even absolutes like the speed of light are not quite absolute it seems.

Secondly, there are all kinds of differences in the state of being conscious, both between different conscious entities and during the existence of any one entity. From this it can be seen that the conscious process is virtually a universal one, in that it merely means responsiveness to external stimuli. To be pedantic, it also means the process of being susceptible to inner stimuli, as in pain or pleasure in animals with brains and sense-organs.

Redefining Evolution

As the word conscious is defined in the previous few paragraphs, it undermines the very concept of evolution. Any responsive system changes in reaction to changes acting upon it. Those changes do not have any inherent merit, beyond being merely consequences. The idea of improvement is a very specialised form of analysis. A human mind can perceive the difference between a shark and a killer whale as somehow a progression because, if for no other reason, the killer whale is more like a human in, say, its intelligence, communication skills, and socialisation. But sharks are older than dolphins, by several hundred million years. They are already phenomenally successful. Did the planet need a warm-blooded, Mensa shark? Well it now has one and I am tempted to ask, 'So what?' This is a case of convergent evolution, a very common occurrence in which quite unrelated species evolve similar adaptations. The responses to external stimuli commonly have a relatively small range of options. Therefore, species are often perceived to be competing with similar strategies, as if they were businesses trying to enter new markets. This is human thinking. But it isn't human *evolution*.

Human Evolution

It is, admittedly, a saga of consciousness, though not in the way we usually mean. When we humans look at evolution as a whole, as a big mountain or a giant tree, with our own gold medal species on the top, we are defining existence by our own appetites. Even those of us who are great thinkers. Maybe especially the big thinkers. Now I must declare an interest at this point. While I would never presume to regard myself as a major mind, I have to admit that I adore thinking and that I am devoted to a certain kind of consciousness. The human mind, when it is being creative, loving, beauty-pursuing, and even especially problem-solving, is a great joy to me. On the other hand, I find human arrogance increasingly offensive. (Especially my own, when I recognise it.)

One feature of the conscious human that seriously bothers me, therefore, is the assumption of racial superiority. The primary feature of the conscious state in our race is that it is so self-directed. We are so full of ourselves that we use the word conscious as if it means self-conscious, forgetting, if we ever knew, that this is only one way of being conscious. And it may, for all we know, be the worst way. To quote Barash again,

'Why should we (or any conscious species) be able to think about our thinking, instead of just plain thinking, period? Why need we know that we know, instead of just knowing? Isn't it enough to feel, without also feeling good - or bad - about the fact that we are feeling?'

The most wide-awake evolutionist is liable to ask, what is the evolutionary advantage of self-consciousness, the kind of consciousness that is apparently almost exclusive to the human race? On the face of it I would have to reply none so far, if only because our current position is disastrous. After more than a hundred thousand years of apparent struggle to survive, when many human types perished, our numbers have risen from a scattered few million up to seven billion in a few centuries, largely due to agriculture and medicine. The cost to the planet has been immense and now it is likely to backfire on our race. That is hardly evolutionary success compared with that of the sharks or, even more so, of the bacteria. But I do not believe in the myth of evolutionary success for any species. Change is always happening, and the fact that the planet earth had no life on its surface about four billion years ago, and is now covered with species of immense diversity, could only be regarded as a success if we knew what criteria were being applied. I can think of no reason why this livening of the planet is good or bad, any more than I regret that our local sun will turn off one day.

Self-consciousness as it is experienced by the human animal is another matter. To answer honestly, I have to take the question, 'Is your self-consciousness a good thing?' in purely personal terms. I have no way of knowing whether it has any value to this species or to any other. For myself, I suppose I am narrowly in favour of it. I enjoy thinking, so it's good. I hate being afraid, so it's bad. I dislike worrying and can't quite manage to ignore the absurdity of the future. So there I am, moderately lacking in dissatisfaction.

Turning again to my recently acquired guru, Dr. Barash, I quote his suggestion of one way in which human self-consciousness could be a useful element in responding to our environment:

'One possibility is that (self-) *consciousness gave its possessors the capacity to overrule the tyranny of pleasure and pain. Not that pleasure and pain are inherently disadvantageous. Indeed, both have adaptive significance in themselves. Pleasure is as a proximate mechanism that encourages us to engage in activities that are fitness-enhancing, while pain should help us to refrain from those that are fitness-reducing. But what about things that are fitness-enhancing in the long run, but unavoidably painful in the short?'*

Well, I might reply, at least there's a choice. Our genes might well benefit from conscious self-control at the phenotype level, and that could theoretically be why we do our dieting and jogging. I don't know and I don't think I much care. Another variant on this rather trite theme is that the opinion of others (real or supposed) could influence our behaviour to racial good effect, thereby improving the survival-chances of our genes if we were perceived as nice rather than nasty.

Notwithstanding these possibilities, I am astonished at how severely our human self-consciousness inhibits our individual or collective common sense. This is partly, if not greatly, due to the emphasis on the self, the conscious idolising of one's supposed own and unique personness. I am inclined to the view that it is our (self-) consciousness that will actually kill us off, and maybe quite soon.

My harping on awakeness, while being central to my personal existence, is externally focused on this advancing doom. The need to be awake is both at the individual level, where we otherwise commit ego-based suicide of the spirit, or at the collective level where we behave like the Romanovs in Russia, basking in their supposed superiority while the proletariat eventually turn against them and allow rogues to massacre them.

Perhaps the greatest paradox of our species is the fact that we are so extremely self-conscious, arguably a huge evolutionary change, which makes us behave erratically and induces us to shut ourselves off from the fears that exist as a result of our consciousness. Coming awake actually entails acceptance of our wonderful consciousness.

Theory of Mind

According to Wikipedia: *'Theory of mind is the ability to attribute mental states, beliefs, intents, desires, pretending, knowledge, etc., to oneself and others and to understand that others have beliefs, desires, and intentions that are different from one's own.'*

A key result of the extremely high human consciousness is claimed to be this ability, and it is assumed that this enabled our species to succeed because it allowed social development and co-operation. As David Barash expresses it in his seminal essay:

'It seems highly likely that those who possessed an accurate Theory of Mind enjoyed an advantage when it came to modelling the intentions of others, an advantage that continues to this day, and it was an active ingredient in the evolution of human consciousness. And it is at least possible that the more conscious you are, the more accurate is your Theory of Mind, since cognitive modellers should be

more effective if they know, cognitively and self-consciously, not only what they are modelling, but that they are doing so.'

My reaction to this is that, if this were true, why have we made such a mess of our individual and collective states of being and our world? I agree that it ought to work like that and that perhaps it actually did, so that we'd have been even worse if that ability didn't exist. One way or another, therefore, the human race is an enigma in its evolutionary position. I don't think that our species has been or is being an evolutionary 'success', but I admit that I don't see evolution as a matter of failure or success. In a way, I don't believe in evolution at all, if it is regarded as a process of progress.

Obviously, life appeared on this planet (as we humans perceive the scenario) and a vast proliferation of different organisms has occurred over millions of years. But it is not at all obvious that there is any direction to this process. And even less is there any evidence of purpose. Our minds may imagine it otherwise, but that is because our minds happen to work that way. We must surely be a unique species in that we consciously congratulate ourselves on having come into existence. It is the same uniqueness that applies to our neurotic attitudes to life and particular to our states of fear and our denial of that fear. It could be argued that self-consciousness is the inheritable characteristic that will destroy rather than promote human existence. It seems to be an accident waiting to happen.

The Lottery of Mutation

However, an accident waiting to happen could be the term applied to every biological mutation that has ever happened. If the theory is right, the diversity of living organisms is the result of genetic mutation and the selective action of the environment. It appears that, in general, the rates of genetic mutations are relatively low and that the effects of mutations are usually deleterious, i.e. they harm the offspring that inherit the mutation. It seems that the general biological rule is to stay the same, because change is risky, but a very small proportion of changes may pay off and produce some organism with greater competitive potential.

In the case of the mutation leading to the origin of hominids, it is not at all clear if that mutation was good in a long-term sense. But one thing is certain, the hominid's self-consciousness has the disadvantage of making the species aware and congenitally worried. *Homo sapiens* is an anxious animal. He is an inordinately intelligent creature but he is always wondering what is going to happen next. His awareness is fixated on the past and the future. And a lot of his attention is devoted to fear, or the overriding of fear. Not necessarily good or bad, this intensity of focus uses a lot of nervous energy and creates a high degree of strategic pondering. It is, necessarily, a quality spread unevenly through any human population. What, I wonder, are the practical consequences of the anxiety-mutation in humankind? How does it function?

The Terror Carousel

Looking at the carousel of five stations of the human cross described in Chapter Ten, I am struck by what must stand at the centre, at the core around which the carousel moves. The five stations are quite logical, even sensible, if we ignore the question of fear. It seems quite proper to be bothered about death, isolation, the responsibility of being free, the lack of meaning, and the absence of knowledge. Who wouldn't find these things troublesome, once recognised? At the centre of the carousel, however, is the metaphorical proprietor who runs the show. This central agency would be a motor in a fairground carousel, a man made engine with the power to rotate the five peripheral vehicles. It would be controlled by an attendant, a human being qualified and capable of keeping the whole contraption in operation. His master would be the proprietor of the whole funfair and above and beyond him there'd be a hierarchy of people with interests in the entertainment business. Then there are the customers, the people who use the carousel, normally searchers after fun. On the terror carousel there are few fun-seekers, and most of us are only pretending to be happy and all of us are afraid.

It is a real terror carousel, therefore, with a metaphorical origin and an unknown purpose, if there is any purpose at all. It is as difficult to identify the proprietor as it is to discover a purpose, even if a lot of customers assert that they like the thrill of the ride.

The most generally accepted idea of who set up the carousel and who now runs it, is called God or Mother Nature. Other names exist, such as The Devil, The goddess Fortuna, The Prime Mover, The Source, and, more often nowadays The Universe. There is discord between goddists and universists, as there is uncertainty as to which of these is primary. Once it was generally assumed that some god or other made everything (including itself) but rational determinism, such as it is, seems to favour the gods as products of the universe, which of course, merely pushes the metaphor further up the line. Those of us who do not claim knowledge, nor favour the possibility of acquiring it, accept the carousel as it is and try to adapt to it, regardless of what or who set it up in the first place.

When you look at the centre of the terror carousel, it is apparently empty. No proprietor seems to exist. But, as a logical being, a human tends to assume that there must be a program. Surely the carousel must run on some system, unless Newton's eminently serious laws might be nonsense, might they not?

What program could it be? To reduce it to basics, bearing in mind recent developments in biology, whereby the genetic basis of the brain and its output, called mind, is blamed for most things, the carousel program would seem to have been designed by chromosomes. Just as all living programs are. We ask, 'What is a chromosome?' Answer, 'A string of genes.' Ask, 'What is a gene?' Answer, 'A sequence of nucleotides, what else?' Ask, 'What is a nucleotide?' Answer, 'Something that goes into DNA.' Ask, 'Where does the nucleotide come from?' Answer, 'We are still working on that. It's an interesting question.' Ask, 'So it happens where?' Answer, 'It happens in the cell, but it's fantastically complicated.' Question, 'You mean we make it in our own cells. It's self-chemistry?' Answer, 'Oh, sure. But you can get it from a TV dinner. Or a lettuce.'

From outer space, some say. Could be. They are only nitrogen combined with sugar and phosphate. The raw materials of the mind manager of the terror carousel are everywhere. They were probably hanging around when life first existed, or before then. So the carousel is a terror contrived by organic chemistry, with the proviso that everything in life is contrived by organic chemistry. Otherwise, it isn't life.

So the Five Stations of the Cross of the Human Condition are just organic chemistry? Certainly, if organic chemistry is accorded its full majesty. What else would they be? And the demoralising inference is that humans, like the rest of the vast continuity of life, are wonderfully an accident of organic chemistry.

The Primate Experiment

Experiment is perhaps too purposeful a word to describe the beautiful dance of meosis, the cellular process whereby mutations become general currency in any population of living organisms. But to get the flavour of the event in which the present version of humankind came into existence, it is useful to think of primates in general. They seem so much to be a hesitant and risky experiment. And however much we may wish to claim humankind as a special, even unique, biological innovation, it is necessary to take into account the close relatives.

The fact that we have close relatives may, in itself, reduce the inflation of our self-importance. Primates are animals that range from humans, through other apes, to monkeys and prosimians such as lemurs. The apes are most relevant to this discussion because they are our closest relatives. Many apes have become extinct over the last million years, as the climate has changed, and there have been some twenty species of humans that have also died out.

On earth today there is just one human species (with a very wide variety of physical characteristics) and very few other great apes, such as the gorilla, the orang-utan, and the chimpanzees. It is a teasing thought that if the early human sub-species had been geographically confined for longer than a hundred thousand years or so, they might now be definite different species, as are the few great apes. But humankind is a travelling animal, and speciation has been held back.

These few species of apes, including us, do represent a major evolutionary experiment because they all have high intelligence and great tool making facility. These are prized possessions of humans and, accordingly, we rate the handful of great apes, including ourselves, as exceptionally interesting and, somehow, valuable. But, apart from the exceptional population explosion of humankind (which is a very brief, recent, occurrence and unlikely to last very long because of environmental factors), the apes have been an evolutionary failure. All but one of the human species have disappeared, while the few other great apes are just hanging on to their precarious niches

(largely because of competition from us)

So, whatever is at the centre of the carousel, it is an unreliable program for the humanoid races. It has failed to establish a sustainable great ape population on earth, but instead, there is a handful of brainy relics and one species, us, that is ploughing its way to non-existence. And we, the cleverest toolmaker ever, with phenomenal communication technology, have no idea how to save ourselves from our own greed and exploitiveness.

We have good cause to fear.

As the saying goes, we are up an existential creek without a paddle. Or on a carousel with nothing at the centre. But do we believe it? Are we in collective denial of the obvious? The Carousel of Terror is emotionally over-stated. Certainly we are justified in being afraid, given the facts of life, sweet and sour nature. But the centre of the Carousel is occupied by nothing more than a mere algorithm, a development program without meaning or purpose. It does not care for us and we should not care for it, except that we should ty to take care of ourselves within the given environment.

The Existential Quintet

- No Meaning
- Isolation
- Freedom
- Unknowing
- Mortality

(Genetic Algorithm)

Evolutionary algorithms have become quite popular in arcane thinking circles. The fact is that our existence is unlikely to have divine origin, nor help, nor hindrance, and also no evident overall significance, just like all other life-forms. Yet it is hard to avoid imagining some direction to the process of evolution. Algorithm is a useful way of placating the inquisitive mind. Yes, there is a design, but no-one has created it. It had just happened. Hard as it may be to imagine, a randomised algorithm is a strictly logical, methodical, process with no precisely determined outcome. That seems to fit genetic evolution perfectly.

Caveat Emptor

As with everything I have ever said or written, all this is open to question: it may be pseudoknowledge. But do me the favour of regarding all statements by everyone, always and everywhere, from popes to astronomers royal, as pseudoknowledge. I have, as it happens, leaned heavily on science and veered away from superstition (or the divine). There is a sort of comfort in this. It has a sort of basic sense, possibly. Though if everything is actually nonsense we could just give up the pointless exercise of thinking. Nevertheless, should the cerebral porridge have a point here, it must surely be that the question-mark is actually a zero. The centre of the carousel is quite empty. Just an algorithm, a set of rules for the sake of rules. There is not even a central consciousness managing the whole contraption. The whole contraption is the program and is called evolution, mindless and directionless.

The human mind finds this too stark and demeaning, obviously. So, since the beginning of our short history, we have put something there to make us feel significant, needed and immortal. The empty centre has been allotted a presence. It is one or more of the following: 1. The archetypal human self, 2. A Superhuman (king, shaman, arch-priest, leader-prophet), or 3. A god or goddess. I have possible missed a few more, But there are enough here to show the principle.

The centre is supposedly secured by having a great presence in it. Obviously this is pure pseudoknowledge, but if it works, so what? Unfortunately there are dire consequences of this arrangement, namely that the Five Stations of the Cross of the Human Condition are incongruent with the central presence. Specifically, it is claimed, Meaning must exist, Freedom is conditional, Mortality is debatable, there is Knowing and we are no longer Isolated. Therefore, logically and inevitably, the Five Stations are denied. They do not rule human life now that the centre is supreme. In my terms, a fool's paradise has been created out of the thin air of human egotism. There are also far-reaching consequences in terms of racial anxiety and global mayhem. If I am right.

CONSQUENCES of Station-Closure.

First, whether we like it or not, they are still there. It is appropriate to give them due consideration, since they go on controlling us while we pretend to have a different overall control-centre. We can start by giving each of them a clearer definition. In doing so it is vitally important to remember that the five Stations of the carousel-cross *are* only Fears, and Fears that we Deny. The basic reality is that all five Stations are built upon mistakes regarding the nature and function of knowledge.

Denial Up Close

The first and the last terrors, **meaninglessness and mortality**, join up like the snake swallowing its own tail, the so-called Uroborus, a paradoxical symbol of creation. Therefore, I have implicitly quoted a comment about fear of death being the same as fear of unmeaning, and I emphasise the connection between them. If there is no meaning then it seems that life is pointless, so dying gets an extra sting in its tail, putting paid to the remotest possibility that there was some meaning in the life that has ended.

The Uroborus, on the other hand indicates a continuity, in which the life force circulates freely. There's no real death as the energy never dies, it merely moves around. But this continuity is not self-boosting so people don't really want to know it. Once again, we have this harping upon the me-factor, the all-important individual ego-self. To escape the clutches of this evolutionary error it is necessary to examine the unmeaning and find just how hollow that is.

Next, the **fear of isolation**, a neurotic anxiety based on the false concept that each of us is not alone in the indifferent universe. Why should we fear that? Of course we are solitary, each of us, each multitrillion mass of microscopic constituents. A strange aloneness indeed, totally ignoring the biological reality of our 'individual' make-up and the importance we claim for it. In what sense would we wish to be unsolitary? It can't be that we fear lack of companionship, or love, or social support. These processes demonstrably exist. They are the wonders of human life at its best. No, the solitariness we bemoan is the problematical need for a cosmic parent. This need is based on the importance of the self, an evolutionary blip, so that we drive ourselves mad looking for evidence that we really are supremely important.

We are not, evidently; or no more than any other animal. The fear of that lack of specialness has to be suppressed, otherwise we would have to face it and change our state of being to accommodate to cosmic insignificance. We would have to alter our concept of power, our competitiveness, and our desire to achieve. Too scared to do that, we redouble our efforts to be special, to merit fame and be vainglorious. To escape the misery of this deep blunder, a way must be found to surrender to true friendship and humility, with recognition of a more profound connectedness.

Then there is the oxymoron of **freedom-fear,** which perhaps beats even fear of death in absurdity. In this case, we as individual poly-creatures, demand freedom, i.e. the ideal of being able to act without repression or suppression from some authority or other. This does, of course, coincide precisely with the fact of isolation. That scares us out of our wits, yet we desire it in the form called freedom. Nevertheless, we are terrified of actual freedom, precisely because of the isolation it implies, but also because it means we are totally responsible for the 'individual' we claim to be. So we repress our fear of the reality of freedom and tend to opt for its cheapjack substitute, licence. Thus we lose both the reality of freedom and the much-desired fantasy of self-respect. The solution to this muddle is that we would have to face and embrace true freedom, and accept the enormous responsibility it requires.

Finally, the quicksands of **knowing versus unknowing**. In the terror of mortality, the big ingredient is that we do not know anything that will relieve our egoic anxiety. So we have to make it up. But this involves a double fear: we are afraid of what we don't understand, death, isolation, etc, *and* we are afraid of not knowing anything for certain. In a way, this Station is the place where all our fears assemble to weep together. We have put together a colossal mountain of so-called knowledge but cannot really trust any of it, especially the material most obviously constructed from the gingerbread of hope. The bastions of religion, philosophy and science, and the homely delusions of common sense and folk wisdom, prove vulnerable under actual pressure of reality. The purveyors of knowledge are a million strong, ranging from priests to professors to sages to gurus, and none of them hold the twenty-two carat gold of knowledge in their crowns: how could they, given the fact that all they have is the evolutionary detritus of millennia in their skulls. For the fear of not knowing to be laid to rest, all the other fears have to be dispelled, plus the overriding need to give up the need for knowledge altogether: we do not need knowledge beyond that which makes us civilised. That does require definition.

Thirteen
The Tree of Innocence

Trees and Terrors

The Carousel of Terror has a terrible kinship with the Tree of Knowledge of Good and Evil, the abominable trap laid for humankind by the maniacal Abrahamic deity. The resemblance is in the nature of the terrors and in their duplicity. For the Carousel of Terror is also a trap, even if we humans do not altogether realise it. Basically we have here two Big-Knowledge systems that make it impossible for us to have a happy existence. They seem to exist to make us suffer. But we have created them for ourselves. They are not poisoned gifts from the cosmos, even if we are foolish enough to think that they are. The fact is that these horrors are optional and the case being made in this book is that we could, and should, refuse both options.

I have said that coming awake is the best way of making the stand against our knowledge-fixation. But this is a hard task. My own progress in awakening has been slow and often painful. I still have a lot more to do, I think, and it adds to the fear of the future if I let the anxiety rule. Fortunately there are handholds to support the struggling progression, and these seem to be innate to consciousness, readily available if I surrender to them. I mean beauty, inner truth, and love as a state of being, the wonderful trio that has sustained the suffering human since mind first appeared in our existence.

The Sublime Trio

More needs to be said about these elements. Beauty, famously, is in the mind. Well, of course, where else would it be? But how do we know it is beauty when we see it? Certainly we will not agree amongst ourselves. I contend that the perception of beauty is a mystical experience in that it can enhance, or at least change, the state of being of the one who perceives the beauty. To some degree, fortunately, the experience of perceiving beauty can be shared, in the sense that an audience of hundreds of people can be collectively moved by a great musical performance or a sublime piece of theatre. Nature may also enrapture us, if unreliably.

Inner truth, as I have called it, is different from the usual idea of *the* truth, which is a will-o-the-wisp. Indeed, much of our life is wasted on a vain search for this commodity. The whole danger of Big-Knowledge, for example, stems from the incorrect assumption that therein resides the holy grail of *the* truth. I maintain that this grail is as delusional as the one supposed to contain the blood of Jesus Christ. It is nonsense, however desirable as an idea. By inner truth I mean something more complex and difficult to comprehend as a mere idea. Most of the great gurus who have their feet on the ground are very keen on inner truth. Maybe truth is a poor word for what I mean. It is certainly used too tritely and mundanely, as in a court of law or a church or a laboratory. I quite like the word essence for this deep reality, and I accept that intuition is also a useful alternative word. I experience truth as a quite shattering realisation of rightness, as in the utter rejection of murder or pederasty, or more happily, as in the sweetness of kind or generous behaviour.

As for love, it is probably the ultimate validation of human existence, so long as it is not merely a degraded form such as desire, lust, greed, and jealous possessiveness. Like truth, love is a polymorphic range of behaviour. I mean love that elevates the state of being of the lover and whom or what is loved. I mean an aura or a charisma enfolding human action. I do not mean love as a commodity or a mere affair.

Art, the Saving Grace

I recently listened to a performance of the 'Missa Solemnis', a piece that draws together all these separate strands: it thrills and astonishes me repeatedly that Beethoven could bear to use the religious text, which I find totally abhorrent, to make music that transcends the trap of dogma and sanctimoniousness. The piece is a blazing testimony to the power of the beauty, truth and love that seem to me to hold out the best chance of achieving true civilisation. It is extraordinary that this composer could take the dross of an Abrahamic tirade and find his own inner resources to create a masterpiece. There are many other examples of this phenomenon, especially in music. Visual art has the disadvantage of seeming literal, and therefore is part of the indoctrination. Some painters and sculptors have managed to transcend that limitation. Unfortunately, however, coercive images of suffering saints and heavenly beings have prevailed in works hung throughout the Western world to impress the masses with mythic illusion. But art so often triumphs over evil doctrine, just as Buddhist mindfulness can defeat hatred and greed. In fact, the identification of the root poison as delusion seems to have been the first brilliant recognition of the dangers from the absurdity of Big-Knowledge and the lunacy of denial in the Terror Carousel.

The Shaman and the Mystic

As with the arts, these two embodiments of transcendence are still with us and still puzzle us with their ambivalence. Are they innocent or are they evil? Big-Knowledge authorities dislike them, which is a good sign. Just as Paganism, for all its impediments, seems fresh air compared with the doctrinal religious suffocation in Christianity, Islam, Judaism, Hinduism etc. It isn't fresh air, of course, even if its gods are of modest stature they are still gods and therefore dangerously delusional. Yet there is in the essence of shamanism and mysticism, as in the old animism, a transcendent possibility similar to that now described as the transpersonal (beyond personal) realm, as if there is a permanent region of consciousness that is forever open to anyone who dares to enter. Indeed, it is probably of the same species as the Void, or Awakeness, that are the presiding spirits of this book.

In using the term, 'Tree of Innocence', I am attempting to identify this transcendent power, which I also see as the origin of genuine civilisation, as opposed to the bizarrely foul potential of the Biblical Tree of Knowledge, hung with hatred and dread. It is no accident that trees occupy the territory. This icon of the plant world has immense power, yet is vulnerable to human power. Gods have been connected to trees for millennia. Long before the invention of the Judaic arboretum called Eden, gods were being hung on trees. The innocent tree was repeatedly incriminated in murderous or suicidal behaviour, as in the cases of Tammuz, Osiris, Odin, Dionysos, as well as Adam and the unfortunate Jesus, or arboreally inclined as in numerous dryads, possibly Pan, certainly Cernunnos, not to mention the omnipresent Green Man.

It seems to me that transcendence, as a way of being, has had an unfortunate history and is still suffering from misuse. The shaman was a good idea in its day, in that the power of nature was embodied in certain members of tribes who would ostensibly use this power for magic or healing. The goodness of the idea was in the concept of self-help, a sort of primitive existentialism. This still goes on in the form of homeopathy, acupuncture, herbalism, and reflexology, whereby there is probably more good than harm in the practices. What these practices lacked and still lack is any true transcendence into glory.

Quite apart from the ghastly coerciveness of the religions, otherwise similar in many ways to shamanism, is their lack of transcendence as opposed to the tiresome litany of sin or duty. I regret to admit that much of humanistic psychology and New Age practices suffer similar flaws. But would we all be better without them? It is hard to say. And what of the modern stranglehold of the drug companies? Are their power and range of products of overall benefit to us and other species? It must be a matter of doubt. I can only look into my own personal experience and say that none of these placebos and wonder-methods do anything for me, and I am left with nature and the arts as my main defence against terminal despair, and especially protection from the twin evils of religion and Big-Knowledge.

Mysticism, however, could be a different matter, depending on how it is defined. I have no doubt at all that mystical experiences are enormous sources of transcendence. But that also depends on what we mean by transcendence. Certainly, mystical encounters, or moments of enlightenment, sudden rushes of comprehension, seem to happen spontaneously. I have had these experiences all my life and I have neglected their importance partly out of ignorance and partly because of my institutionalised scepticism. It is time to look and listen.

The Source of Transcendence

I am immediately in trouble. To a large degree, this useful terminology has been appropriated by religious theory. It is assumed, automatically, that the words refer to the divine, supposedly the realm beyond the physical world. But this is typical: every attempt to explore or describe exceptional perception suddenly hits the barrier of religious certainty. It is as if I am not permitted to talk about the full range of consciousness if I do not accept that the highest level must belong to some god or other. I have, for years, tried to have my cake and eat it by referring to non-religious spirituality. I am told that there is, obviously, no such thing.

I have the freedom to dispute this, if I so wish, and I do dispute it in the following terms: I do not know if there are gods, or a God, nor whether such beings would be non-corporeal, nor whether they, should they exist, dwell beyond the physical world, and, if I care at all about that uncertainty, it is only to the degree that I find the whole subject beyond contempt. I imagine and hope that sounds a whole lot worse than mere atheism. I am angry about religion because it is a barrier to civilised spirituality, which, properly defined is what I regard as the only way to exist.

I experience religion as the ultimate corruption of our consciousness and I am constantly surprised by my own vehemence. In the cold light of day, so to speak, I regard religion and the religious as crazy and irrelevant. Then I upbraid myself because I am loosening my grip on my own truth and sanity. I am a militant protestant even against the mildest Protestantism. Yet I think I am wasting time and energy. I have total sympathy with the British Humanists in their campaign against Goddism, just as I stand shoulder to shoulder with the members of Republic in their fight against monarchy. But I think it is a pointless battle, because the targets are deeply embedded at the centre of the omnipresent human delusion.

Instead, rather than futile protest, however justified in the fullness of human consciousness, I recognise that my task must be to explore what I have named, for want of a better term:

Secular Transcendence

It is a long exploration, with occasional flashes of enlightenment. At first, my lifelong encounter with what seemed to be my own inexplicable excitement, led me to mystical inclinations. That roundabout description fits with the idea of the labyrinth, a place of complex wandering in search of some objective, itself often mysterious. Worse than this, I was rarely sure if I was in any kind of labyrinth as opposed to mere personal confusion. After all, however I might burn with ambition, excitement or curiosity, I could easily persuade myself it was just ordinary life rather than extreme experience.

What is ordinary life and what is extreme experience? Are they merely opposite ends of the same spectrum, say, or just the two extensions of the Normal Distribution Curve? Or is there a change halfway across, not just a gradation but a shift of essential nature? Even science and mathematics have hit upon such shifts, as in the Catastrophe Theory, whereby there is a sudden change in an otherwise smooth process or it may be described in modern Chaos Theory, in which something precise and durable suddenly comes out of apparently total muddle. Even the wayward plod of evolution includes these lurches into a new dimension, though the time-scale may be astronomically huge.

The everyday changes that we take for granted may also be fully transcendent, in the secular sense, because of the strangeness of the change when we really pay it attention. The extraordinary behaviour of water, for example, when its liquid form suddenly crystallises or changes into vapour. We may explain it in terms of molecular behaviour, but it is still astonishing that molecules of any substance can convert their behaviour so drastically. The process of photosynthesis is widespread and routine, we think, but it is an extraordinary flip of the molecular coinage when it happens. We have become inured to the reported (or actually experienced) switches of reality following intake of hallucinogenic chemicals, without really taking in the fact that for the person involved a major change of reality has occurred. And I almost dare not admit that I have bent metal with a protracted caress. It is not that difficult, but rather wonderful, even when done as a conjuring trick by professional fraudsters. The fact is that our mundane reality is actually rather unstable, or fluid, depending on your concept of what is properly normal. There is also, for those who endure it, the quite astounding experience of falling in love. How transcendental is that process, whereby the entire behaviour of a complex multicellular multi-organism, changes absolutely as a result of a person to person interaction that is often instantaneous?

The Amateur Sceptic

I have dabbled in scepticism since I gave up being a choirboy. Before then I was prone to dazzlement of most kinds, though I was unaware of choice. Afterwards, I realised I was primarily responsible for running my life and it was an uncomfortable feeling. I adopted scepticism after a few unpleasant events before my age reached double-figures. Grammar School honed my powers of disbelief without quite dimming the susceptibility to dazzle. Such dazzle as happened tended to set into fixed impressions, and they are still with me, despite all the scepticism I could muster. Some of these dazzlements I categorise, with some hesitation, as mystical experiences.

How does a person know what is a mystical experience, as opposed to mere excitement, even ecstasy, or a devastating disappointment. Is it a difference in kind, that is a qualitatively distinct event, or is it a matter of degree or intensity? It could be justifiably claimed that it doesn't matter either way. Absolutely or relatively different, it may be enough to experience the transcendental as such, and to incorporate the beauty or truth of it into one's life without straying into the errors of knowledge or belief.

My New Reality

When I wrote 'Mystikos' I still hankered after certainty, and I can now see how this need devalues everything. Certainty is the opposite, or enemy, of innocence in the same way that religion defiles spirituality, while spirituality itself is just a state of being rather than a universal absolute. Therefore, I am in a different mind-set from that governing me in 'Mystikos', when it really seemed to matter to me if the apparent mystical experience was a separate species of consciousness. Different questions arise in this changed mind-set, the main one being: what effect can the actual experience have on my existence. And there is a subsidiary question: can these experiences be accumulated into a new mode of behaviour in myself?

This being the case, I can re-examine my possible mystical experiences in a new way, i.e. not whether they are genuinely other-worldly, as only my ego would care about that (like the malady of wanting to be famous), and pursue the infinitely more valuable route of wondering how far they go to dispel the misery of the Terror Carousel and the crushing inconsequence of religious and scientific Big-Knowledge. I will begin therefore, with the reference to 'Mystikos' in which a shimmer of enlightenment seems to be penetrating the sceptical gloom.

What is It?

In the first few pages of the book I tried to define mystical experience and identify the character of it in terms of grace, ecstasy, unity, love and going beyond self, together with feelings of unusual depth, and intensity, joy or grief. If I compared my own subjective sense of the mystical with other sources I found considerable correlation: my words crop up everywhere in so-called spiritual or transpersonal contexts.

There were others, however, that connected with my perception yet seemed to have too much subjective judgement, such as a sense of harmony, intuitive understanding, and all-inclusivity, as opposed to clearly emotional effects such as extreme beauty, intensity of fear or vulnerability, suspension of time, transformed awareness, and. enhanced vividness of sensations.

There were also many impressions of a paranormal and extrasensory nature, which seem to me to have too great a subjective judgement. Phrases that were not consistent with mine referred to specific iconic beings or processes. I had experienced some iconic presences, but never anything that I could or would call god, world soul, angel, or any other religious vision. I gathered that such specifically divine events were more likely to happen to someone already inculcated with religious beliefs and that, as I rejected religion when very young, I was not primed for such experiences.

This raised an important issue. I might have expected mystical experience to be both precursor and content of religious experience. But it did not seem to be so, at least not with any consistency. I have continued to be surprised by the attitude of religious authorities to mysticism. Where I might have expected enthusiasm, there has been a measure of apathy sometimes mounting to antipathy. Now I see why this is the prevailing mind-set of religious authorities, as mystical experience must seem to them to break the rules by making direct connection with a realm that they regard as their special preserve. But that should be no surprise to me, as religion is and always has been more about worldly power and ruling than it would care to admit.

For me, personally, it is a different and much more significant issue. I had not realised that my animosity to religion was of the same psychological ilk as my own ambivalence towards the mystical. It was also a control issue for me, though I would have been horrified to see that connection. I needed to *know* where I was in these experiences. I needed to know whether they measured up to the mythical absurdity of absolute fact. I therefore robbed myself of a whole realm of experience. This I am now correcting, to a state of being that is largely what I mean by innocence.

The Pond

Uley fishpond in Gloucestershire, a few stones'-throw from the great bulk of Uley Bury, an Iron Age hill fort, I discovered in my wandering childhood and I became entranced by the impedimenta and process of coarse fishing. The equipment was minor: bicycle, rod, tackle, and bait. It was two miles from my parents' house, just far enough for me to feel free and sometimes frightened. That particular mystikos lasted until I was about thirteen years of age. Was it actually a series of connected mystical experiences?

In 'Mystikos', the book, I used a list of generally agreed elements of mystical experience and measured my fishpond occurrences against it. In general, it seemed true that the fishing process had strong mystical content. I should mention that it was private property and that I was trespassing, No-one else fished there, to my knowledge. It was surrounded by trees on two sides with open meadow in between. It could be very dark there, especially in the evening, and it was silent except for occasional sounds of wildlife. The expanse of green water was probably a couple of acres and the main fish was roach. I longed to catch a fish and when I did I was scared of hurting it, so here was great ambivalence. The red float was a talisman, magical in itself, yet an enemy too in that invaded the secret world of the fish.

Here's a summary of the experiences checked against the 'official' list of genuine mystical experience.

1. Unity: I was part of the whole and I felt that the whole belonged to me.

2. Self: identification with nature, plus a feeling of mystery and apprehension.
3. Knowledge: I didn't feel I knew everything but a sense of coming home.
4. Love: No sense of all-embracing love or of being deeply loved.
5. Beauty: extraordinary beauty and everything equally beautiful; plus fear.
6. Bliss, Joy, elation, wonder, awe, discomfort with sheer intensity.
7. Time: stoppped, flow of past into future.
8. Some sense of contact with normally hidden reality.
9. Realness: more real than ordinary experience.
10. Life: everything animated, strong sense of consciousness and energy.
11. Immense presence or power in immediate natural vicinity.
12. Heightened awareness, clarity: very sharp and even painful.
13. Vision: strange light and vivid colours and shapes.
14. Sound: very sensitive to silence and sudden bird noises.
15. Can't remember bodily sensations except ordinary ones.
16. Fusion: maybe some synaesthesia, not sure.
17. Extrasensory perceptions: probably not, at the time.

These seem to add up to moderate extrovertive mystical experience. However, it is probably necessary to look at the context and the durability of memory, to get the full mystical relevance of this pond. I suspect that there can be a sustained mystical state, spread out over months or even years, with periodic flowering of greater intensity. The Uley fishing-trips were acts of worship, I have no doubt, if the object of idolatry is accepted as nature itself. My sense of being by the pond, watching my float mesmerically, is of a child possessed by a profound vision.

Taking a Position

When I wrote 'Mystikos' I was obviously searching for a position to adopt, as it has always been important to me to have clarity and coherence in my overall mind-set. In practice, this has been difficult to achieve and probably at best unnecessary and at worst destructive. The genuine experiences described in that book are not categorised as truth or fiction, and I was uncomfortable with that hesitation, as I saw it. I now think that the scrupulous havering diminished the book, because I realise that the idea of veracity is itself tainted with falsehood. It was as if, having fallen in love, I was questioning whether I was *justified* in feeling as I did. This is a product of our age: although still encumbered with Old Big-Knowledge we try to re-accredit ourselves by obtaining proof of all kinds and pack them into New Big-Knowledge, as if we had somehow moved forwards. I now think that my reprocessing of my own genuine mystical experience invalidated the actual experience.

The undeniable fact, and it is just that, is that I had the experiences described, however reservedly, in the seventeen chapters of 'Mystikos'. They actually occurred. It is factitious to doubt them as occurrences. But it is perfectly correct to question whether they mean something not demonstrable or provable. The shift in my perception, now, is that the *meaning* of the experience is of a different order from that of the experience itself. Also, and perhaps more important, is the effect the experience has upon me and my consciousness. It need not be the subject of a doctoral thesis: it does need to be integrated into my psyche. It isn't taking a position, the academic or analytical process, because that is a vainglorious exploration, compared with the relatively humble acceptance of a wonderful happening.

I will return to 'Mystikos' in subsequent chapters, as other considerations arise.

The Academic Position

My background is a mixture of wilderness and cultivation. The world of nature has always enthralled me and often alarmed or disgusted me. It is the mainspring of my psychic behaviour. On the other hand, I was some twenty years in places of education and learning. I became a scholar with some reluctance because of the repressed vainglory I found in academia. Then I opted for thirty years of business endeavour, which was probably my biggest mistake, because it combines the worst of human conceits, being powerful and changing the world.

So I come back with relief to the blood-stained pastures of Mother Nature, where beauty and horror dance an endless foxtrot. I instinctively know and understand this arena, and I know that my mystical experiences are the transcendent influences from this terrible and exquisite environment. It is, therefore, with something approaching nausea, and some bewilderment, that I scan the following summary of the academic postures around supposed mystical reality:

Two overlapping ways of understanding the consciousness expansions of mystical experience are distinguished. Filtration theorists, such as Henri Bergson, William James, and Aldous Huxley, believe that access to previously subconscious material takes place when neurological or psychological valves open. Psychophysical theorists draw on mind-body metaphysics to explain how consciousness can reach into the world at large. Several metaphysical alternatives are considered, including dualism, dual-aspect theory, and neutral monism, but idealism realist explanations, and more recently, T. L. S. Sprigge has raised idealism in connection with nature mysticism. A panpsychic form of idealism that reworks Leibniz's monadology is a particularly fertile option. It not only addresses the deeper unitive and noetic facets of extrovertive experience but may also shed light on the relativity and holism of modern physics.

No doubt an accurate picture of the academic position on mystical consciousness, but where does it get us? It is so obviously the same Big-Knowledge approach that still obstructs our fragile attempts to make full use of our intelligence at all its levels. There are a few areas of new enquiry that, while interesting psychologically and maybe philosophically, still remain embedded in the same old mode, whether religious or scientific, the mode that enlarges the presumption of human *discovery* to preposterously titanic proportions.

Panpsychic Idealism

Let us suppose that this field of study/opinion is anywhere near a truth of some kind, and who can tell, anyway? I picked out the name of Professor Sprigge because I found the Guardian obituary on him by Jane O'Grady in 2007. He sounds an interesting and rather good person. Here are a few quotes:

'The trend in current philosophy is to believe that everything is exclusively physical. Timothy Sprigge, who has died aged 75, kicked against that - claiming that the underlying essence of the universe is mental. Physical qualities by themselves, he said, are like the musical score as opposed to music's heard sound, and he insisted that philosophy has been distorted by the way philosophers ignore subjectivity. He independently formulated the "what is it like to be a bat?" question about consciousness which Thomas Nagel later made influential, but for Sprigge subjective consciousness was the wellspring of metaphysics.'

'Panpsychism (as he argues in his major work, 'The Vindication Of Absolute Idealism', 1983), has an ethical upshot - enabling, and requiring, us to empathise with other humans and animals. It "bids us recognise that what looks forth from another's eyes, what feels itself in the writhing of a worm... is really that very thing which, when speaking through my lips, calls itself 'I'." For Sprigge, living his metaphysics imposed duties that were often agonising (when he attempted to wear plastic, instead of leather, shoes). It also made him tolerate very opposed viewpoints, and try (as chair of the Advocates for Animals in Edinburgh) both to reason with animal rights extremists and to temper animal experimentation.'

'Sprigge was deeply religious, but had too much integrity to adopt a consoling personal-God package. A Unitarian in his later years, he believed in a god you could not pray to and a religion stripped of superstition. Yet, though he was maverick and unfashionable, a metaphysician, pantheist and idealist in both technical and ordinary senses of the word, he picked out what has become the key topic in current philosophy - how consciousness fits into the world. His doggerel on FH Bradley could apply to himself: "Said that soldierly mystic called Bradley /Please don't take my system too sadly /It's really quite fun /Thinking everything's One /We should all feel unreal very gladly."'

For all his philosophical obscurantism here was a very bright and good man who was on the cusp that I am trying to address. This is the choice we may make between being clever explainers and exploiters on the one hand, and not-so-clever understanders and sympathisers on the other. I am not sure where the following pair belongs.

Quanta and Tubules

Finally, in this reference/deference to academe, there is the collaborative work of Penrose and Hameroff, which speaks for itself as follows:

*What is consciousness? Some philosophers have contended that "qualia", or an experiential medium from which consciousness is derived, exists as a fundamental component of reality. Whitehead, for example, described the universe as being comprised of "occasions of experience." To examine this possibility scientifically, the very nature of physical reality must be re-examined. We must come to terms with the physics of space-time - as is described by Einstein's general theory of relativity - and its relation to the fundamental theory of matter - as described by quantum theory. This leads us to employ a new physics of objective reduction: "OR" which appeals to a form of quantum gravity to provide a useful description of fundamental processes at the quantum/classical borderline (Penrose, 1994; 1996). Within the OR scheme, we consider that consciousness occurs if an appropriately organized system is able to develop and maintain quantum coherent superposition until a specific "objective" criterion (a threshold related to quantum gravity) is reached; the coherent system then self-reduces (objective reduction: **OR**). We contend that this type of objective self-collapse introduces non-computability, an essential feature of consciousness. **OR** is taken as an instantaneous event - the climax of a self-organizing process in fundamental space-time - and a candidate for a conscious Whitehead "occasion" of experience. How could an **OR** process occur in the brain, be coupled to neural activities, and account for other features of consciousness? We nominate an **OR** process with the requisite characteristics to be occurring in cytoskeletal microtubules within the brain's neurons (Penrose and*

Hameroff, 1995; Hameroff and Penrose, 1995; 1996).

The Other Ways

George Gurdjieff offered the Fourth Way. It combines what he saw as three established traditional ways, or schools, those of the mind, emotions and body, or of yogis, monks and fakirs respectively. He eschewed reliance on any one of these because the whole awake being of a human required all three. It was not always clear that his teachings lived up to his ideals, but his Enneagram was, and remains, a useful concept for unbundling the thick fascia of infantile attitudes.

Carlos Castaneda, in his long series of novels featuring the wisdom of Don Juan, the Yaqui Indian, describes just two realities, the tonal and the nagual, Mesoamerican entities with magical shape-shifting powers. Rather than simply the folk-religion interpretation, in which tonal and nagual are both shamanic, he takes the more psychological view in which tonal is everyday existence, including everything ordinary, while nagual is everything else. In my understanding of this idea, the tonal is what we all accept as normal or common sense, while to access the nagual we have to come awake into a new form of consciousness. We have to develop a new kind of attention compared with ordinary attention, thereby becoming liberated from the shackles of conventional living.

The Abrahamic religions. At times it is almost possible to see that these regimes have tried to break out of the very restrictive chrysalis that their origins impose on them. In Judaism, Christianity, and Islam, each employs much the same method of escape as each other, but the solid case of the chrysalis will not yield. It is a great pity. As is the dependence on an imaginary transcendent authority. These behemoths grind down the nations of humankind and are therefore the worst part of our past and the most threatening aspect of our future. If only they could change. The kindness implicit in some Christian teaching and the sense of honour flourishing in original Islam could theoretically transform our existence. But they won't. The chrysalis is too thick. Or what emerges is a rapacious, carnivorous, dragonfly and not a transcendent butterfly.

Buddhism and Taoism and Epicurianism also seek a liberation from ordinary suffering by different kinds of mindfulness. There was huge potential in these spiritual philosophies. I don't understand why they have had so little effect. Unless, of course, the world would have been even worse without them. It may also be a chrysalis problem, in that the genius of the original minds has not developed and produced a true imago. More's the pity.

Mystical and Mundane Choices

The wonderful things I have experienced are nullified if I try to process them into some traditional mode. Like Gnosis, you get it or you don't. But somewhere in the whole mix, the mystical breakthrough is always possible. It is an interesting exercise to imagine where in the following mix it might otherwise occur and give a person transcendence and even transfiguration: the arts, sport, travel, alcohol and drugs, love, compassion, kindness, ambition, aggression and competition, encounters with the vast panoply of nature, and any other emotional diversions from the travails we inherit with our species identity.

Is there some way even our engrained habits of thought and behaviour could move to a better state? My own view is that it is possible but I doubt our willingness to make the leap required. I am sure, however, that mystical insights could help anyone to move to greater awakeness which may not be gained in any other way.

Fourteen
The Giant Hare

The Spectral Lagomorph

Continuing with reference to the book, 'Mystikos', I want to pursue other aspects of mystical experience, particularly to look more closely at the phenomenon of the Great Continuity, the main subject of the early part of 'Freedom River - The Infinite Beginning', the book that preceded the present volume. I argued there that it is a grievous error to see any organism in simplistic terms only, as if it were just an isolated and unitary being. Of course, an organism such as you, the reader, or me, the author, is unitary, even uniquely so, but that is a limiting perception. Each of us is also a universe of different entities, some that are our cells and ten times as many that are migrant organisms living on or within us.

Thus you and I are simultaneously singular and multiple. We are ourselves Great Continuities and we are each part of a greater Great Continuity, and who knows how far the overall continuity extends into space and time. For me, the sublime reality of that cosmic inclusivity is near enough to the woolly idea of The Divine but does emphatically not warrant the invention of a Supreme Being, unless it is the Great Continuity that is supreme while in no sense any kind of unity.

A Christian friend once gazed fixedly at me and intoned emotionally, 'We are all one'. I asked him exactly what he meant. In a sense he was just singing from my hymn-sheet. But I felt the claustrophobic enclosure of his religious faith pulling at me to enter a sacred vestibule. No, clearly he didn't mean his close connection with a dung-beetle or a Clostridium bacterium. But I do. Nor, much as he admired blackbirds and silver birch trees, did he see himself as having shared identity with them. I do. And increasingly so. Spinoza set us all free by recognising Nature and God as identical. We still fail to take the lesson to heart.

The tiny speck of the vast continuity I wish to discuss here is not real at all. At the least it's super-real, as while it fails to turn up on the greensward of our native land, perceptible to our five wonderful physical senses, it has stood a foot or two away from me, towering over me, invisible and yet eerily present. The encounter, the first and most specific, is described in Chapter Two of 'Mystikos', under the heading, 'In Search of the Effable', an ironic phrase, as I was obviously pursuing the unspeakable, though not the red-coated, fox-hunting, gentry as labelled by Oscar Wilde ('The unspeakable in pursuit of the uneatable').

It was a hare, zoologically a lagomorph, twenty feet tall, who spoke soundlessly to me as I plodded gloomily across a wide expanse of grass on a summer day. For months, even years, I had been oppressed by the waste and savagery of nature. I had become a birdwatcher, for whom the facts of life are bloodier than they are for a botanist, my chosen profession. Plants die too, but it was the annihilation of sentient creatures that seemed so unfair. I didn't really mean unfair, being an atheist and biologist who was convinced that there was no good intention whatsoever in the universe. But I seemed unaware of my own perversity: here I was, a *part of nature*, feeling affection and sympathy and regret, so how could there be no good intention in a world containing me?

Maybe it was this inner logical muddle that made the hare manifest itself. I needed a lesson and my subconscious, or something, was giving it to me. Irony piled upon irony. Hare-coursing was a human activity that I had long regarded with loathing. I saw the hare as an innocent victim of human depravity. I still do. But that giant was no victim. Its sub-verbal message was blunt and forceful. I was told to mind my own business. The giant hare wasn't disagreeing with my criticism of humankind, far from it, but I was told to focus on my own problems and let the animals deal with theirs.

This did not mean I shouldn't help animals where it was feasible. My guru-hare meant something more subtle and more searching. I was in serious need of sorting out my messy mind-sets. That was the big lesson. It showed that my problem was in myself not in the vagaries of nature - except the vagaries of my own nature and to some extent the cruelty of man.

Who Is The Hare?

It has a long history and much significance in various countries. Hare symbolises, for example, death and rebirth, ambivalence of creation and destruction, self-sacrifice, trickstering, good luck and bad luck, the witch's familiar and the Virgin's footstool, thievery, magic and maybe amorality. It was naive of me to settle for my experience solely in terms of caring for the welfare of all animals, though it has that connotation. The broader interpretation of its appearance by my side is that it commands me to face the manifold chaos, uncertainty, destruction and dispossession of my being, and of being in general, and still be open to life and even to spring ecstasy.

Furthermore, and full of meaning, was the new idea that mystical experience is not just a magnificent theatre of out-of-this-world, or beyond-this-world, events, but an irresistible master of learning, a great guru at our elbow or on our shoulder. I like to get benefit from my activities and as far as mystical experience is concerned, even if its benefits are 'only' greater awareness and understanding. That would be more than enough for me.

Hare knows pain and death and loss and terror. If nothing else, human beings hardly worthy of the title make sure this fine animal knows these agonies by inflicting coursing with hounds upon him. Yet he longs to live and does so as long as he can. And he tells me to dry my tears and mind my own business. Here is the core of nature mysticism for me. There is extravagant beauty everywhere, but it is in my eye. It is not inherent in nature. On the other hand there is horror, but it is also in my eye, not inherent.

I am an alchemical vessel, in which the experience I have of nature has to be transformed into my own being, whether I see good or evil in front of me. Therefore, I, like any other human, have the responsibility of transforming raw experience into an inner vision. Sometimes, there is help, as with the Giant Hare. It doesn't much matter where he comes from or who he is. The fact is he arrives and is experienced, as if on a ray of infinite light. So the experience I choose to call mystical, as in the case of the great hare, changes my psyche and therefore my life.

Background and Foreground

Considering the nature of human consciousness, which is similar to, but more self-inflating than, that of other mammals, an obsessive concern with survival is an inevitable species characteristic. The self-inflation factor is key, and is probably too complex to be understood by the consciousness it dominates.

The hare, and the other creatures we are fortunate to live amongst, have laws of behaviour that have evolved over millions of years. Or so our scrappy knowledge informs us. It seems that our lagomorphic neighbour has few options in his existence. His mandate is simple: get born, live, breed, and die. That is apparently all he is programmed to do. The frenzy of spring, the racing and boxing, are mere adjuncts to the breeding. He is simply an accidental automaton casually constructed by the female Frankenstein called Mother Nature. He is purposeless, pointless and expendable. Such is life. The reductive view. To a degree, the human view, if our treatment of most other animals and so often of each other, is anything to go by.

Alternatively why do we suppose the human animal is any different? Could we be wrong about the hare and even more wrong about our own species? How sure are we of our opinion, biological or anthropomorphic? As the world seen through the lens of religion becomes modified by the evolving lens of science, our Big-Knowledge becomes more, not less, uncertain of what life is. The relatively new interest in the mysterious phenomenon of consciousness increases the size of the mountain of questions we have heaped up in our brief history. And if we were ever truly innocent we have thrown away that birth right.

Innocence and Consciousness

Are they opposites? Starting from the assumption that the hare, and all other animals, are innocent because they lack self-knowledge, human consciousness must mean that we lack that innocence. If that is true, are we not alone in the great spectrum of organisms in being guilty of bad behaviour and warranting brownie-points for good behaviour? Possibly, possibly not. Who can judge that contest? Yet there is a sense in which we have traded innocence for awareness, as if that mad biblical tale had a shred of truth. We can't have it both ways. If we are more intelligent, or conscious, or aware, or prescient, than even the brightest of our fellow creatures, then we do carry a burden of sin which grows by the day, the sin of misusing life as a whole.

There is some truth in this but I prefer a different logic. Innocence does mean lack of guilt and it also means lack of knowledge. If the tree of evolution were a model of increasing consciousness then it would be a tree of culpability, but that is because the metaphor is wrong.

Evolution is not tree-like, as the biology picture-books tend to indicate. Evolution is a change-process going in all directions at once. It is neither progress nor regress nor improvement nor disrepair, but all of these at the same time. It can hardly be a process of increasing consciousness when so much evolutionary energy is taken up in the production of new species of microorganisms, whose consciousness is rather basic to say the least. But of course one of the changes is this rather sudden spurt of consciousness that began with certain of the mammals and a few other species such as the octopus. It is an evolutionary change, certainly. If it has a special glamour it is because human animals consider themselves both conscious and superior.

Without claiming any of this interpretation as absolute fact, I would also add that consciousness (or its synonyms awareness, mind, intelligence, whatever) can be seen as a burden as well as a prize possession. It could be argued that the human race is uniquely blighted by this unfortunate characteristic. (Or not even uniquely if chimps and elephants and orcas have a lot of it as well.) Anyway, it causes us a lot of trouble. It is a very mixed blessing, this consciousness. For a start, it seems to be the cause of doctrinal religion, which makes life tricky, even dangerous, for most of us. It is the basis of the Terror Carousel. We are the only species to make war on itself on a gigantic scale. We have almost wrecked the planet. None of those things could have happened if we had not been very conscious. After all, it is consciousness that has made us supreme makers of tools and weapons. Chimps make do with twigs, we have computers and farm machinery.

Homo neuroticus

While humankind may not be the only species to show them, the following negative states are typically human:

Anxiety, sadness or depression, anger, irritability, mental

confusion, low sense of self-worth, phobic avoidance, impulsive and compulsive acts, lethargy, unpleasant or disturbing thoughts, repetition of thoughts and obsession, habitual fantasizing, negativity and cynicism, dependency, aggressiveness, perfectionism, schizoid isolation, socio-culturally inappropriate behaviours.

These are official neurotic symptoms, and it must be at least probable that we have them because we are conscious, or that we are conscious because we have them. Is it not also likely that they are connected to an obsessive concern with survival? Perhaps they also show that humans are self-inflated. This condition might also be too complex to be understood by the consciousness it pervades. But it is the power-generator behind our worst misery while its positive opposite is the source of our creative genius. Hare has neither. Is he, therefore, more fortunate than you and me? Is there good reason for regarding our great consciousness as our primary involuntary mistake of speciation, and envying hare for his superior peace of mind?

The Hominid Enigma

Taking an evolutionary view of our neurotic species, we have enough scraps of genetic evidence to surmise that our genotype is exceptionally out of kilter with our phenotype. It is apparently quite common for there to be lack of co-ordination between the effect of the evolved genes and the existential needs of the creature involved. Genes are typically regarded as mechanical units carrying information that affects cell-development. So they are not viewed as purposeful in any way, which is why the term selfish gene is ironic. As survival-proteins they have built-in mechanisms for reproducing their own kind. And sometimes they make a copying- error and the resulting mutation, while usually harmful, sometimes leads to new creations. So they are creative' as well.

I cannot guarantee the veracity of the preceding paragraph, but it seems to me to summarise the position well enough for my next suggestion: if they are reproducing information-units, then why not regard them as living organisms? Our cells, like those of any living organism, are home to numerous kinds of invaders and lodgers. Why shouldn't genes be seen as living organisms occupying the nuclei of cells of another organism? Suppose I choose to see them that way. Then, in my opinion, my genes could be living organisms that carry the information that determines my nature. They are living godlets within me.

Viruses

These are the nearest things to living genes and there is a deep-set area of scientific Big Knowledge that says viruses are not proper living organisms. This is the alive/non-alive cusp and there's no need to straddle it intellectually because it is acknowledged that viruses behave as if they are alive once they occupy a living cell, and they can even revivify a dead cell. There must be a case for seeing viruses as potential genes, at least of the cytoplasmic variety. I don't care either way. But what is vitally relevant to the discussion here is that DNA is not simply an inert, disinterested passenger on the train of life. In some sense, beyond my comprehension, a gene could be regarded as having some sort of life purpose. This at least makes me wonder if the teleology question has still hardly been asked, let alone answered. And it seems obvious to me that my genes could be aiming in one direction while the rest of me is pointing somewhere else. It extends the concept of the Great Continuity by an enormous leap, which adds emphasis to the foolishness of human assumptions about knowing how everything ticks.

Time the Destroyer

Now it seems to be a fact, established in modern genetics, that genes have a kind of use-by date. A gene that is created in one space/time may be in tune with its host, by which I mean that they are both broadly favoured by the prevailing environment. In a different space/time, say a million years later and in an inhospitable location, they may be out of sync with each other. What was a symbiosis between gene and phenotype (the organism as a whole) ceases to exist.

Take a simple example: *Homo sapiens* was a new species a few hundred millennia ago, not long in evolutionary terms, and it didn't do very well. Survival and reproduction were hazardous ventures for man and gene. Now, there are billions of humans and the species faces a future in which it would be better if our numbers were smaller, say one or two billion globally. But the old symbiosis soldiers on. True, something has changed, as the global replacement rate has reduced to around two per breeding pair. But the numbers continue to rise anyway. Other factors operate, obviously. But the minute inner godlets are actually as threatened as the phenotype. Whose job is it to change the picture? Consciousness is conspicuously failing to save the situation, whereas it was a primary factor in our species survival two hundred thousand years ago. Human consciousness is havering, unable to update the survival-mandate. The problem is partly our conscious fixation on personal existence.

Die and Let Live

It is probable that the human imagination, even, or especially, in less intelligent humans, exaggerates the importance of this personal survival. The evolved need (for the phenotype) to stay alive long enough to reproduce, because necessary for the genes' survival, has perhaps become overdeveloped in the human. In addition to the common biological awareness shared in some form or other with all animals, the human animal is presumed to have additional awareness such as a conception of the future and ideas of personal destiny or significance. This could have led to perception of existence in extremely self-referential terms. And it may not be a genetic factor at all, as consciousness can override the genetic mandate.

Indeed, the extraordinary inflation of the sense of *self* has, in humankind, distorted what might otherwise have been a normal animal life. It can be seen as a bonus or a curse. Positioning oneself on this good/bad polarity is crucial to one's serenity of being, as most of our imaginative activity demonstrates. It is also pivotal in matters of death and survival. (The non-human animal may not have such a burden of consciousness/awareness and therefore has no need to position itself on an irrelevant polarity.)

We could start by asking whether it really matters very much if we live or die, remembering that there are now so many of us on this planet. As already intimated, the situation has changed dramatically compared with, say, the early Stone Age, when only handfuls of human creatures occupied niches here and there, the whole of Europe having, say, a population equivalent to that of a modern English village. Eleven thousand years ago, before agriculture developed, the world population is estimated as about three million people. Even as late as the time of Buddha (2500 years ago) the entire human population of the world was probably less than the present population of England, say 50 million.

The Value of a Human Life

Almost nothing could be harder to judge, at least by a human observer. Contrary to theoretical ethics or religion, a human life may be judged on a scale from beyond price to utterly worthless, depending on circumstances and the judge, and the value may be at any point in that spectrum. There is also the fact, largely kept in the background of our minds, that the entire present population will certainly have died by the early part of the next century. We are absolutely temporary. We will probably be replaced, while in the short term, our numbers will probably increase, giving the illusion that life goes on. Which, of course, it doesn't for the phenotype, and only temporarily for the genotype. Even our species will become extinct at some time, as all species do.

Yet we perpetuate the myth of a human life being sacred, and that human rights are immutable, while we go on slaughtering billions of our fellow creatures. Of course, there is a sense in which life *is* sacred, but in a metaphorical, poetic or spiritual sense. For that to manifest, all life must be considered not just that of the human. In fact, the ruthless expansion of human populations is desacralising life as a whole, as it involves the death and destruction of the rest of the biosphere. As for each individual human creature, the value of a life is as long as a piece of string, i.e. it is an indeterminate quantity.

Power and Mythology.

In writing the book entitled, 'Creatures of Power', I had intended to explore the overwhelming problem of religion, but was suddenly aware that the problem of power was far worse than the problem of religion, bad as that is. The two mind-sets work together, of course, so that it's not always easy to say where the trouble lies.

I can only guess how it began. There must have been a time when human behaviour was similar to that of any other puny but resourceful mammal. In other words, this early man was little different from the creatures he stalked as a hunter. Perhaps he was similar to the modern hyena, an opportunistic thief of bigger predator's kills. Or maybe his unusually high level of cunning enabled him to win where any similar animal would have failed without the extra brain-power. Power, in one way or another, was the critical factor in his survival as it is in any new mammalian species. He must have been aware of this and deliberately developed it. He would have become addicted to the miracle of power.

Then, at some stage he utilised power, of brain and/or dexterity, to build shelters, store food, make weapons, and communicate with his companions more effectively and specifically. He somehow discovered how to use the great power of fire. Maybe he used plants as medicines. He began to imagine, to have ideas about his dreams, to see the world as having an intelligence that could harm or enhance him - after all, he must have been aware of the power of his own intelligence, why not look for evidence of that intelligence in other animals, or plants, or just in the elements? Which is where the hare came in.

A Special Consciousness

The human concepts of survival and death have become invalid, generally, when the sheer diversity of behaviour is taken along with the knee-jerk ideas about value. This is the context for considering a new personal approach. It is clear that existence for most of us is relatively unsatisfactory, positioned on a mathematical Normal Distribution Curve, probably. At one extreme of it there are the sybarites, the naturally joyous, the privileged who are content in their splendour, the stars and the famous (if they are happy) and the ones with faith and hope in themselves and their destiny. They probably comprise some five per cent of the world population. At the other end are the people in poverty and squalor, the sick, the hopeless, the criminals, the victims, the starving and the dispossessed. Perhaps they are much more numerous, say thirty-five per cent of our species. The remaining sixty per cent will be a hump of forty per cent bunched together in its middle, with a high crest at the centre, and these are the ones who are reasonably content with their lot. To one side there will be ten per cent who are generally very pleased with life, and on the other side, another ten per cent with some degree of dissatisfaction or distress.

In this approximate distribution there will be many religious people and many atheists of one kind or another. It is unlikely that they will match the general curve, as religion or non-belief can be involved in happiness or it's opposite. What is also virtually certain is that awakeness, true spiritual awareness, will be sparsely represented and unpredictably situated. It would be reassuring to me to know that there was great awakeness amongst Buddhists and Taoists. But at best I suspect only slightly higher incidence. In fact, I have no idea where awakeness is likely to be greatest in the Normal Distribution Graph.

I know many Christians and Muslims would claim a state of awakeness, and some must have it. But most do not behave as though they are really awake. Indeed, there is a case for saying that religious certainty cannot occur alongside true awakeness.

Much of my work has involved exploring that depressing reality. Atheists, on the other had should be more awake, but I doubt if most of them are, as Atheism is a form of doctrinal certainty for many non-believers.

The problem in the religious mind is its certainty, because however comforting it may be to know for sure all you want to know, there's no room for new data. The store is closed except for loyal buyers of the same wares. That is a practical description of the state of being asleep.

Innocence and Awakeness

Earlier I questioned the connection between innocence and consciousness and felt that they were antagonistic rather than synergistic. Careful definition of the two words is necessary because I think the true value of being human is destroyed by the interaction of these two areas of experience. In other words, the words are utterly critical. I wish to identify innocence as the primary focus of the process of mind and spirit, from which the ultimate wonder of awakeness can be derived. So, to get to what I mean, I have to be sure of the meaning I am using. But innocence is a seriously misused word. Or maybe it is just hackneyed and therefore without any meaning at all. Most words are like that. Therefore, a verbal meditation on the word innocence. For a start I will add a capital, as I am talking about a very special form, Innocence, as if the letter 'I' were also critical. I think I mean, **'I do not know'**.

The trouble with consciousness is that it grows or collects knowledge, often indiscriminately. I know highly conscious people who carry colossal bundles of knowledge and who can't put down the bundle for a while and walk free. This is another way of approaching the phenomenon I am trying to call Innocence. Without the crate of knowledge, a person can walk into the open country with wonderment. But this metaphor is troublesome because some knowledge is essential to survive a walk in that country. In any country, actually. As it is for the hare and his fellow lagomorphs, a basic survival kit is really necessary. Being human, there is a prodigal knowledge appetite derived from thinking, 'If knowledge protects me, I must get as much as possible'.

Consciousness is not, in my opinion, all it is cracked up to be. Indeed I regard the various forms of Big-Knowledge as drugs, some Class B, which can be useful, some Class A, which are toxic.

Innocence, therefore, could be linked to a freedom from any dependence on questionable knowledge. In that case Awakeness could also be defined by its independence from toxic knowledge systems. Thus Innocence and Awakeness have a close relationship. But putting the two together brings an enormous additional advantage: awakeness is a powerful alternative knowledge system.

How could this be? We have learned to expect Big-Knowledge from religion, science, philosophy, pedagogy, and a shop full of other commodities. As far as mysticism is concerned, this is seen as alternative Big-Knowledge from a different set of practitioners. Now there is this third source, commonly termed inner truth, intuition, or plain old shamanism.

The answer is that when early man looked upon himself and this world he was basically a mystic and a shaman - that is in his off-moments when he wasn't killing or copulating or fooling around. We haven't changed in two hundred millennia. We still do the same things. We have just professionalised it all. And learned how to make tools and weapons. The third source of knowledge has been driven into the shadows. We call Innocence naivety, ignorance, or, more positively, freedom from guilt. We have side-lined it as a way of being, just as we have buried mysticism and shamanism in a grave called Paganism.

A New Definition

It now seems to me that the key to human awakeness is Innocence, and it is the source of mystical and practical perfection of being. Of course it still means the same as before, but the other meanings seem to me to have acquired a new basis. I refer to my earlier discussion of Original Sin: but I would now like to add that it is not just an Abrahamic error of perception. All humankind has an inveterate lust for gods, and this insatiable desire co-exists with our egoic terror. The Carousel of Terror stands in every human-occupied territory. I would use the term sin to encompass all our neurotic agony and ecstasy. Our species is hooked on sin and the obsession destroys our lives. But we can opt out of sin, in concept and in practice. We can convert to the transcendent level, above and beyond sin, a realm called Innocence.

Sin, therefore, is the monster at the centre of our individual and collective labyrinths, and it is far removed from the Biblical nonsense. Innocence is not a state of slavery to some god-system or other. Innocence is at the essence-level of humanity at its best. It does include good behaviour, how could it not? But it is not naive, in the way that populist politicians and academics are naive, puffed up by the importance of their minds. Innocence means regarding all other life forms as our neighbours and being careful and polite towards them. There is respect and surrender in the idea of Innocence.

When I say, 'I do not know', I am breaking many social conventions, especially the one that demands that we should stay abreast with the news. But in most cases I truly do not know anything. I have a pile of information. I can go to the TV, the newspapers, the internet, and come away with a stack of information. But what, really do I know? It is just what other people are saying, as if they knew. All this information, covert or overt, is viewed as power, as in 'Knowledge will set you free'.

Worst of all, there is this presumptuous knowledge about the future. We cannot be other than Innocent regarding the future, because it does not even exist, Knowledge of the past is fraudulent because most of the past is unrecorded or subjectively selective. Knowledge of the present is at best fleeting. Innocence and Awakeness are enduring, if we care to make them so.

So, in the end, the hare wins all around. He is all of a piece, his genes and his phenotype and his environment are approximately, though dynamically, in balance. He is, above all, perfectly innocent. He deserves our respect. And our deep affection.

Fifteen
Superstition

Excessively credulous belief in and reverence for the supernatural
Such is the online definition. As a self-confessed experiencer of what seems to be mystical, I have tried to avoid excessively credulous belief, whatever that means, and I do have a reverence for what might be called the supernatural, which I prefer to call the natural. On the other hand, neither religious Big-Knowledge nor Scientific Certainty works for me. I am confused, I admit. As the many preceding pages demonstrate, I am not even convinced that reason is always a good guide to the cosmos. I think this is why I find it worthwhile, despite my distrust of history as a Big-Knowledge subject, to imagine what my early ancestors made of their world. It is my clear impression that they were really very superstitious. And probably without the kind of reservations and doubts that I have today.

Superstition is still with us, however, in many forms. It is the central urge in all the religions, obviously. Calling it faith or belief doesn't alter the fact that religion exactly fits the opening definition. Perhaps the only argument about that would be the word excessively, if only because I, for one, could not be sure what would be adequately or moderately credulous. The word credulous means too much readiness to believe, anyway, so that excessively is tautological.

What is Natural?

In reality, everything that exists is natural. So what could possibly be unnatural or not-natural? Is a belief in God natural or supernatural, for example? It is such a widespread behaviour in humankind, anyone could be forgiven for thinking it natural. But it is at least questionable if any other life form on this planet has this habit. We are a very recent, and despite our over-population, a numerically minute part of the biosphere. We could therefore be said to be an unnatural beast compared with all the naturally godless beasts around us. We have taken natural fear and desire and escalated them to the unnatural extreme of superstition. That seems to be a fair assessment.

Natural, unnatural, or supernatural, it was perhaps humankind's first serious mistake. It might even have been the biggest of our mistakes up to now, judging by the harm that continues to follow from our religious practices. At the beginning, the perceived power of the spirits was shamanic and, as such, was extremely influential but also unpredictable. Shamans became practitioners of shamanic power who gave certain guarantees, yet cleverly blamed their clients for failure. It is a trick still in evidence today. It is part of becoming a professional to be able to share blame, as well as benefit, with the client. The priest's confessional cell has a double action: it gives solace to the sinner and power to the absolver.

So superstition gained power and credibility through the resourceful minds of the shamans and the neediness of the early believers, and no doubt the placebo factor was already well-established in primitive spiritual medicine. Then, the extraordinary idea, god, entered the life/death equation, turning everything into a cosmic hierarchy rather than a living landscape. I cannot help seeing this as an act of ludicrous infantilism, even if I recognise and even sympathise with the dependence mentality of humankind.

It has been alleged that god occurs in all cultures in some form or other, as if that proved that deity was a necessity for humankind. I see it quite differently and this is not just a matter of argument, but a decisive element in deciding whether or not the human animal is capable of true maturity and awakeness.

Descent into Power

I am not sure if it is possible because there is no reliable knowledge to show the whole picture. We do seem to have remained an infantile, if brilliant, species. But it seems to me that the need, or awareness of the need, for a higher reference-point must have originated in magical or shamanistic practice sometime in the Stone Age. As I have said, the key word is *power*, and power manifests in many psychological terms such as will, charisma, magic, or spirit. In the Stone Age, these factors must have become important and eventually the collective term for spirits of this kind must have been *gods*.

Therefore, the idea of a *species* of gods is much less overwhelming than the perversion that has quite lately come into the human mind as a single, unique, all-powerful monogod-over-everything. Christian traditionalists have claimed monotheism as having always existed, but they would say that, wouldn't they? More likely is its invention in the Middle East around one thousand BC. It is a truly monstrous mind-set, leaving humans and all other animals in the position of slaves or serfs to a grandiose, mythical, celestial, overlord. That was probably not the way religion, or even just spirituality, figured for people living, say, fifty thousand years ago. The gods, plural, were everywhere, for them, just as the elements of nature are everywhere for me and my contemporaries. These are the shady presences on the edge of existence recognised by Spinoza as Nature and sensibly disregarded by the great Epicurus.

We are not infantilised by such beings, and although they are rather silly ideas, they are fairly harmless compared with the vast destruction brought upon ourselves by belief in entities such as the Abrahamic monogod in his various impersonations. It is a phenomenon of power, the democracy of ourselves among animals and spirits warped into the fascist dictatorship of a single supreme colossus. It is this perversion of power that has ruined human existence for some thousands of years. The process is iterative, too, in that attempts to retain the democracy of spirits have been repeatedly frustrated, as in the destruction of numerous Pagan cults by the Christianised Romans.

Hierarchic Inflation

Hierarchy does certainly exist in nature and it is apparent that natural power structures have been magnified gigantically by human societies, while adding unnatural god-fixation into that social structure. Concreted power structures have become crushing misconceptions whether religious or secular. The idea of a fixed hierarchy is a cosmic error. How have we been so stupid as to give ourselves into the clutches of this insane, metaphorical, monster? In essence, power is merely the capacity or potential for action of some kind. All living things have to employ power to survive. Generally speaking, the power used in this way is more or less appropriate to the task, otherwise there is too much wastage and inefficiency. Admittedly, though, natural processes do tend to be wasteful. Particularly in the reproductive process, where offspring can be far more than seems necessary, although there is usually an approximate balance with the level of predator activity.

It could be argued that nature often tends to overdo the application of power. This could be identified as the loophole through which human animals have pushed the energy of power to absurdity. It seems as if the relatively immense brain potential in the human is another inherent wastefulness of nature, even an evolutionary error (of which there are many throughout the natural world). The short history of the hominids is, in any case, hardly one of resounding success. All the human species have died out, leaving only *H.sapiens*, which was also on the edge of extinction for a prolonged period. But, in one sense, the mutational gamble has paid off. The intelligence of this particular hominid became a formidable survival power, once the potential for co-operation was hitched to tool-making and used for growing or breeding plants and animals for food.

On the face of it, power proved to be the elixir of human life. In a sense, it became an object of worship. Power became a magical or godlike commodity. It was something to be fostered, developed, and used in large quantities. Then the trouble started, just as it seemed that an existential problem had been solved.

Rampage

Appetite and fear are intimately connected to power in the human animal and maybe in animals generally. Power may be used to achieve adequately or it may, at the extreme, be exerted for infinite goals. The human way, like a fox in a coop of chickens, is to go wild with lust for anything. In our present world, for example, the reasonable goal called 'security' is the excuse for a global industry of espionage, surveillance, sanctions, torture, and astronomical expenditure on weapons-systems. A need is escalated into an immense, insane, greed; and power is the means (and the goal) of satisfying that greed.

Power is inherently liable to be manifested as bullying. It even finds itself employed excessively in putatively good enterprises as in the immense spending on health or the perverse stimulation of fertility.

Once humankind realised the theoretically unlimited scope for using power, then it became our primary mode of behaviour. The consequence is a state of imminent collapse of the human population, either in individual countries or, potentially, on earth generally.

Master-Species

Belief in our natural supremacy, our god-given right to rule the earth, blinds us to our folly. But not all of us are duped. Some people have recognised the absurd catastrophe that superstition and power have conspired to make, yet most human creatures just go on behaving as if nothing could go wrong. They believe they are special beings and that they are protected by a benevolent superpower of some kind, if only, and most ludicrously, the universe itself. This belief is deeply embedded in the human psyche where, paradoxically, it is encoiled with a complementary anxiety that something could go wrong if we don't have enough power to prevent it. So we strive for even more power.

I grew up in a country which had an empire. In school, the geography lessons were set against a giant map showing red patches, like blood stains, all over the mercator projection. By one means or another, the myth called Great Britain, basically a bunch of small islands in the North Sea, had gained hegemony over many countries, including India, Australia, Canada, and huge tracts of Africa. The British Empire was a perfect example of superstition married to power. It was a mini-version of the human domination of the rest of nature, this absurd mastery of half the human world by a few Britons. It is paralleled by the structure within Britain, or in most other nations, of about 2% of the population governing the other 98% in terms of ultimate power.

The element of superstition pervading our empire was that we British were inherently superior to all other tribes of humans. In our case, the Christian version of God was the authority from the celestial sphere, and He had supposedly devolved his power onto one British individual person, Queen Victoria or one of her ancestors or progeny. While almost immortal, that little female had been empress of one of the greatest empires ever concocted on the earthly sphere. The whole irrational fantasy was propped up by a cultural hierarchy at the centre, in which aristocrats, public schools, and a servile lower class, enhanced the arrogance of British adventurers. Other countries, France, Spain, Belgum, Germany, Portugal, etc. made similar efforts to carve up the world for themselves. And it was by no means the first time one human tribe had made the whole world its oyster.

As I grew up, the British Empire disintegrated. Yet its elite clung on to both the superstition and the power. Today, the shreds of our past glory are still flapping in the wind. It is still our fantasy that Britons are superior to non-Britons. We still try to brandish power. At the same time the constituent parts of Britain itself are following the empire into disintegration. This is a natural process and it occurs throughout the world. Britain is not even unique in its instability. But what I perceive in the processes involved is a serious failure to use human ability creatively. By chasing the unicorns of superstition and power, Britain, like all other nations, is missing out on its real potential. It would be funny if it were not tragic.

The British Comedy

Our Island's sad history and extremely uncertain future notwithstanding, the politicians still dive and duck and posture. There is no awareness that coming awake and tuning in to the Great Continuity would bring personal relief and even collective salvation. The monarchy/oligarchy is fake and the false make-up and on-going break-up of the UK under natural destructive pressures are possible portents of further national decline ahead. It is a comedy, already seen on the world-stage innumerable times. Why do we do it? It must surely be an inbuilt error. It may be an existential failure in the half-alive genes? Or is it just a weak collective intelligence? Human behaviour could just be very badly programmed.

Histodramas

Superstition is institutional in our British culture, even if half of us are godless. In some ways superstitious impulses are regaining ground that was lost in the Enlightenment. It is especially endemic in the social media and in TV competitions. Everyone seems to crave wealth or fame as if by some inalienable human right, which is itself a facet of superstition. And the urge for freedom and self-determination has become overwhelming, under the battle-cries of democracy, rights and equality. We are still looking for unicorns as desperately as ever.

Everything has changed and nothing changes. A TV programme on the Plantagenet dynasty of English monarchs who ruled dictatorially from 11th to 15th centuries illustrates the power-perversion very well. The power of the monarch was assumed to be directly conferred on the human by the divine. And power was typically translated into territory, money, or success in warfare. So when a king won a battle he was considered to be ordained by God and his policies accordingly approved. A similar but more apocalyptic result of military slaughter was the Roman Emperor Constantine's enforcing of Christianity upon the world because he'd seen a cross of light in the daytime sky and an inscription telling him to use the symbol in all his battles. We continue to be entertained by lavish programmes on royal dynasties all of which claim divine authority. Why this interest in power and fantasy?

Preposterous, even hilarious, as it is, one third to a half the population of the modern world still labours under the Christ-delusion, while its connected god-delusions control the wills of most of the other half. At the same time, the equally toxic superstition about identity continues to wreak havoc everywhere, with a dozen or more wars going on at the present time. There is serious trouble in the collective human psyche and the unknown future looms dangerously. Most sinister of all is the fact that these superstitious power-inflated myths are deliberately inculcated into the developing psyche of the young humans.

The Plight of the Individual.

Anyone wishing to explore the effect of these fixations on the individual could do worse than study existential psychopathology. Not only does each person have to contend with societal pressures, often involving extreme coercion or systematic brainwashing, and actual laws prohibiting freedom of thought or action, but there is also in each of us the deep anxiety, even terror, of ceasing to exist.

The individual stratagems for dealing with this fear are mirrored in the society's thought, belief and behaviour. To add to the existential distress and confusion, there is inconsistency in both the society and each individual. Most damaging of all, the very stratagems that try to neutralise the fear are sources of deep neurosis and that appears as a different problem from the straightforward hysteria about dying. The ideas in existential study are reflected in other, unconnected, methodologies, especially those of the humanistic and transpersonal psychologies, and the vast, flawed, realm of Jungian ideology.

As mentioned elsewhere, I have some respect for Enneagram analysis, where the personality is regarded as a puppet facade unwittingly created by every person in reaction to early environment stress.

The theory is that the personality needs to be dismantled to resurrect the hidden, true, essence of the actual, real, person. It is one of the ways, also, of coming awake, by which I mean the liberation of personal being from mendacious habit and self-deceit.

Dealing With Death

How can any of these concepts or methods bring us down to a safe landing on solid earth regarding the complex, idiotic, ambivalent, repressed and denial-dominated subject of mortality? And how can we reasonably maintain a respect for mystical experience and the ill-defined realm of spirituality, on the one hand, and humility about our inevitable ignorance on the other? If the best methods are those that actually face the reality of mortality, and the worst methods are those that deny or obscure the reality of death, the life history of humankind could have been and still could be very different from that which has happened.

That much is evident and incontrovertible, if truth is preferred to lies and awakeness is better than asleepness. If we have any chance as individuals, or as a species, to become free and relatively unafraid, then facing the monster in its lair is the only option. The monster is not death, but the refusal to acknowledge death at the deepest psychological and emotional levels of consciousness. We may think we do that. Plenty of people assert their honesty about mortality. But the reality disagrees with them when they look deeply into themselves.

Mortality: Poor Solutions

The cure is worse than the disease, maybe? The solution to the problem of death, specifically the fear of it, is formed by human imagination and implanted in our beliefs and behaviours by cultural pressure. That it is entirely false is usually ignored or refuted. Of course, we need to think we know the answers and we need to feel we are on the right track, too bad if it is the wrong track

There are three separate mind-sets, ideas which are widely accepted and implemented across continents and through time. These belief-systems are:

1. The unitary manifestation that matters is the **ego, or self, or personality**. And it is this trinity or the constituent parts of it that have to be asserted and developed to offset and neutralise our inherent tendency to be infinite creatures. In addition, there is a backstop, with titles such as **soul, spirit, or oneness**, which may be the eternal element of human existence, though it is hard to demonstrate and as vague as consciousness itself.

2. Following from 1, there is a secret, but entrenched and widespread, individual and/or collective conviction of **specialness.** No matter how much we know or rationalise, no matter how many deaths we witness, it is impossible to imagine something as special or important as I/we being utterly extinguished. As in the soul idea, or maybe in our bequests to others, or in monuments and artifacts, I/we will survive somehow.

3. I/we are protected from death by the presence of someone or something, like a guardian angel, or God, or a special person, or an organisation, or just something we don't need to name (often now, ironically, the Universe!). So long as this **Ultimate Rescuer** is there for me/us there is no need to worry about mortality: this is a safe place, or so we persuade ourselves.

It may seem odd that people could delude themselves in this way. But it should be remembered that consciousness is layered, and much of it is hard or impossible to haul into conscious awareness. Any of us may be irrational, even delusional, sometimes, or consistently in certain mental niches. Apparently one of the favourites in Sigmund Freud's joke-book was the statement by a man who said, of himself and his wife, 'If one of us dies, I shall re-locate to Paris'.

I admit that there would be little point in striving to overcome these mistaken concepts, if we became unhappier as a result. It could be argued that the Self, Specialness, and Ultimate Rescuer sound like good solid defences against cosmic angst. But are they? And is happiness, like love, a relative term, to be used sparingly rather than bandied about as a universal panacea?

These ideas and the attitudes based on them are explored in the next chapter in terms of the ego, the self, and the personality.

Sixteen
The Ego-Self-Personality

The Triple Trap

In terms of death and survival, these are not very serviceable entities. Neither are they particularly helpful in any other aspect of life. The reason for their inadequacy is their basic crassness. This is a big claim, I admit, and it is important to examine it carefully.

Earlier in this book, and in others such as 'Ways of Being' and 'Beyond Belief" I have challenged the idea of unified existence and also the fictional personality we each present to the world. The craving for personal validation and individual immortality finds full expression in the paradox of selfhood and is manifested in a set of beliefs and behaviours we put out as the real *me*.

The first error, a truly egoic mistake, in this is that the human being is not a unity in any sense at all, but, as explained fully in 'Freedom River, The Infinite Beginning', a moving population of myriads of microscopic bits and pieces. Not only are there trillions of cells of different kinds, but the greater proportion of our constituent cells are immigrants, not human at all. Those cells that are genuinely of human origin are also extremely complex, as are the millions of sense organs and genetic units in the human body. Our much-vaunted intelligence and consciousness are also diverse and rich with inexplicable happenings and behaviours. It is indeed miraculous that this microscopic universe presents itself as a sort of unity, as it is almost an infinity of different constituents.

The second (double) fantasy, the energetic thrust of the ego, is the conviction that we are individual selves, with genuine identities manifesting as personalities. In fact, the self is at best a useful fiction in that it is convenient to manage life as if it were a coherent and logical process, but the so-called self is repeatedly shaken by catastrophe because it is actually a mixture of more or less disparate and variable elements.

Thirdly, the personality is a psychic construction made in very early childhood to deal with an apparent world and which is owned for life by the person as if it were a real being. It is the enduring substance of egotism. There are some useful disciplines that have analysed this phenomenon and work with the personality to minimise its dangers and maximise its usefulness for a happy life.

The ego is therefore a compendium of all three, and seems to latch on to any one of the ingredients to suit a particular situation.

Uncovering the Truth of the self or personality is extremely difficult for most people. The biggest problem is the vested interest we have in the embedded fiction. We have no wish to learn the truth. It has been buried deliberately, albeit unconsciously for most people. It is a deliberate lie but not an inherently malignant lie. It is only the results that are toxic. To some extent the self or personality are similar devices to the shadow, the constellation in the unconscious where we have each buried unwanted material, such as impulses or memories that are very disturbing, or desires and phobias we can't admit into conscious awareness. In the case of the shadow, the unconscious mind has a trick up its sleeve, and it makes us commit errors or accidental confessions, often in dreams, so that we are occasionally shocked into recognition of the buried truth.

Fortunately, there is also the possibility that the unconscious may rebel against the fictional self or personality. This potential can be used to bring the reality to the surface. It is the main work, for example, of psychotherapy or psychiatry, which in various forms are used to help a person recover the true nature of their being. Often, this work, as in the long process of psychoanalysis, seems to go nowhere except into deeper obscurity or ignorance. But that is the problem: the patient is in the territory of the unknowable if the need to bury the truth is strong enough. It is what makes everyday knowledge inherently suspect and usually false, and causes Big-Knowledge to be an enormous obstacle to true civilisation.

Psychologically and philosophically, it might be asked, therefore, 'Why not leave the sleeping dog alone?' This is, indeed, the critical existential question. It is easy and grandiloquent to say, 'The truth shall set you free!' but in practice this is hard to achieve. I think the key question is whether a human being is stable and contented, or neurotic and miserable. The secondary issue is whether or not the lives of friends, lovers, and family members are enhanced by the individual concerned. Nevertheless, aside from these criteria, there is the fascinating issue that is deeper and more enigmatic: has the human concerned made the most of potential power for full awareness, for, in fact, becoming fully alive?

It is this last category that interests me most. For myself, and for the people around me who care about it, I would like full awakeness and therefore as *true* a life as possible. By true, I don't mean an abstract perfection of knowledge, but a stripped down clarity of being, where self-deception is minimal. The need for this is a powerful tool in the work of finding the inner reality, because it is positive and creative, whereas other motivations are weakened by the fact that they may be seen as merely healing processes. This can be yet another form of self-deception if the healing is just about feeling good, or the bliss of loving and being loved, or making one's psychological or emotional nest cosier (desirable as that may be).

The Process.

This book is all about the failure of Knowledge, ordinary or Big, to make human life civilised, beautiful, loving and true. It is necessarily directed towards the Void which is the future. But there is no grand educational program that can take an unawake person to full awakeness, to a First Class Honours in Personal Maturity. It is best to proceed humbly, each step being a new awareness of one's world. We can only grasp each opportunity as it arises rather than attempt wholesale change. Some people have tried and still try the frontal assault, by Zen for example, or endless meditation. You may be sure that the self or the personality will resist change and it is futile to expect quick, across the board, progress. Learning programs such as the Enneagram can be a useful background actvity. But constant and open-minded vigilance are key, coupled with the utmost honest scepticism. I will try to illustrate the process with two generalised examples of primary development strategies.

The Healer and the Soldier

The sense of self and the personality of these bipolar opposites, while superficially so different, have a similar basic motivation. Both are using power to alter the world, i.e. they are controllers and change-agents. The will tend to have strong egos and be very deliberate in their effect on other people. (In the Enneagram system they may belong to the 8-5-2 triad, in which Enneagram Type Eight is the action-man, Two is the keen helper, and Five is the cautious observer'.)

The Healer is apparently motivated by the purest of love and sympathy. The self and the self-image are positive and kindly. But the steel at the centre is the determination to change people and to collect kudos by the work done. The healer claims lack of self-interest and all his effort is alleged to be selfless; his personality is driven by love and humanity. That may be, and often is, true but the motivation is not so simple. The downside of the healer self/personality is his own neediness. He wants what he offers, often to a neurotic degree. He can also become messianic in his determination to make a difference, which means he is asleep to his own deficiencies.

He is also likely to be fixated by one or more of the alternative therapies, sometimes to an obsessive degree. As a homeopath, an acupuncturist or a reflexologist, he may proselytise as if peddling a sacred religion. He may lose any sense of proportion or relativism in his overwhelming zeal. These traits are present in many vocations, by no means only in the layers-on of hands. A wide range of professions are liable to attract the healing propensity. The healer self/personality can turn up in practitioners of medicine, in teaching, or politics, and also in some forms of parenting or the vague and diverse class of social work. Increasingly, it may also find strong expression in people who care about the environment or the biosphere, as well as lovers rather than mere users and consumers of other creatures.

The Healer's Wound

While the healer self/personality may function as the better kind of human being, the downside elements of his dedication may apper as an irritating smugness or piety, and the inner stresses are often seriously neurotic. The problem is that being such a good person is hard work and involves very egoic behaviour, albeit masquerading as selfless. A healer, or giver as he is often known, may become very spiteful if frustrated. It is as if good behaviour as a career has an inherent flaw, if it is a duty rather than a joy. In other words, if the practitioner is not fully awake.

Inevitably and even necessarily, it is a challenging task for a healer self/personality to emerge from the sleep of automatism. Such an individual is deeply convinced of his own rectitude and can see no virtue whatever in questioning his fervour. What he does is evidently absolutely right so why doubt its validity?

Healing the Healer

What possible advantage to this perfect person would be self-doubt? How could he benefit from undermining his own certainty? He will already protest that he is only human and never fully effective because he is too aware of reality to make the mistake of excessive self-congratulation. He is trapped by his own convictions as are all unawake people and it is questionable whether his nature could cope with the freedom of losing those convictions.

The benefit of freedom to the healer self/personality would be immense if he could accept it. The responsibility he has been carrying for others would become his own personal task: he would be able to turn to his own being as the primary focus for his skills. He could change from mere self-indulgence to full connectedness to others. He would, in effect, become part of the natural world instead of a fanciful exploiter of its resources and its needs. Most of all, perhaps, would be the intense joy of true intimacy with others, having removed the barrier of his own superiority.

The Soldier, although obviously different from the healer in the form of self and personality, has remarkably similar problems. In general, a soldier tends to aspire to the so-called archetype of the hero, unless he is the lowest form of mercenary. As a heroic aspirant, the soldier is motivated by concepts of bravery and service. His inner references tend to be determination, orderliness and willingness to suffer or inflict suffering in some higher cause usually laid down for him by his superiors. He is, in effect, a paid servant of the collective will, the will to battle for the collective gain or survival. Just as the healer self is theoretically dedicated to kindliness and humaneness, the soldier self, as hero, is in service to restitution, order, or punishment of the enemies of the collective. Unlike the healer, the soldier is prepared to suffer injury or death in his calling.

On the face of it, therefore the soldier self/personality is even more unselfish than the healer: he risks all for his people, who are often totemised as a monarch or dictator. When he is killed, the people mourn him, when he returns from battle his people idolise him. I suppose the key word for the soldier must be *glory* compared with *wholeness* for the healer. This is the theoretical stance of the soldier, the soldier as hero.

The Selfish Hero

In practice, even if heroic, the soldier self/personality is hardly as unselfish as he portrays himself. The love of adventure, the thrill of taking risks, are fairly typical characteristics of most boys and maybe a few girls too. There is a fight going on, one in which the bored youngster looks for a way out. There is also the phenomenon of Narcissism, in which a human individual needs to indulge in a form of self-worship. In this milieu dressing up in uniform has positive attractions, paradoxically mimicking the very mundanity that is being shunned. Then there is natural aggression, too, an energetic resource ideally suited to soldiering as a follow-on to contact sports.

On top of all this, despite the huge implicit risk of being a soldier-hero, there is the comfort and safety of fellowship and following orders in an organised regime. In the less salubrious forms of soldiering, there may be the lure of looting and rapine, in some times and places condoned by the collective authority as the inevitable consequence of armed conflict.

There are many other ways of behaving like a soldier without actually being one. In some sense, soldiering is what men, in particular, tend towards as a way of being. For example, the police, fire, rescue and lifeboat services may all attract the soldier type. Also, unfortunately, the criminal organisations can also be irresistible to the anti-heroic mind-set. The rather bizarre concept of honour amongst thieves does, however, imply the soldier self/personality in the general sense. The soldier can all too easily become a murderer, a thief, a rebel, a tyrant, or a dictator.

Civilising the Soldier

What, then, are the deeper perils of being the soldier self/personality in the sense of unawareness and automatism, the state of being that may be fundamentally false and therefore potentially disastrous to the individual or collective? It is perhaps easier to see the dangers here than in the healer, who seems so serene and humane. The soldier is paid to be violent, therefore violence has to be accepted as a key feature of the person. On the other hand, there is in this self/personality an inbuilt conflict, because the hero type must be able to choose when to be aggressive and when to be kind. He will often be in a situation where conciliation or even gentleness are the qualities required. This means that the individual concerned has an extra awareness task even when lost in the nature of his type.

In some ways this could be useful in the process of becoming truly awake, also, whereas the healer has quite a secure and comfortable life in his assumed role, the soldier has a tough existence, one way or another. It is surprising how much misery a soldier type will accept in his chosen self/personality. But of course there is also the brotherhood factor and the belief in his own valour.

Too Many Soldiers

Taking an existential view, I would say that the soldier self/personality is far too prominent in the human race today. Even if relatively harmless as in sport and athletics, it is still aiming in the wrong direction as far as awakeness and self-awareness are concerned. It depends on what we really want as a well-lived life. There must be serious concern that so much human energy is devoted to aggression or its less violent cousin, competition. As to the latter, the human blueprint does seem sullied by the triviality of what we choose to praise, the fatuity of fame-obsession.

When, as is inevitable, the soldier reappears from battle in a dire condition, often shaken to his core and hardly capable of ordinary life, we praise him and are sorry for him, but are ourselves asleep as to the culture that permits and even encourages such a sacrifice. The soldier self/personality does often continue to display heroic qualities in his damaged being, and it still seems too much for our or his imagination to admit that everything has gone wrong.

Hero in Chains

So, *someone has to do it,* is the ultimate defence of the soldier's life? Collectively, given the propensity of our species to aggress and rampage, there is some sense in this slogan. But does the individual who offers himself as the sacrifice have full comprehension of his behaviour? And, do the rest of us understand what we expect of the hero-victim? In terms of personal freedom, the soldier is in a permanent prison. Is that not a greater crime than any other?

How would a soldier self/personality benefit from giving up his career-choice; at the deepest level of his being? It would be hard to refute all the fine values he offered to himself when he signed on to willing sacrifice. He may suffer from guilt, or a sense of failure, even humiliation, and the fear of cowardice. Why would he suffer these withdrawal symptoms as a matter of choice? It is a question, in one form or another, that arises for anyone choosing to come awake to reality. For the soldier, it would be his greatest conceivable victory but could he see, believe in, and live with that victory?

States of Freedom

Are there *any* people not sheltering under the leaking roof of self and personality? And could they help the rest of us if we asked them? I think there are such people but are they easily recognised? It can be difficult to identify such a rare creature.

I have recently read an artcicle on W.H.Auden whose hidden life displays the qualities required by this unsatisfactory existence of ours. Behind his gruff and often rude exterior there lurked a kind and compassionate man. He put himself down yet repeatedly helped others. I am impressed by the fact that he refused to shift his moral stance despite being side-lined for a Nobel Prize. Some other poets seem to have the same inner sweetness. John Clare, for example, Keats unquestionably, and even the curmudgeonly and great Philip Larkin.

At its best, poetry is a route to awakeness. So is music. And fine literature. The creators of these works need not be paragons, and they often seem to be conduits for a greater love and wisdom than they could ever practice in life.

Female Saints

There is no way of being certain about this, I think, but on the whole it seems that female humans are more likely to live an awake life than males. My experience suggests it is true, but how could I be sure? It may be that men are lumbered with the worst of the hormones, testosterone, and are recipients of the macho culture that has ruined the world from the beginning. I know that both sexes can be horrible, but I would still feel happier in a world more open to the female spirit.

Saints as a species regardless of gender, are not easy to understand. So often they are tied to a deistic fantasy which makes it impossible to assess their real worth. But secular saintliness has to be one way to rethink our human world. Are we so cynical and selfish that we are not able to dedicate our existence to the good? As things stand, we seem only able to extol power. That must be the worst thing to do. Power is our worst enemy. Yet we do worship it. Is this our Achilles heel? Are we such fools?

Just think of a world in which the primary value was goodness. That would be an extreme variation in the evolutionary labyrinth. But self-consciousness is our primary innate characteristic. We use it wilfully and often criminally. But the way of the secular female saint would be pure goodness and it could only be achieved by transcendent self-awareness. It would be worth trying.

Seventeen
What Comes Next?

Top Predator scores 150 Billion

The number of animals eaten by humans every year is estimated as 150,000,000,000. It is not clear what animals are included but presumably it is mainly mammals, birds and fish. US data for 2008 are reported online as: cattle 35,507,500; pigs 116,558,900; chickens 9,075,261,000; turkeys 271,245,000; broiler chickens 9,005,578,000. These numbers are publicised by Animal Liberation Front. Whatever the actual detailed numbers, the data indicate that 7 billion humans must be the top predator level. The other factor is that we humans have done a lot to eliminate other top predators such as the big sharks, big cats, and other mammalian competitors.

Humans have some powerful enemies, such as insect-borne disease, sundry bacteria and viruses, and, it must be admitted, ourselves. We kill a lot of our own kind, if not usually for food. And we have a range of self-destructive habits such as drug addiction, over-eating, and an enormous use of resources to make our lives safe and enjoyable. Looked at biologically, the human species, for all its huge power, is now in a precarious position.

Some years back I wrote a book now titled 'The Global Gamble', which predicted the downfall of our species. It was a serious attempt but highly fictional. I foresaw a decline in human population as a result of several trends, and by 2055 I put our numbers as a very small fraction of what they are today. The human world in 2055 is one I'd rather enjoy, in theory, because most of the struggle and conflict we have now would have disappeared in my small utopia of survival.

I still tend toward that idea, as an ideal, though Big-Knowledge being as it is, I know the actual world in 2055 could be very different from my crystal-ball vision. I wish it were otherwise, but I cannot see how humankind, the top predator, can possibly hang on to his position. Indeed, I suspect that the decline will be rapid and horrible.

The Crowded Dish

I used to be a microbiologist, with a special interest in fungi and symbiosis. I thought that plants made a better job of life than animals. Not the fungi, as it happens, because these organisms are neither plants nor animals in modern classification, and they lack the salient skill of plants in being unable to manufacture their own food from sunlight and simple inorganic molecules such as water and carbon dioxide. A plant is a genius compared with the animal which has an extraordinary struggle to feed itself by eating other life-forms. Of course, plants are primary foodstuffs for many if not most animals, but they probably suffer less pain than the creatures that browse on them.

As for the fungi, they have some interesting strategies, one of which is to form close mutually beneficial relationships with plants, these marriages being called mycorrhizas. Trees, usually with mycorrhizal partners, are successful life-forms without needing to be predators, nor, indeed, herbivores.

Therefore, but for the questionable importance of animal sentience, or its higher form, consciousness, trees have been outstandingly effective in colonising the planet, generally without significantly harming it - quite the reverse, considering the immense benefit they confer upon all life. Tree-worship is not just a new age fad, because trees deserve it. Most plants are similarly benevolent, with only the occasional type that uses poison or spines to protect itself from hungry mouths.

Microbiology studies the needs and foibles of tiny life-forms which nevertheless mirror the needs and achievements of large organisms.

Fungi or bacteria can be cultivated on a nutritious substrate in that grail of the laboratory, the petri dish. But when the substrate becomes used up or fouled with toxins the microorganism dies. Nothing can save it. It has eaten itself to death.

The Petri Planet

Trees and other plants can also suffer the same fate as the microorganisms. It is a general fact of nature that when space or food or water is inadequate, life is destroyed. It is often caused by crowding by sedentary organisms, but frequently also a hazard to mobile animals. Many, many species have become extinct on this planet and often because of lack of space, food, or water. Sometimes it is death by competition or predation. It can be caused by changes in the environment for which the phenotype or genotype of a species is ill-prepared, the unsurvival of the non-fittest.

The big predators are extremely susceptible to most of these changes, with the added hazard of needing an adequate supply of their prey. Predation is, in effect, a high-risk strategy. And the bigger the predator the greater the risk. As the human animal is a large and numerous predator, it is especially vulnerable. Humankind, have some advantages over lions and crocodiles and orcas, one of which is facultative omnivorousness. We humans can live and flourish without meat. We can become herbivores or, more fashionably, vegans. Admittedly, given the gigantic number of animals we devour, replacing them with vegetarian alternatives could be difficult. But it's an option which may become a necessity.

In any case, if all the requirements of the human predator are considered, there is great cause for concern. There is an immense water-need in the human population, and water is beginning to look a limiting factor. Humans are not well adapted naturally to high or low temperatures, and devices used to moderate the climate are costly. We have a generally large energy need, which is also costly. Much of the human population uses artificial transport, again very costly. One way or another we are resembling the failing microorganism in the petri dish.

How Long?

We have no way of knowing how long our species will survive on this planet. My guess of forty years or so did not assume extinction. But there are reasons to suggest that we have already passed the critical stage, in that some calculations conclude that we have already used too many resources to maintain our position on earth. We have passed the point of no return, it is said, and so we are bound to die out. Well, that seems quite probable, but we cannot know for sure until it has nearly happened.

What is even more interesting to me is whether there are yet any signs of what might replace us. Lateral thinking is needed, because we are far too prone to suppose it has to be something like us only better in some way.

If, as I suspect, the human experiment has been a failure, then the new regime, if there is one, should be as unlike us as possible or such a paragon in our mould as to be a pipe-dream. As we are talking about the future, there is almost nothing we can say about the probabilities, except that humankind might well be coming to an end. Robots that are superior versions of even the most advanced human are the sort of solution that reeks of the incense of reincarnation fantasy. Why would such a monster be a good idea? What would it be good at? Loving? Artistic creation? Empathy? Who would program it to such prodigious behaviour?

The Contenders

Perhaps it's my past profession that makes me say it, but I quite favour the microorganisms or the plants, or both in symbiotic partnership. Why should the new lord of the earth be even a vertebrate let alone a humanoid? I also back trees as a wonderful mainstay. But the human opinion is irrelevant. No human would be on earth to observe the new Great Continuity of Life, and this gives us a good opportunity to wake up to our perfect unimportance. We might even make a better job of living as we go under.

I can look at the presence or absence of people on the planet in two ways. First, as a human, I am totally disorientated by the thought that my species is likely to disappear. I can't really believe that it's possible. I live in a human world. Second, there is the simple reality of nature's way of dealing with failure, as far as I can see and understand it. The universe itself seems quite implacable. What can happen is likely to happen.

My preference, insofar as I am arrogant enough to have one, is that I would like humankind to stop its bad behaviour and become as near perfect as possible, thereby surviving and improving in quality of life. I don't know why this matters to me, but it does, and to an overwhelming degree. But my feelings are irrelevant. My awareness has to be my guide. I am aware that trees, insects and microbes are likely to be the great survivors, and I wish them luck. As far as animals are concerned, they'd have a great opportunity in the absence of humans, but they would go on facing the challenge of indifferent nature. I wish them luck, too.

The Sting in the Tale

This is the beginning of Amazon's description of a new book by an expert on jellyfish:

'Our oceans are becoming increasingly inhospitable to life - growing toxicity and rising temperatures coupled with overfishing have led many marine species to the brink of collapse. And yet there is one creature that is thriving in this seasick environment: the beautiful, dangerous, and now incredibly numerous jellyfish. As foremost jellyfish expert Lisa-Ann Gershwin describes in "Stung!" the jellyfish population bloom is highly indicative of the tragic state of the world's ocean waters, while also revealing the incredible tenacity of these remarkable creatures. Recent documentaries about swarms of jellyfish invading Japanese fishing grounds and headlines about armadas of stinging jellyfish in the Chesapeake are only the beginning - jellyfish are truly taking over the oceans.'

Bearing in mind my own strictures on Big-Knowledge, especially as applied to the unknown vastness of the future, the story of the advancing jellyfish comes in the category of threatened climate change. They are both probabilities not certainties. But they are high probabilities. This opinion is based on the fact that both global warming and prodigious growth in jellyfish populations are apparently already happening.

Big-Knowledge about the past also holds that jellyfish have been in the oceans for a long time. As Wikipedia puts it:

Jellyfish *or* **jellies** *are the major non-polyp form of individuals of the phylum Cnidaria. They are typified as free-swimming marine animals consisting of a gelatinous umbrella-shaped bell and trailing tentacles. The bell can pulsate for locomotion, while stinging tentacles can be used to capture prey.*

Jellyfish are found in every ocean, from the surface to the deep sea. A few jellyfish inhabit freshwater. Large, often colourful, jellyfish are common in coastal zones worldwide. Jellyfish have roamed the seas for at least 500 million years, and possibly 700 million years or more, making them the oldest multi-organ animal.

On this basis, these animals are extraordinarily successful survivors. What has now happened is that a combination of sea-warming and over-fishing, both achievements of humankind, has enabled jellyfish to extend both their range and numbers in the world's oceans. Therefore, they could be the next top predator, and possibly the natural successor to our species. And we have prepared the way for them. Professor Tim Flannery has just written about Lisa-Ann Gershwin's book in the New York Review of Books as follows:

From the Arctic to the equator and on to the Antarctic, jellyfish plagues (or blooms, as they're technically known) are on the increase. Even sober scientists are now talking of the jellification of the oceans. And the term is more than a mere turn of phrase. Off southern Africa, jellyfish have become so abundant that they have formed a sort of curtain of death, a stingy-slimy killing field, as Gershwin puts it, that covers over 30,000 square miles. The curtain is formed of jelly extruded by the creatures, and it includes stinging cells. The region once supported a fabulously rich fishery yielding a million tons annually of fish, mainly anchovies. In 2006 the total fish biomass was estimated at just 3.9 million tons, while the jellyfish biomass was 13 million tons. So great is their density that jellyfish are now blocking vacuum pumps used by local diamond miners to suck up sediments from the sea floor.

The jellyfish would not have an easy life. They would presumably be restricted to the oceans, although rivers could be a secondary habitat. Land creatures would benefit from the absence of human beings and should be relatively safe from jellyfish so long as they kept out of the water. Plants would get the world back. But, being constitutionally carnivorous, jellyfish could run out of fish to eat and might have to adapt to a greater degree of cannibalism than they already practice. As a top predator, they'd have limitations as we do, but of a slightly different kind. It should be remembered that there are a lot of different species of jellyfish, unlike us, so that considerable differential evolution would be much more feasible for them that it is for us. Whatever the problems, nature would sort them out, as usual.

Philosophical Implications

Big-Knowledge faces a gigantic upheaval. It is a specific human activity, this collecting of information about everything and collating it into a world-view. Clearly, it would stop if humans disappeared altogether. Any knowledge left in the world would be enshrined mainly in the innate nature of the organisms which remained after we ceased to exist. That is still a very large amount of knowledge, but it is not the kind we have accumulated in religion, science and philosophy. The world will lose all of that, and it is impossible to imagine that the world will suffer in the slightest as a result. Big-Knowledge was always just for humankind.

Nevertheless, as the human race goes under, there will be muffled cries about the failure of the gods to protect us. At present, many, perhaps a majority, of human beings do presume to be under the aegis of gods, or God. How would they react to the gradual realisation that neither gods nor nature nor the universe have the slightest concern for the fate of humanity?

If it happens, many would reply, with more or less absolute scepticism that they could not be so wrong. Well, maybe they are right. Maybe we will be saved. No-one can be sure either way. We must have faith and hope, the believers would declare. What if they are right?

A Practical Strategy

What if they are wrong? Isn't there something we ought to do, just in case God lets us down? How would it be if we took a long, hard look at ourselves and the global environment and decided to optimise our chances? It may be argued that we are already trying to do that, but it is not remotely true. We have, wrapped up in a muddled form in our famous Big-Knowledge, some vague conception that something needs to be done to secure our future on earth. Some even favour leaving it and going somewhere else.

Being practical, as if we actually did own the planet and it was recognised to be falling apart in terms of our environment, we would have the option to decide and implement a survival, even a prosper, strategy. But, so far, we have merely demonstrated our ineptitude. There is virtually no sign of any useful action to avert possible or probable human apocalypse.

Maybe we should all study the jellyfish. Not just in terms of being a threat to us, as that is not the main issue. We have a large raft of unpleasant hazards sailing towards us. The jellyfish are only one. But they have a second, more valuable, lesson to teach us, if we will pay attention. It is that nature is not a friend to humankind, nor any other kind.

Nature is an implacable force of logic. If you think nature is evolving towards collective super-consciousness, as some people do, don't forget that it is extremely unlikely to be a process directed towards human benefits. It is obviously just as inclined to favour the jellyfish, while they follow natural, implacable, logic. Or the myriads of bacteria, the half-alive viruses, or any of the dead-or-alive genes. Nature is the essential *logic* of the universe. Humankind has a small dose of it in their basic nature but they are amateurs compared with the whole, relentless, thrust of the Great Continuity, the terrible and beautiful reality of the cosmos.

Epicurus the Great

He shall have the last words of this book. In paraphrase, he said that of course there were gods, but they were completely irrelevant and not in the least interested in human beings. We should ignore them completely. It was entirely up to us to make life good and be happy.

www.ingramcontent.com/pod-product-compliance
Lightning Source LLC
Chambersburg PA
CBHW050325170426